PRAISE FOR COURTNEY E. MARTIN'S
LEARNING IN PUBLIC

Lessons for a Racially Divided America
from My Daughter's School

"Is it possible to integrate with integrity? To advance justice one school choice at a time? Courtney Martin the writer asks such questions. Courtney Martin the mother, neighbor, and citizen lives them. *Learning in Public* is a powerful, unflinching chronicle of responsibility-taking: what it feels like, what it costs, what it makes possible."
—Eric Liu, CEO of Citizen University and author of *Become America*

"An honest, searching, and progressive book that will spark debate."
—*Kirkus Reviews*

"Writing with equal passion as a journalist and a mother, Courtney Martin interrogates the history and the moral contradictions of 'elite parenting,' gentrification, and school choice. She lives the question of how to chart a new way forward with her daughter in their neighborhood. This is a kind of modeling our society needs—as openly messy as the work of remaking our world."
—Krista Tippett, host of *On Being* and author of *Becoming Wise*

"In a vivid, meticulously reported, and unflinchingly honest way, Martin describes choosing a school for her eldest daughter in progressive Oakland and navigating both unconscious and explicit biases that force her to confront her privileges and fight against them. In the end, she concludes that the main barriers to true integration in public schools are well-meaning white mothers—without finger-pointing or absolving herself as a white savior."
—*Oprah Daily*

"Martin reveals the tensions that progressive parents grapple with when choosing schools for their children in a limited market for 'good' schools. She inspires us to ask necessary questions about race, class, and education in a country that has not yet achieved justice for all."

—Dr. Dena Simmons, founder of LiberatED
and author of *White Rules for Black People*

"Martin brings to her perspective on her daughter's education a self-reflection that goes well beyond her one daughter and their one family, or even their one school, placing instead the story of her white family in the racial history of the United States and the gross disparities seen in the American public education system. This reflection is what allows *Learning in Public* to live up to its title."

—*Shelf Awareness*

"This is the story of what school segregation, a nationally important issue, looks like through the lens of one family's experience."

—*Literary Hub*

"Correcting the harmful legacies of racism in America is generational work. *Learning in Public* invites us to walk the long road of this process in beloved community. Martin refuses to settle for the comfort and false certainty of simple answers and static moralizing. Instead, she insists on the painful discomfort and joyful awakening of transformation that's possible when we live into the biggest questions we have through the most personal choices we make."

—Mia Birdsong, author of *How We Show Up*

"*Learning in Public* by Courtney Martin rules, and I hope you read it."

—Garrett Bucks, *The White Pages*

"White parents want to be instruments of change, yet we don't want our own children to 'suffer.' We want to raise anti-racists, yet we segregate our kids in 'good' schools dominated by families that look like us. Martin wrestles with all of these hopes and conundrums in ways that are personal, heartfelt, and, especially now, profoundly necessary." —Peggy Orenstein, author of *Girls & Sex* and *Boys & Sex*

"If you have ever wondered what school choice means for White families who profess racial justice and understand that, in the United States, with whom we learn is as important as what we learn, then this is a book for you. Martin understands that the choices White families make about how and with whom their children live and learn is a way to share in the doing of justice across racial divides. Honest, human, real, and necessary, *Learning in Public* is a triumph." —Noliwe Rooks, author of *Cutting School*

"There is so much love in these pages. Martin's capacity to empathize with and challenge White parents' notions of what is best for our children and our communities is what makes this book so compelling and necessary right now. She's a master at calling out our bullshit while still calling us together." —Whitney Kimball Coe, vice president of the Center for Rural Strategies

"I'm so grateful to Courtney Martin for writing *Learning in Public*, for so many reasons. For one, I now have *the* book to hand to my White parent friends when they start talking about what school they're going to choose for their kids. Two, Martin shows White people in particular how to walk the walk *and* talk the talk—and how neither process is easy, orderly, or what we expect, and hope, it will be. Three, she reminds us that being a 'good parent' and a 'good citizen' isn't about knowing all the answers or being the smartest one in the room. It's about being willing to *not know.* To be curious, to listen, to try, to fail, and to accept that morality is messy. With *Learning in Public*, Martin offers the kind of radically vulnerable intelligence that we can all use much more of." —Kate Schatz, author of *Rad American Women A–Z* and *Rad Women Worldwide*

LEARNING IN PUBLIC

*Lessons for a Racially Divided America
from My Daughter's School*

COURTNEY E. MARTIN

BACK BAY BOOKS
Little, Brown and Company
New York Boston London

Back Bay Books / Little, Brown and Company
Hachette Book Group
1290 Avenue of the Americas, New York, NY 10104
littlebrown.com

Originally published in hardcover by Little, Brown and Company, August 2021
First Back Bay paperback edition, August 2022

Back Bay Books is an imprint of Little, Brown and Company, a division of Hachette Book Group, Inc. The Back Bay Books name and logo are trademarks of Hachette Book Group, Inc.

The publisher is not responsible for websites (or their content) that are not owned by the publisher.

The Hachette Speakers Bureau provides a wide range of authors for speaking events. To find out more, go to hachettespeakersbureau.com or call (866) 376-6591.

1914 Emerson Elementary School class portrait (page 99) courtesy of Oakland Public Library, Oakland History Room
1956 Emerson Elementary School class portrait (page 100) courtesy of Eileen Suzio

ISBN 9780316428262 (hc) / 9780316428279 (pb)
LCCN 2021931461

Printing 1, 2022

LSC-C

Printed in the United States of America

For Maya, who is one of my greatest teachers already.

*And for every kid who isn't her. Who deserves
just as much.*

It is not a racial problem. It's a problem of whether or not you're willing to look at your life and be responsible for it, and then begin to change it.

That great western house I come from is one house, and I am one of the children of that house. Simply, I am the most despised child of that house. And it is because the American people are unable to face the fact that I am flesh of their flesh, bone of their bone, created by them. My blood, my father's blood, is in that soil.

—James Baldwin, *I Am Not Your Negro*

How exactly do you cure bad blood?

—Yaa Gyasi, "1932"

CONTENTS

PREFACE

W HEN I WAS A little girl, I went around and asked my neighbors for donations for the homeless. They handed me their loose change, and I listened as the metal hit the glass bottom of the jar satisfyingly.

I didn't actually know anyone who was experiencing homelessness. Or even anybody who was serving those who were. Where I live now, in Oakland, people who are unhoused are everywhere—under the highway a block away and even closer, under the stoop at the Glorious Kingdom Primitive Baptist Church across the street from our house. Once even in our black cherry Prius in our driveway, as happened when my husband, John, left it unlocked overnight.

John found an elderly Black man sleeping in the passenger seat, my daughter's favorite book on CD—*Man on the Moon*—in his hand. John tried to wake him gently and asked him to get out. The guy looked up, clearly disoriented, and said, "Ah, sorry, man. Is this mine or yours?"

"Ours," John said. "It's ours, man."

Even at seven and eight and nine, I was confused about why some things were ours—my family's, my friend's, my neighborhood's—and some weren't. Even in that far less unequal time, there were dramatic differences between what I'd heard called the haves and the have-nots. I was a have. I was born into a "have family"—not a trust-fund family, but a have family nonetheless.

I had a hunch that being a have had something to do with being White. And no one made much of an effort to explain it to me. We weren't supposed to notice race—not others' race, for sure, but not even our own. That would be racist.

I look back at that little White girl—frizzy hair, pile of friendship bracelets on her wrist, magenta high-top Chucks on her feet—and I feel love and outrage. She was overcoming her shyness, circling the block in a misguided attempt at redistribution. From whom and to whom, she wasn't exactly sure. But she sensed something.

She needed truth. But she got loose change.

Unsure of what to do with the money, racked by guilt that she had asked for it but had no idea where to take it, she buried that jar of change in the dirt near her playhouse in the backyard.

This book is about the jar of good intentions that so many of us carry around these days. We set it on our bookshelves next to our copies of Ta-Nehisi Coates and Isabel Wilkerson. We put it by our tasteful succulent gardens next to our BLACK LIVES MATTER signs or on our nightstands. We stare at the ceiling in the dark, genuinely wondering why it feels so hard to be on the right side of history.

I left that sweet neighborhood in Colorado Springs when I was eighteen and went to Barnard College, in New York City. In new forms, I did lots of circling the block. I went to protest marches. I read slam poetry at the Nuyorican Poets Cafe. I made a short film about gentrification in Harlem. I joined the campus hip-hop club. I studied abroad in South Africa and lived in a township with a Black family. I graduated and moved to Brooklyn, as one does, and lived there for a decade. I wrote a book about activism.

The White moral life remained elusive. I was almost getting used to the idea that I would never have it, that it was a definitional impossibility. To have White skin and economic security in America was to be tangled up in the sin of what historian Aristotle Kallis calls the "hierarchy of human life."[1]

And then I became a mother.

And it was as if the universe dared me both to give up altogether on this quest for the White moral life, which felt like frivolous intellectual bullshit in the face of my kid's real needs, *and* simultaneously to double down. The gift of adulthood is not a mortgage, I realized, but the freedom to pursue a moral life on your own terms, even if you are White, especially if you are White, and to let your children witness you trying.

This is the story of that trying.

A NOTE ON THE MAKING OF THIS BOOK

I HAVE AGONIZED OVER the ethics of telling this particular story at this particular time.

Journalists claim that they are objective, that once you interview a person, you have every right to use anything they've said. That's obviously bullshit.

Memoirists claim that they are subjective, that once you've witnessed or experienced something, you have every right to tell it your way. That's obviously bullshit.

So here I am, somewhere in between, trying not to give you, my reader, or the people who got entangled in my decisions any bullshit.

I changed the names of all the kids except my own, and most adults, too. (Maya and Stella are already in the public record because the poor fools have a writer for a mom; don't worry, I'm saving up for lots of therapy.) I kept the names of people who are public figures.

I showed sections of this manuscript to many of those described in these pages, which wasn't always easy. I tried to write no angels or villains, which wasn't always easy. I believe that our kids will do better when we, grown-ups, do the hard stuff of seeing one another's humanity, even when we passionately disagree, and telling the truth about our own confusion and failures within education.

I've capitalized ethnic designations throughout the manuscript, including White. I'm following the lead of sociologist Eve L. Ewing, who writes that by not capitalizing White, we conspire with the myth that White people are "normal, neutral, or without any race at all, while the rest of us are saddled with this unpleasant business of being racialized."[1]

This book is very much about racializing White people, myself included. I attempt to write with a "white double-consciousness," as the philosopher Linda Martín Alcoff puts it, which is to say, I attempt to see myself "through both the dominant and nondominant lens, and recognize the latter as a critical corrective truth."[2]

I got feedback from many friends, among whom are brilliant anti-racist organizers, professional editors, and experts in education. I learned so much from them. You will see footnotes throughout the book from one critical friend in particular: Dr. Dena Simmons. Dena, a Black woman, and I met a decade ago when I was reporting my book *Do It Anyway: The New Generation of Activists,* and have since developed a rich friendship. She supports schools, districts, and other organizations at the intersection of social and emotional health, racial justice, and healing with her organization, LiberatED. By including her feedback here, I'm essentially "showing my work" so you can learn from my mistakes and shortcomings. This thing, after all, is called *Learning in Public.*

I believe that writers, especially White and/or privileged writers, need to reach for more honest ways to think about our own power when crafting stories and about our own access to those who decide what stories get told. It is my experience that much of what we claim is journalistic convention is a way of skirting our own discomfort with hard conversations and our accountability to the people we write about.

Rabbi Abraham Joshua Heschel writes: "It is in deeds that man [person] becomes aware of what his life really is, of his power to harm and to hurt, to wreck and to ruin; of his ability to derive joy and to bestow it upon others; to relieve and to increase his own and other people's tensions.... What he may not dare to think, he often utters in deeds. The heart is revealed in the deeds."[3]

The process behind the making of this book, not just the thing itself, is my deed. I hope it reveals my heart.

PART I
CHOOSING

The quality of light by which we scrutinize our lives has direct bearing upon the product which we live, and upon the changes which we hope to bring about through those lives.

—Audre Lorde, "Poetry Is Not a Luxury"

1

LIKE MANY NEW PARENTS, I took wandering walks in our neighborhood when Maya, my first of two daughters, was a baby. I would listen to podcasts—So. Many. Podcasts.—and think about how my life had been obliterated, in both good ways and bad. In retrospect, I think I had postpartum anxiety—vigilance about her health that left me exhausted and unrecognizable to myself. I just couldn't turn my physiological volume down. The walks didn't solve the problem, but they helped. I walked by our neighborhood public school over and over again.

I first noticed the giant vine with sweet purple flowers covering the tall wrought-iron fence. It cascaded down in a pleasing V-shape, shielding the kids playing inside from view. But if I walked a little farther, I could see the blacktop, where mostly Black and Brown kids were running, jumping, screaming, doing what kids do when they are finally released from stuffy classrooms that contain their days. I would pull out an earbud so I could listen to the sound of their joy.

As the months wore on, I noticed more about the school. There were beautiful murals everywhere, a couple of playgrounds, a huge redwood in one corner of the campus. There was a neglected Little Free Library, often stuffed with books that kids would never pick up—Preston Bailey's *Design for Entertaining* and *Modern Architecture: A Critical History* by Kenneth Frampton.

There were also, I noticed, a few White kids running, jumping, screaming, doing what kids do. Not many, but a few.

I was genuinely confused. Temescal, the neighborhood where I moved with my husband, John, when I was pregnant, was multiracial. My daily strolls left the impression that there were plenty of multigenerational Black families in the neighborhood but also lots of White newcomers, too. Where did most of the White children go to school?

In Colorado Springs, Colorado, in the 1980s, I went to my neighborhood school. Learn where you're planted. No big fuss. I'd never heard the phrase *school choice*.

I'd come to find out that learning where you're planted was never as innocent as it seemed and also was from an era long gone. Our neighborhood school with that towering redwood and the murals and the beautiful children shouting—Emerson Elementary—was "failing," according to all the official weights and measures. Wondering where the White kids were on that playground was the start of a journey of a thousand moral miles.

2

L̲IKE A GOOD MILLENNIAL parent, I turn to the Internet. On GreatSchools
.org, the go-to source for school rankings particularly among White
affluent parents, Emerson gets a 1 out of 10. Maybe that's why there
aren't many White kids on the playground. The rating, it turns out, is
mostly based on standardized test scores.

A Scantron form filled with a seemingly infinite number of tiny bubbles
from my own school days flashes through my head. I was mediocre at
math. I scored well in English, but my dominant experience of those
tests was thinking up the thirteen ways one could make an argument for
how each answer could be the right one.

The text below Emerson's ranking reads: "This school is rated below
average in school quality compared to other schools in California.
Students here perform below average on state tests, are making below
average year-over-year academic improvement, and this school has below
average results in how well it's serving disadvantaged students."

If I were a different kind of person, I probably would have looked
this information up before we moved into our house. But I hadn't.
When we moved cross-country from Brooklyn to Oakland, I was a
couple of months pregnant, and all I could think about was finding an
obstetrician.

When John got what appeared to be his dream job in San Francisco,
I agreed to move, but only on the condition that we land in Oakland,
which reminded me of my beloved Brooklyn (where I'd lived for over
a decade after college). San Francisco always struck me as too White

and too self-satisfied. The East Bay has more of a ragtag feel that I liked—mom-and-pop bookstores and Rastafarian vegan eateries and hipster coffee shops. What sealed the deal was getting wind of an opening in a cohousing community in Temescal, a neighborhood we'd both loved after visiting frequently over the years. I'd always been intrigued by intentional living, and this was our chance to try it. We'd been so in awe of our luck at landing a space in a cohousing community and so freaked out by buying a home for almost $500,000 that we didn't think about much else.

But here I am, four years later and all that mortgage paperwork behind me, with a new test: Getting my kid into the "right" school. She also has a two-year-old little sister, Stella, which means that getting Maya into the "right" school gets Stella into the "right" school; twice the pressure.

I return to that little phrase in Emerson's ranking—"compared to other schools in California"—and decide to quickly look up the other two schools that I've heard neighbors and friends talk about. First, Chabot Elementary, a happy green circle with a 9 out of 10 inside. Second, Peralta Elementary: same, same. I guess this means Chabot and Peralta kids don't struggle in the face of those damn Scantron forms (do kids even still take those tests?). What is happening at these two schools that isn't happening at Emerson? And does it matter if my kid doesn't get whatever that magical thing is?

I decide I'm not going to tell John about any of this. At least not yet. He's all gut when it comes to big decisions like these. He'd see that "1" and run in the other direction, as I'm sure do most White parents in our neighborhood. He might even say, "So, which is the school with the highest ranking, and how do we get her in?" Which, again, is a logical, and I'm sure common, way to approach this whole thing.

But it's not my way. I have a gut of my own, and it's telling me that this is one of the most important decisions we're going to make, not just as parents but as citizens.

3

L IKE MANY CITIES THAT have become hip, Oakland is attractive for the very reasons it is also plagued by inequity and hypocrisy, and the resentment born from both.

It has cultural cachet via its rich history (birthplace of the Black Panthers and Bruce Lee) and its contemporary treasures—great, relatively affordable food (including BBQ, Burmese, and Ethiopian), fantastic music venues, gorgeous beaches and hikes within a short distance of the city center, and so much else.

It's the second most racially diverse city in the nation (nearby Stockton is the first).[1] According to the Census Bureau, there are over 400,000 people living in Oakland, and 35.5 percent of them are White, 27 percent are Latinx, 23.8 percent are Black, and 15.5 percent are Asian. The median household income, despite being in proximity to all the tech money of San Francisco and Silicon Valley, is just $73,692, and 16.7 percent of people are living in poverty.[2]

Oakland is also known for being profoundly progressive. In Alameda County, only 10 percent of the population identifies as Republican, so pro-choice bumper stickers and billboards for weed-delivery services abound, and Pride marches are packed. There's a general consensus, so widely held that it's rarely articulated explicitly, that its residents are anti-Trump, anti-yuppie, and anti-racist.

Oakland, like so many cities, is also deeply segregated—not by accident, but by design.

The World War II era defined Oakland's contemporary neighborhoods in many ways. A predominantly White region became far less so during the boom times of war, when the population as a whole increased—almost 100,000 new people arrived between 1940 and 1945, many of them from the South—and the Black population went from 8,462 to 21,770.[3] All these new Oaklanders had to live somewhere, of course. Enter the Federal Housing Administration.

The federal government built more than thirty thousand public housing units in the East Bay. Black families were steered toward poorly constructed housing near the shipyards where they worked, near railroad lines, or in the flatlands. White families were steered toward new suburbs and farther inland to the hills, where the houses were sturdier. Richard Rothstein, author of *The Color of Law,* writes: "Racially explicit government policies to segregate our metropolitan areas are not vestiges, were neither subtle nor intangible, and were sufficiently controlling to construct the *de jure* segregation that is now with us in neighborhoods and hence in schools."[4]

The flatlands and the hills are real places but also mythic constructs in the Oaklander's imagination. The hills are quiet and full of money; spacious homes built vertically clutch the earth that reaches for the sky, with views of the Pacific and industrial Oakland far below; you need a car to get down and around. The flatlands are, well, flat as hell. You can ride your bike block after block, find vibrant murals alongside abandoned grocery carts filled with what look like all of someone's worldly possessions, grab an IT'S-IT ice-cream sandwich at the corner store, and have a sweet chat with the guy behind the counter. The homes, at least the original homes, are pretty small. It's never quiet. But the sun almost always shines.

Almost every American city has hills and flatlands—the part of the city where the White and upwardly mobile folks go, and the part where the Black and economically marginalized stay. We find ourselves on one of these dividing lines, not by accident or desire, but by design. Our cities were planned this way. Which means our schools are planned this way. As the educational historian Jack Schneider writes, "Buying a home means buying a school."[5]

Between 1961 and 1966, Oakland lost 10,000 manufacturing jobs, and people fled.[6] The city's overall population fell by about 23,000 between 1950 and 1970; the majority that left were White.[7] A group called the Oakland Redevelopment Agency spearheaded new construction in the middle of historic, and almost entirely Black, West Oakland, as well as the expansion of Interstate 880, which cut through the neighborhood. Between 1960 and 1966, more than 7,000 housing units in Oakland were destroyed, and almost 5,100 of them were located in West Oakland. Many of those displaced moved to East Oakland.

Amid this destruction and the outrage that followed, together with the larger fomenting of the civil rights movement, the Black Panther Party was born. It was founded in 1966 by Huey Newton and Bobby Seale, both students at Merritt Community College. Newton and Seale were intellectually radicalized by their involvement in the Afro-American Association and other groups on campus and by reading the words of Malcolm X.[8]

But it was their paid jobs running youth service programs at the North Oakland Neighborhood Anti-Poverty Center that first planted the seed that caring for kids, what they would come to call "survival programs," could and must also be part of the revolution.

Their famous free-breakfast program, established in 1969 at St. Augustine's Episcopal Church in West Oakland, quickly grew. Eventually Black Panthers were feeding tens of thousands of kids in the U.S.—from Des Moines to Detroit—before they went to school every morning. It wasn't just about meeting a fundamental need; it was also about shining a light on how inadequate the government efforts were to show up for hungry children—the most innocent of America's victims.[9] Put to shame by the Panthers, the federal government eventually committed to feeding kids breakfast at schools with high poverty levels. A direct line can be drawn between Newton and Seale's vision in 1966 and the little carton of milk that sits in front of kids every morning in Title I public schools today all over the country.

Black Oakland wasn't the only community being radicalized. In the Fruitvale neighborhood, Latinx folks were organizing, pushing back against police violence and army recruitment, and creating community clinics and other programs to weather increasing poverty. The Brown Berets, as some activists were known, collaborated with the Black Panther Party on bringing free breakfast to their kids.

In the 1970s, '80s, and '90s, the city hemorrhaged jobs—particularly in manufacturing, transportation, and utilities—as was the case in so many industrial cities.

More White families left (90,000 between 1970 and 1990), and now quite a few Black ones have, too. Downtown Oakland was gutted—department stores disappeared and storefronts stood vacant for months. There was a sense that the radical sparkle of the late 1960s, the cohesiveness of so many communities, was fading. Oaklanders were strained by the systematic disinvestment in the city—again, not a naturally occurring phenomenon but a choice on the part of policy makers from the federal level on down.

Where there is economic deprivation, there is collective vulnerability and precarity. Oakland was brutalized by gang-controlled drug operations and violence, starting in the 1970s. By the end of that decade, Oakland's per capita murder rate was twice that of New York City.

But in the 1990s, crime began to decline steadily. After three decades of the city's population dwindling, Oakland got bigger again—going from about 339,000 in 1980 to over 430,000 in 2010.[10] The Latinx population surged, and recent immigrants from a wide range of countries showed up. Oakland Chinatown, which had also been decimated by the creation of Interstate 880 and years of disinvestment, started to revive.

The East Bay—like so many cities across the U.S.—grew attractive to White and/or privileged folks who might have passed it over in earlier decades. There was a resurgence of interest in living in cities, particularly by those whom the economist Richard Florida dubbed "the creative class"—designers, artists, writers, photographers, architects, and the like—who clustered in urban centers once eschewed by their parents.[11] They valued walkability, not white picket fences.

Today in Oakland, the creative class is everywhere—people who sometimes seem to have no job at all other than hanging out at coffee shops all day, taking conference calls in the back garden, and drinking espresso. But it also has a tech layer—the dot-com boom led to an abundance of jobs for recent college grads. Google, Facebook, and other tech behemoths started chartering buses back and forth to Silicon Valley. Before long, downtown Oakland was experiencing its own little tech building boom.

When our cohousing community was founded in 2000, the land and the buildings on it (which at the time were pretty decrepit but would eventually constitute *five units* of varying size and value, plus a bunch of shared amenities) went for an asking price of $110,000. When we moved in, in 2013, we were lucky to get our 1,300-square-foot unit for just under $500,000. Today, it is valued closer to $1 million.

Neighbors gossip about all the underwhelming homes that sell for close to or even over $1 million, all cash. Even my friends who are lawyers and doctors talk about never being able to compete in a housing market where a cash offer or an offer over asking price has become a prerequisite. The tech money feels like a noxious, odorless gas, seeping into every major financial decision in the Bay Area, even for those who have nothing to do with the companies directly.

Of course White middle-class precarity is nothing compared to experiencing poverty. In Oakland, only 41 percent of residents own a home, rent has skyrocketed (a two-bedroom will run, on average, nearly $4,000 a month),[12] and there is an infamous dearth of affordable housing units (even as luxury condos are being built at an unprecedented rate, high, high into the sky).[13] True instability—the I-can't-make-my-rent-and-buy-food kind, the I'm-one-car-accident-away-from-losing-my-home kind—is a thought experiment for the vast majority of White Oakland, not a lived or even an adjacent experience.

We, White progressives, *love* Black Oakland; we just don't actually know anyone who is Black who is from Oakland. We move here, at least in part, for the music, the radical politics, and the laid-back vibe, but we are estranged from the actual humans who made it what it is. The multigenerational Oakland families that arrived in the 1940s and were pointed toward West Oakland by the federal government? The silver-haired Black Panther grandmamas who saw the Victorians around them go from being unaffordable at $25,000 in 2000 to positively alien at over $1 million cash in 2020?

We don't know them.

Sure, we have Black friends, but they tend to be the Black upper middle class—the software engineer who rides beside us on the bus to Palo Alto, the woman who went to our same college, the nonprofit director whose radical rhetoric we cheer on at an otherwise predominantly White polite dinner party.

We've moved here for the progressive cred that proximity to a "real" American city offers, but we don't know the names of Black families who lived in Oakland before it was hip. We don't know the taste of their food or their sense of humor. Their particular pains or dreams.

4

I HAVE ADOPTED A sort of parasitic approach to parenting. I befriend maximizers (people who tend to weigh every single option before making a decision), and then I watch what they do: What kind of car seats do they purchase? At what age do their kids make their first visit to the dentist? What kinds of rules do they have for screen time? A satisficer to the core (meaning I am typically satisfied with a little research and a "good enough" choice), I watch and then copy the more diligent parents (usually mothers) around me. It leaves me slightly uninformed on a range of parenting topics, but it saves a lot of time and energy. At first glance this seems like the perfect hack for choosing a school, too.

Before Maya was potty trained, I'd gotten the message that there were two schools I was supposed to want my children to go to: Peralta or Chabot. The bizarre, but I think fairly common, thing is that I don't even remember a moment when I learned that this was what White and privileged parents did in Oakland. It was as if the knowledge wafted into my brain during breezy playdates or seeped into my bloodstream via the breakdown of the BPA-free plastic plates in my house. The directive was—as it is with hegemony—so powerful, I don't even remember when it entered my consciousness.

Studies show that most parents look to their friends when trying to make educational choices for their kids—what psychology and marketing professor Robert Cialdini coined "social proof."[14] We want to know what those around us, those who look and shop and talk like we do, think is the safe thing to do. Especially when it comes to our kids.

The majority of my White friends seem to be proceeding as if "How do we get our kids into Peralta or Chabot?" is the right question to be asking. There are a few other schools that White parents reference as "up-and-coming" or "hidden gems": Kaiser, Glenview, and Sequoia. A few are touring Park Day, the neighborhood private school, and various charter schools.

Even the friends who most often proclaim to be committed to racial justice—the kinds of people who direct nonprofit organizations or run political campaigns for progressive candidates—don't seem to be considering Emerson.

I'm told that I should register our interest in Peralta or Chabot with the Oakland Unified School District (OUSD) enrollment office before the deadline for applications—that this is what is called "school choice" (such an innocent sounding phrase, isn't it?). We get to choose up to four schools. We should definitely *not* put Emerson, our zoned school, on that list, I am warned, because then we will definitely get it. (Our feelings about Emerson are irrelevant; this is now a game that must be won.)

We might get it anyway. Even if we don't put it on our list. It's not time to freak the fuck out, I am reassured by parents who have already been through this complex dance of avoidance (and quite likely freaked the fuck out). It is time to start buying doughnuts. Lots and lots of doughnuts. It makes logical sense that the enrollment office will assign Emerson to us at first, just to see if our will is weak; it's under-enrolled, and everyone wants to get into the other two schools that we chose (the demand rate for Peralta is 149 percent and for Chabot, 205 percent).

We will show them that our will is not weak. We will show them through emails and phone calls and in-person visits to the enrollment office, said doughnuts in cheerful pink boxes in hand. We will exhaust them with our soft power. We will, if necessary, come up with convoluted rationales for why Emerson is not a "good fit" for our child, who is gifted, highly sensitive, a Scorpio, the big sister of someone who is these things, allergic to things, scared of things, and did I mention highly sensitive? The rationales can and will become very creative—like a Mad Lib of terrifically fragile White children.

None of this, mind you, is formally written anywhere. The official OUSD website takes the party line: Enroll your student in "4 easy steps!" The steps are: Explore, Apply, Confirm, and Register. When I hit on the FAQ under Apply, I am transported to a Google doc with the revealing name "Public Facing—OUSD Enrollment FAQs" (where is the "private facing" one, and what does it say?). The answers are short, plucky, clearly designed to ward off the doughnuts and the soft-power approach at any and every turn. Under "How can I learn more about public schools in Oakland?" there are two disingenuous recommendations: (1) "Look for schools based on program offering or by location," and (2) "Contact schools of interest to find out the best times to visit and learn more."

I am reading a handbook written in the invisible ink of obfuscation and maneuvering so that I might get my already deeply advantaged White kid into the best possible school, while kids with less White, less rich, less available parents are not. (White people believe passionately, and erroneously, that we are the busiest humans on Planet Earth.) These less resourced parents are also talking to their friends and neighbors and doing whatever they can to get their kid a shot at a great education, but their handbook says nothing about doughnuts or highly sensitive children.

Elite parenting is a process of piecing together the unwritten rules about how to advance your child through a broken system. The system itself is rarely considered. School choice becomes a game of telephone, where you pass along the questions you are supposed to be asking and the answers you are supposed to be satisfied by. It's a strategic scramble, not a moral investigation.

5

Thirteen Ways of Asking the School Question
(after Wallace Stevens's "Thirteen Ways of Looking at a Blackbird")

Where do we want to send our kid to school?

How does that choice align with or depart from our values?

Does that even matter? (I mean, does integration *actually* work?)

What is a school?

What is education for?

What are we afraid of?

Who are we—as parents, as (White) people—and what does this
  choice say about that?

(To us? To everyone else? To Maya?)

Where will Maya learn and feel loved?

Where do Oakland kids learn and feel loved?

6

I'M FILTHY WITH FRIENDS and surrounded by caring neighbors. I have ten women whom I can text right now to ask which diaper cream they think actually works (Weleda) or whether earthquake insurance is worth it (nah). So far, I haven't found one White friend who is seriously considering our neighborhood public school.

Maybe the repulsion to Emerson is the result of living in the shadow of Silicon Valley and the comparison it invites. Even if we're economically secure by any rational calculation, even if we're rich, for that matter, we have a way of feeling always in danger of becoming noncompetitive. What if we are unable to buy a house or get our precious children the most humanizing, beautiful educational experience possible? What if we are actually ordinary or, worse, helpless? Or as philosopher Alain de Botton writes in *Status Anxiety*, "Amid such uncertainty, we typically turn to the wider world to settle the question of our significance."[15]

The wider world, for White and/or privileged Oakland, is economically freakish. While the average worker in the city makes a bit over $40,000, the average Facebook employee makes well over $200,000 a year, with a luxurious suite of benefits (at least luxurious in a country that has no federal paid family leave). When you sit in birth class beside someone who is not only getting paid six times what you are but will enjoy six full months off work, paid, while you have no paid leave at all, it's hard not to feel envious and small.

My friends with little kids are too stressed and too wrapped up in their own feelings to entertain any but the most strategic questions. But whenever I bring up school choice and racial equity with White parents who have older kids, a resigned malaise settles on their faces, and they almost always sigh audibly. These parents of pimply, emotionally manipulative teenagers appear to see me, the parent of ratty-haired, emotionally raw toddlers, as well intentioned but also in need of humbling. Just keep your kids off drugs, they seem to be saying with their eyes. That's enough work for one parenting lifetime.

At a potluck dinner, I bring up with a Black friend my conflict over enrolling Maya at Emerson. I've been listening to *This American Life* episodes on the anniversary of *Brown vs. Board of Education* by the brilliant journalist Nikole Hannah-Jones. I've been thinking about integration. And my friend says, "Don't send your kid to a shitty school on my account!"

The record scratches in my brain. I want to ask her a million questions, but this is not the time for me to do my usual annoying thing of being way too serious at a really fun party. My friend's words echo in my head for weeks afterward—unprocessed, so powerful.

I flash back to anxious preschool tours. I can't help but wonder: Are all those White parents going on all those tours actually part of the problem? Is the real issue not that parents of color should be on the tours but that school tours shouldn't be a thing at all? Are these anxious White and Asian-American parents the ones who are wrong, while everyone else is just trying to live a decent life?

Every person has to come to terms with—even if just for themselves—the gap between what they believe and how they live their lives. And if you happen to be a parent, the gap can feel particularly wide and meaningful, the rationalizations even more garbled and urgent. Ultimately you're not answering to just your own conscience but to your children, too. They will want to know—they might already want to know—why you did what you did. Why send them to this school? Why make the sometimes soul-crushing effort to get them into clean clothes and in these particular pews on a Sunday morning? Why live in this neighborhood? Why befriend these people but not those? Why care so deeply about certain rules and let other things go? Kids ultimately care, not just about how you shape them but also how your shaping of them shapes the world.

I suspect that White economically privileged and well-intentioned people have shirked our moral responsibility to the common good for decades under the cover of responsible parenting. In a time of eroding public institutions and soaring economic inequality, we have normalized private solutions whereby our children won't have to endure the most broken American systems—public education, health care, the courts. By doing so, we've inadvertently created one of the country's biggest problems: increasing and unconscionable inequity. We act mystified by this inequity, all the while propping it up with our choices.

Or as the poet and essayist Hanif Abdurraqib, puts it, "Not everything is Sisyphean. No one ever wants to imagine themselves as the boulder."[16]

7

MEET JOHN, MY HUSBAND, Maya's father. He's the handsome guy sitting on that Eames chair in the corner, with beautiful thick hair that he shampoos expensively because his mom never let him use her fancy stuff as a kid, light brown eyes you can get lost in, dark eyebrows, and a back a little lopsided because his parents lost track of his scoliosis.

When we got engaged, we decided that we each would get to pick three things that we wanted at some point in our marriage. His: a Dyson vacuum; a weekend convertible car; and a train caboose. (Like a real train caboose, yes, to make a clubhouse "for the kids"; he searches for them on Craigslist and eBay almost every night.) Mine, thanks for asking: one of those floor-to-ceiling bookshelves with a ladder; a claw-foot bathtub; and a week alone by myself every year. So far, he's got the vacuum, and I've got the bookshelf (with no ladder), so we're getting there after nine years, slowly but surely.

At this very moment, John is huddled over his laptop, catching up on work after the girls have finally gone to bed. He's trained as an architect but has spent most of his career advocating for architecture and design for the public good instead of for the small sliver of people who can afford it. He's run nonprofits, as he does now, persuaded wealthy people to be more philanthropic, written books, and challenged the nearly all-White boards of organizations that uphold architecture's classist, racist, sexist roots.

But honestly, he's not much help with this school thing. He's not a boulder, exactly, because he's not blocking the way. And for this I am very grateful. I can imagine how hard it would be to persuade a fearful partner that considering a "failing" school was justifiable.

But he's not pushing anything up a hill with me either. He's not making spreadsheets or perusing GreatSchools.org. He's not waking up in the middle of the night, flooded with worry that we've missed all the tours. His running buddies aren't sweating it out while talking about school admissions strategies.

He's the kind of guy who, if he's into something, he's *really* into it, like all-out obsession (Eames furniture, classic cars, and his daughters—writ large—fall into this category), and if he's not, he's 100 percent not (this category features some of my own obsessions, like long, sad movies, sociology, and dance parties).

But I think his lack of attention to our family's school choice is about more than his all-in or all-out personality. I think it's also due to his class background and educational history. John started working at the age of ten so that he could escape his very full house (he is one of six kids, plus Grandpa lived with them for years). There was a lot of love but also a lot of noise. And Johnny, as they called him with their heavy Wisconsin accents, didn't like noise. He was sensitive and precise and a highly strategic kid, a kid who put his Legos in his mom's saucepans, and then slept with them in his tiny twin bed so no one would mess with them.

After caddying for three years at a country club, he turned to flipping butter burgers for a while at a joint owned by one of the wealthiest couples in the suburbs where his family lived. Shining golf balls and slinging burgers, thus began his shrewd, almost anthropological journey in understanding how rich people behave. He became an Honor Caddy in record time because he endeared himself to one of the rich guys, whom he asked for rides to the golf course; that way he could bypass the line of his bored teen peers waiting on the picnic table to be the next to caddy. He just smugly strolled onto the first tee with the rich guy who gave him a ride.

John went to mostly White Catholic schools, where he never felt smart enough or athletic enough. He managed the basketball team, something his own father had also done when he was young, earning his dad a full ride through college. Freshman year, the mostly Black team adored and made fun of John in equal measure. They once took him to the clothing store in downtown Milwaukee where they all shopped—it was called Johnnie Walker's—and dressed him up in Karl Kani jeans and Cross Colours T-shirts. They all laughed together as he emerged from the dressing room and spun around. Or at least that's how he remembers it.

He got into the University of Minnesota on a probationary basis. His high school grades were mostly Cs. And then he discovered this thing called architecture, and for the first time ever, his internal world mirrored the external world. The way his mind worked, which he'd never before even known was a recognized type of intelligence, suddenly had a home, a building on a college campus where he could carve out his own future for the very first time. He graduated summa cum laude, at the top of his class, and was the commencement speaker.

In other words, John has had a perfect storm of experiences that make choosing a school for his daughter a frightening prospect. He never wants her to feel unseen like he did. He never wants her to feel dumb like he did. Basically, he never wants her to suffer.

I've done some really absurd things in the spirit of preventing my kids' "suffering"—like so many red-eye flights (less time away) and nursing them both with a sort of religious fervor. I was the one who had to sit on the porch and drink an IPA while John listened to Maya cry when we finally decided to sleep-train her.

Which is all to say, I get where he's coming from deep in my bones (or uterus or something) *and* I still don't want to make this decision from a place of fear. I tell him this, collapsed into the couch across from him, huddled over my laptop, reading Nikole Hannah-Jones's moving essay in the *New York Times* about choosing where to send her daughter to school.

"Babe, I don't want to make this decision from a place of fear," I say.

"Yeah, I get that," John says genuinely but absentmindedly. He doesn't look up.

Nikole Hannah-Jones, the nation's most read and most respected journalist on education, struggled with the question of where to send her Black daughter to school and writes about it with a powerful blend of personal narrative and historical analysis. Maya was just three years old when the piece in the *New York Times* came out. When I first read it, it felt like an intellectual pleasure, a sort of abstract provocation. Now, two years later, I hang on every word.

Even Hannah-Jones struggled. She writes: "I'd be lying if I said I didn't feel pulled in the way other parents with options feel pulled. I had moments when I couldn't ignore the nagging fear that in my quest for fairness, I was being unfair to my own daughter. I worried—I worry still—about whether I made the right decision for our little girl. But I knew I made the just one."[17]

I look over at John, tapping away at his keyboard. He has a Jesuit heart—a heart that rebelled against the trappings and hypocrisy of the Catholic Church but was nevertheless shaped by the deeper waters. No matter that the jocks and the geniuses got all the attention; John still absorbed the message that good people are of service to larger goals, not just to their own betterment. He hammered away on Habitat for Humanity houses, paid off friends' debt in secret, and never met a quiet child he didn't fall a little in love with.

But I'm guessing school choice is too fraught for him; it's too painful to revisit his own school days or imagine Maya experiencing anything like them.

"Did you know school integration hit its peak in 1988? That's when you and I were in, what, second grade or something?" I ask.

"Crazy," he responds.

"It says here that 'the difference in Black and White reading scores fell to half what it was in 1971. As schools have since resegregated, the test-score gap has only grown.' And listen to this: 'The improvements for Black children did not come at the cost of White children. As Black test scores rose, so did White ones.'"

Nothing.

"Babe, isn't that interesting?" I prompt.

"Sorry, can you say it again?" he asks, finally looking up from his screen. I reread the words.

His bottom lip protrudes, and he nods his head, "Wow, that *is* interesting."

"And now Black children are more segregated than they've been in half a century," I go on.

"Jesus. That's crazy," he says. Then, after a few moments, he adds, "I've told you how badly I did on tests, right?"

"I think so."

"Like pathetically bad. I got a 20 on my ACT, three times in a row. That was out of 36 at the time."

"Damn."

"I hope Maya isn't as bad at taking tests as I was. I mean for her sake. I don't care if she doesn't score well, but I don't want her to feel bad about it," he says.

There it is—the no-suffering instinct.

"We can explain that we don't care, that it's not one of our family's values. We can reassure her," I reassure him.

"Yeah, that's a good idea."

"So what are you thinking on the school stuff?" I ask.

"Honestly, I'm not thinking about it that much," he admits. "It seems like you are."

"Yeah, I'm thinking about it a lot. Like a lot, a lot," I say.

He smiles at me and there's a whole paragraph in that smile. Something like: *I love you, you big nerd, but don't make yourself crazy with this. And yes, you can take the lead. I'll follow you. I trust you. I'll surrender. But don't let our baby get hurt. And don't make me feel patronized about this shit. And did I mention I love you, you big nerd?*

He turns back to his work. I turn back to my article. Hannah-Jones: "True integration, true equality, requires a surrendering of advantage, and when it comes to our own children, that can feel almost unnatural."

8

I look at Berkeley Parents Network—a place where you can find out all you'd ever want to know about how terrified White parents feel about schools but also find a *New Yorker* contributor to teach your kid about Greek philosophy or where to order Gripe Water from Canada (real examples).

Emerson Elementary has a long list of entries dating back to 2004—most from neighborhood parents with incoming kindergarteners who are inquiring about people's experiences. They're not exactly glowing. Some are careful—talking about how much potential the school has, how beautiful the garden is, how "vital" the neighborhood is.

Others are unabashedly racist: "I'll be honest and say that the kids are rough, to say the least. I'm not in this situation, but it seems that the other parents may keep their kids out of Emerson to protect them—and I'm not saying that to be snotty. You truly would not want your child [your White child] to be exposed to a lot of the behavior that I see as they [other people's Black children] walk through the neighborhood after school."

There was an effort circa 2006 to get a bunch of parents in the neighborhood to band together and send their kids to Emerson. The Yahoo Group where they coalesced (so 2006) is no longer functional. One entry reads: "Do check out the Yahoo Group (even though it is mostly me talking)."

The case that the neighborhood parents tried to make was this: "The school has its share of challenges, but it also has some things going for it, including its small size, a decent facility, and a new principal who is dynamic, experienced, and committed. We hope to generate interest in and support for the school by bringing together neighborhood families—will you join us?"

Apparently "you" wouldn't. By 2011, when the pleading messages dropped off, there were only 18 White kids at the school of 278.

No one ever says a word about the racial identity of their own or anyone else's children in this thread. But the implications are clear. This is White and privileged parents messaging to other White and privileged parents about a Black and Brown school. One woman, the same one monologuing in the Yahoo group, asks her imagined White audience: "Should we all 'bite the bullet' together and consider Emerson?"

Bite the bullet. To force oneself to stop hesitating and do something unpleasant, as if this mostly Black school is some kind of cross to bear.

By 2008, the once plucky parents have taken on a defeated tone: "It's been a mixed bag. Efforts to restart a PTA faltered. There were some deeply disheartening racial divisions that kept the PTA from flourishing. On the other hand, there are some parents who are trying to revive the efforts. Hopefully, Emerson's time will come."

It is as if they are suggesting that until a critical mass of White children exists on the campus, Emerson hardly exists at all. Which is sort of true, at least when it comes to the space-time continuum that White parents exist on. A few of my friends—all White parents—offer to send me the spreadsheets they've been making about which schools are out there and when the tours are. I scroll through them expectantly. Emerson is nowhere to be found.

9

Everybody wants the best for their kids. Everybody wants the best for their kids. Everybody wants the best for their kids. Everybody wants the best for their kids. Everybody wants the best for their kids. Everybody wants the best for their kids. Everybody wants the best for their kids. Everybody wants the best for their kids. Everybody wants the best for their kids. Everybody wants the best for their kids. Everybody wants the best for their kids. Everybody wants the best for their kids.

10

I DECIDE TO SIT down with my neighbors Mary and Tom and hash it out a bit. Mary has co-owned and run a children's clothing store in town for decades, and Tom is a lifelong public school educator, specializing in helping the most challenged kids learn to read. They have three boys in their twenties, including one set of identical twins.

They're Christian, but unlike the evangelical Christians I grew up surrounded by in Colorado Springs, they live like Jesus, make radical decisions, like sending their youngest to the "failing" elementary school in the neighborhood.

We sit in their sunlit kitchen and drink tea. Mary has a glow about her. She's one of those women who are sturdy in their knowing, plain-spoken, and often quiet. Gray, curly hair pokes out in every direction, and unfailing kindness rests behind her eyes. Tom is steady, too, but with more of an edge. He's mad at the world, as he should be. He's been reading a lot of Wendell Berry and Bill McKibben. He's been tending to his own little plot of land for twenty years. He's disappointed by the excesses he sees all around him.

I explain that we're thinking about sending Maya to Emerson, but the test scores suck and none of our friends seem to be seriously considering it. I tell them about the doughnuts. I tell them that the conversations I'm having suggest that all parents are charged with getting the best for their kids regardless of their values or beliefs, and that's just not sitting right with me.

"It shouldn't be!" says Tom. "How do I get the best for *my* kids? How much crap have I already swallowed by even asking this question?

"Let's play this out: if *best* means I need to get into the best preschool, then it also means I need to get into the best elementary school, and middle school, and then high school."

Tom's still going: "And then my kid needs to work super hard to get the best grades so that he's one of the top two or three percent. So he can get into Cal or go to Harvard. And there's only a couple of spots. And I always have to be the one that brings the doughnuts. And so by saying I need to do the best for my child, you're, like, putting him in this dog-eat-dog mindset and then running it through for, you know, maybe twenty years."

Holy shit. I don't want to run it through. I want nothing to do with that cascade of mounting pressure, building on itself year after year. With this approach, my kid would be the dam, broken from the weight of it all.

"In some ways, that's essentially the Christian definition of sin," he goes on. "Because I'm the center and everything has to respond to me. Like I'm the God; it's me that everything needs to fit around."

"And you turn your kids into gods, too," I add. "You can cast it as self-sacrificing, because you're the parent and you're doing anything and everything you need to do for them, but it's still kind of an ego projection, right?"

Mary is nodding and quietly affirming: "Right, yes."

"I mean, I think Maya is precious, but not in the sense that she deserves more opportunity than any other child. I need her to see me doing whatever I can to make sure as many children as possible have opportunities," I say.

"Plus, it's an important education for kids to grow up with other people who are really different than them," says Tom. "Which I didn't."

Tom grew up in a mostly White community with a hypercompetitive father who pushed him and his sisters hard in sports and school. But there was, as he would learn, no actual finish line. It left him feeling "like a rat in a maze."

I'm reminded of psychologist Alison Gopnik's work on parenting. She points out that many of us—particularly White and privileged people—approach the role of raising humans like carpenters. In short, we try to carve them into our own image of what a successful adult looks like. Her suggestion? Think of yourself more akin to a gardener—you create the right conditions and let nature do the rest. "Our job as parents is not to make a particular kind of child," she writes in her book *The Gardener and the Carpenter.* "Instead, our job is to provide a protected space of love, safety, and stability in which children of many unpredictable kinds can flourish. Our job is not to shape our children's minds; it's to let those minds explore all the possibilities that the world allows. We can't make children learn, but we can let them learn."[18]

If you plant your kids in a monoculture, you can expect less richness, right?

When Tom became a father, he knew he wanted to be a gardener, not a carpenter. He wanted something slower, smaller, more sustainable. He craved community. That's why he, along with a dozen or so other families from his church (predominantly a White and Asian-American congregation), teamed up to create a cohousing community about twenty years ago in what was then still a predominantly Black neighborhood. Tom and Mary's youngest son, Dave, was eight. Many of the other families had even younger children. When the adults cleared the land, which was bought from an old Italian family, with their own hands, their toddlers ran around picking up metal scrap, playing hide-and-seek in the construction site. They prayed over the dirt. They argued about what kind of tree—fruit-bearing or not—to plant in the middle of the land. They prayed some more and decided fruit. That persimmon tree is the one that drops big juicy orange orbs at my daughter's feet each October.

Living in cohousing hasn't always been easy or what they expected. Originally, all the parents intended to send their kids to Emerson. They would work together to make it great, just like they did with the land. But it didn't work out that way.

11

Rucker C. Johnson, a professor of public policy at Berkeley, has the most comprehensive data set on the long-term impacts of integration. He and his team looked at 868 desegregation orders enacted between 1954 and 1980 and overlaid them with data from school districts on school quality as well as nationally representative longitudinal data on life outcomes. In his seminal book, *Children of the Dream,* he described his findings as "empirical gymnastics that enable us to land the triple back flip and land gracefully and solidly on two feet to provide a definitive answer on the effects of desegregation."

That answer: "The medicine called integration works."[19]

Black and Brown kids who went to desegregated schools from kindergarten through high school completed more than a full additional year of curricular material than Black and Brown kids in segregated schools did. Even a five-year exposure to court-ordered segregation translated into economic benefits down the line: "A 15% increase in wages and an increase in annual worktime by roughly 165 hours, which combined to result in a 30% increase in annual earnings," plus a "decline of 11 percentage points in the annual incidence of poverty in adulthood and about a 25% increase in annual family income."[20]

Income, of course, is not tantamount to a life well lived. Johnson writes, "It has often been said that the currency of inequality is best measured in differences in life expectancy and quality of life—and in this way, the reciprocal of poverty is health."

Black kids with access to integrated schools had better health as adults—on par with those seven years younger. They were less likely to deal with hypertension, cardiovascular diseases, or obesity throughout their lives.[21]

White kids who attend desegregated schools have no learning losses. Their long-term earnings don't go down. Their health is not hampered. And there is some evidence that their ability to empathize, appreciate other cultures, and think collectively is improved.[22]

The long-term effects for White children who don't have access to integrated schools have also been documented. Segregation begets segregation. Johnson writes: "Whites who were not exposed to diverse schools during their K–12 years were more likely to have no racial diversity among their friends in adulthood...and to live in neighborhoods without racial diversity."[23]

Integration has the most impact the earlier and longer kids experience it, in what Johnson calls the "dose-response relationship."[24] My four-year-old and the other four- and five-year-olds in our neighborhood are the perfect age to begin soaking up the positive benefits of being in an integrated classroom. By the time kids are middle school– and high school–aged, many are already tracked, so even if you have a school that looks integrated on paper, inside the classrooms you will find profound racial and economic segregation.

Johnson writes: "In sum, these findings tell us a simple thing: integration, when implemented in a holistic fashion, has the power to break the cycle of poverty and can benefit all groups, regardless of race and ethnicity. Like the vaccines that have saved millions of lives in the medical field since they first appeared on the scene, integration is an unmitigated good."[25]

12

Maya looks identical to me when I was her age. Memories of my own elementary school days are creeping into my dreams, like my brain has decided to light up long-dormant synapses that suddenly seem relevant again.

This is what I remember: the thrilling ping of a marble hitting the bottom of my first-grade teacher's bright yellow ceramic smiley-face jar. This meant that the whole class had behaved well and we would have a pizza party. The shame of sitting on the green bench outside the principal's office. That is where you went if you'd done something truly terrible—like stomping dramatically to your cubby or throwing food in the cafeteria, both of which I did, despite being pretty well behaved. The satisfaction of being good at timed math tests in third grade. Dropping my underwear on the way to the swimming pool on a field trip and pretending they weren't mine when the teacher held them up. Troll dolls at recess in cardboard box dioramas. Leaving a hard-boiled egg in a small pocket of my backpack for weeks, wondering why a stench followed me everywhere. A gaggle of kids, riding our bikes around the leafy neighborhood all summer, hitting garage sales and the pharmacy for pixie sticks, and hiding in little caves of fir trees in the nearby park.

What I haven't truly registered until this moment is that all of these memories are filled with White kids. I grew up in a predominantly White neighborhood of Colorado Springs called the Old North End by locals. It was and is filled with Victorian homes and wide lawns, and is within walking distance of downtown—though no one except Daniel

Escovitz's mom walked, which we all thought was *very* weird; apparently she had lived in a place called New York City, where it was very normal to walk for, like, twenty whole minutes to get somewhere. Fathers were doctors and lawyers. (Mine was the latter.) Mothers were industrious but largely unpaid. (Mine included.) Only my very best friend, Megan, had divorced parents.

Whiteness was the water in the North End, at Steele Elementary, and in my parents' social circles. Color blindness was the dominant ideology. I don't remember ever learning about race or racism, but I do remember being told that everyone was equal and there were no differences between us and people of color. To mention race was racist, I somehow understood. So I didn't. We didn't. We talked about racism as a historic phenomenon, something that Martin Luther King Jr. and Rosa Parks fought to end. They succeeded, I assumed.

I distinctly remember the way my grandmother, with her big blindingly white curls and her "programs" on TV, used to pronounce the word: *ray-shist*. It seemed to be something that belonged to her generation—like throwing the detritus from a picnic on a park lawn, or twilight-sleep births. Something from the past. Something embarrassing and wrong with how other White people used to be.

The only contemporary justice issues that I remember learning about at school were environmental. We wrote our own play when I was in fifth grade about the depletion of the ozone layer. The lessons at school, as I remember it, were never about systems and all about boosting our individual empowerment; we were thought cute in our little White kid anger, stomping around the stage in lab jackets, raging about recycling. As a result, I knew more about the rain forest in Brazil than I did about the neighborhoods south of ours.

I can think of three non-White kids at Steele Elementary out of probably around three hundred. There were two non-White teachers, but it never registered with me that they had a racial identity at all. Just as I didn't think of myself as having a racial identity. In 1988, at the peak of integration, I was eight years old and in the second grade, stomping to my cubbyhole, reciting my righteous lines from the stage, never once wondering where all the Black or Latinx (we called them Hispanic back then) kids were.

It turns out that racial development is a process. And my development was stuck in the first stage for a pretty long time. Janet Helms, a Black psychologist who thinks about racial identity and how it gets formed, created the framework for White racial development in the 1990s.[26]

In the first stage, you are basically oblivious, interacting with very few people of color, and when you do, you do your best to pretend as if nothing is different about them. Think Stephen Colbert's pompous persona on his long-running late-night show, who said, "I don't see race. People tell me I'm White and I believe them."

Some Americans are forever destined to tiptoe around people of color and otherwise enjoy an "innocent" consciousness as they go about their preposterously White lives (growing ever more preposterous as our nation's demographics shift). These Americans aren't upset about racial dynamics; they don't even register them. To them, *White supremacy* is an academic term, something they've heard of but don't worry about, since they would never use the n-word, and they love their kid's Black teammate as if he were their own son (never mind the interior experience of said teammate).

According to Helms, sometimes something can occur in the White person's segregated world that pierces the veil. For me, that was North Junior High School, where my Latinx classmates locked themselves inside bathroom stalls so they could beat the shit out of one another over some boy without adult interference. *Why?* The honors classes were overwhelmingly White. *Why?* The lunchroom, filled with the odor of personal pizzas, where the kids from the Old North End sat together at one table, the kids from some other neighborhood—I didn't even know where—at others. *Why?* I played basketball with Black girls and Latinx girls and a Native American girl. But I never went to one of their homes, and they never came to mine. *Why?*

Then a man named Rodney King was beaten by cops in L.A. People break store windows and steal things. People scream into the television cameras. Black people are mad as hell. Their anger scares me, but I also understand where it is coming from. The grainy footage is horrific. All this White witnessing. All these stomachaches. None of the context that you don't even know you crave. Helms calls this stage "disintegration."

During this stage, obliviousness is displaced by unease. Guilt and shame. On the one hand, you still identify as someone who is not racist, and yet you are beginning to reckon with your own internal contradictions. You struggle here. You flail now. Do you choose what Helms calls "own-group loyalty," where there is some other explanation for the behavior of cruel children and violent cops, namely Black inferiority and flawed behavior? Or do you choose "humanism," which would suggest that something about White people needs to change?

The latter is daunting if you really follow the trail: if White people need to change, that means there is something wrong with your neighborhood, your family, your parents, even. Sometimes you regress from the pain of these questions and go into what Helms calls "reintegration"—doubling down on the idea that all of this anguish is invented by weak people, people looking for an excuse to blame personal failure on the bogeyman of racism. I wonder, as I read Helms's description, if we don't have a whole country wrestling with its own soul in this stage.

Ideally, one moves on to "pseudo-independence," what Helms defines as the first positive stage of racial development for White people. White people acknowledge that racism is contemporary and real but still see it as something that must be confronted by people of color. The culprits are men in white hoods carrying tiki torches. It's unfortunate, but it has little to do with them.

It strikes me as unsurprising that many of us get stuck here; I'm guessing I wasn't the only White kid with a string of unanswered *whys*. Our communities, our families, and our schools have made such an anemic effort, if any at all, to answer the moral questions of White children. So many of us stop asking them.

Then there's the "immersion/emersion" stage, where White people finally acknowledge our own whiteness as constructed, powerful, and problematic in a million ways big and small. We try to rip the scales from our eyes. We try to find other White people who have done that.

We taste the liberation of not caring about White-defined values, like perfection and efficiency. We taste the anguish of critique (our internal refrain: *Don't be fragile, don't be fragile*) and of realizing that the work will never be done. We quite likely annoy the shit out of everyone around us by talking as if we invented the notion that White people could be anti-racist, too (Helms didn't say this; I did).

The last stage, "autonomy," is about the elusive and happy marriage of a "positive White identity" with anti-racism. I'm sure as hell not there yet. Even that little phrase—*positive White identity*—feels like it has no file in my brain.

I was raised by proudly progressive parents. I went to public de-segregated, if not integrated, junior high and high schools. Why has it taken me forty years to inch toward "autonomy," much less realize that "racial development" is even a thing? Why didn't I grow up talking more directly about race?

I ask my mom. She says, "Honestly, we just didn't know how." Fair enough.

We are each a product of our own upbringing, charged with inching our moral evolution forward a few steps beyond our own parents' comfort zone or capacity. Unlike *their* own parents, mine knew they didn't want to raise racist kids, but they didn't yet understand that countering racism isn't just about *not* doing things like being an asshole to individual people of color, but about doing things, too. Things like maybe not living in such segregated neighborhoods. Things like maybe sending your White kid to a Black-majority school.

13

I'M CHATTING WITH A few moms in the living room of a neighbor's house during a three-year-old's birthday party. One, a Japanese-American mom who works in progressive politics and sends her older daughter to Chabot, says, "Oh, so Maya has a November birthday. That means she can do transitional kindergarten, right? Are you all considering it?"

Adrenaline floods my body. We've left our shoes at the door, as is the custom of the house. I look down at my feet for a minute and realize there's a hole in the toe of my ratty old socks. This makes me feel even more exposed.

"Yeah, actually we're thinking pretty seriously about sending her to Emerson," I say. I'm still working on saying this in a way that doesn't sound like I'm giving a speech at the Washington Monument and waiting for applause. Or while sitting in a dunking booth, waiting to be plunged into freezing cold water. Just saying it.

The mom's eyebrows go sky high. "Wow, really? But just for transitional kindergarten, right? And then you'd send her somewhere else once kindergarten starts?"

I've only recently realized this is a thing. Not all of the public elementary schools in Oakland have a transitional kindergarten (TK) program, designed to serve kids who have fall birthdays. The thinking is that these kids end up feeling a little too young for kindergarten but too mature for preschool at a certain point. Chabot and Peralta don't have TK programs, so some parents "bite the bullet" for TK at Emerson, knowing they will get their kids into one of the "good" schools once it really matters.

"No, if we enroll there, we'll do so with the intention of staying. I mean, who knows, we'll have to feel it out..." I trail off.

"Oh, wow, that's so *interesting*. Good for you for considering it," she says, as if I already deserve a cookie for even letting the thought cross my mind. She, apparently, gets a cookie, too: "I mean, we did. We definitely considered it."

"Did you?"

"Oh, yeah. We thought about it, but, you know, it just didn't seem like a great fit for our daughter," she says.

Another mom, this one White, chimes in: "I *actually* went on a tour."

"Oh, wow, really? What did you think?" asks the Japanese-American mom.

"I show up, and the secretary, who I think was supposed to give the tour, isn't anywhere. There are no other parents. I'm checking my calendar. I'm, like, I could have sworn this was when they said to come by, and, like, ten minutes later, the receptionist is finally, like, 'Oh, yeah, I can give you a tour.'"

You would have thought those ten minutes were ten days, as if she were wandering the desert of the courtyard, her nails growing brittle from lack of water.

Japanese-American mom: "And? What was it like?"

"It was...I don't know...just sort of what I expected on a lot of levels, I guess. It was fine. It was a school. But there was something about it that just felt so chaotic. The classrooms were sort of small and dingy. Kids seemed to be all over the hallways, which I found sort of suspicious. Some teachers had made a really valiant effort to spruce up their classrooms. It was clear they cared. But, I don't know...it just didn't instill a lot of confidence in me. And I really couldn't figure out how to plug in. I wanted to help, you know? Here I am, captive audience, neighborhood parent with resources and skills, put me to work in some way, and it was clear they really didn't know what to do with me."

Japanese-American mom: "Yeah, that's disappointing. I've heard that."

"The garden program looked really sweet," the White mom adds, like she's handing me a consolation prize. "And I'm sure if you were really there, day in and day out, you could do so much good."

"Well, maybe," I say. "I'm going to go on a tour soon, so we'll see." My insides: *What is this conversation? Why aren't you existentially tortured by the fact that our kids get the best of everything, while those kids, in that school, are just a pit stop on your pity tour of Black Oakland? Just because your kid didn't go there doesn't mean the school stopped existing!* My outside: Chill, millennial mom in ratty socks, drinking a LaCroix, keeping it friendly.

14

ROUGH. CHAOTIC. NOT A great fit. Rough. Chaotic. Not a great fit.
Rough. Chaotic. Not a great fit. Rough. Chaotic. Not a great fit. Rough.
Chaotic. Not a great fit. Rough. Chaotic. Not a great fit. Rough. Chaotic. Not a great fit. Rough. Chaotic. Not a great fit. Rough. Chaotic.
Not a great fit. Rough. Chaotic. Not a great fit. Rough. Chaotic. Not a
great fit. Rough. Chaotic. Not a great fit. Rough. Chaotic. Not a great
fit. Rough. Chaotic. Not a great fit. Rough. Chaotic. Not a great fit.
Rough. Chaotic. Not a great fit. Rough. Chaotic.

15

W HEN SOMEONE MENTIONS SCHOOL integration, most Americans think of *Brown vs. Board of Education*. It's good that it is a readily available reference point for many Americans. But it's also the kind of good that is so incomplete as to be dangerous. If all you know of integration is *Brown vs. Board of Education*—and this is all I knew for a long time—you've heard a misleadingly upbeat line about one-fourth of a long, mournful song.

In 1954, Thurgood Marshall, a Black lawyer, successfully persuaded an all-White U.S. Supreme Court to unanimously agree that separate educational facilities were not and could never be equal. Marshall famously said, "Unless our children begin to learn together, there is little hope that our people will ever learn to live together and understand each other."

Brown vs. Board of Education actually changed very little. What's important about *Brown* is the philosophical ground that it broke. Though *Brown* officially called for the desegregation of schools "with all deliberate speed," it did very little to change the material lives of children or the composition of the classrooms they attended for many, many years. Remember, the peak of school integration in America doesn't come until 1988. There was no speed. Not by anyone's definition.

From 1955 to 1964, almost no integration occurred. The gavel descended, but no real plans had been made, nor was there widespread political will to act on them even if they had existed. The Civil Rights Act of 1964, best known for prohibiting discrimination in public places and for making employment discrimination illegal, had two clauses related to education. And then the Elementary and Secondary Education

Act of 1965 ushered in a new era of federal education spending—from a few million dollars to more than $1 billion a year. But still districts remained largely segregated. The question of how to realize Marshall's beautifully articulated vision in a deeply divided America remained unanswered.

A breakthrough came in 1968—if *Brown vs. Board* was the moral moment for desegregation, *Green vs. County School Board of New Kent County* was the strategic one. The Court moved beyond *Brown* to establish that not only were districts mandated to let Black and White children learn side by side within individual classrooms but they also needed to ensure comprehensive integration within school communities. The "*Green* factors," as they came to be known, included five key areas: faculty, staff, transportation, extracurricular activities, and facilities.

The Green factors jump-started desegregation, especially in the South, where the majority of districts were segregated based on the laws of the state, by right (or, as it is often called, de jure). These laws were explicit and unapologetic, and when it came down to obeying court order, they had nowhere to hide. Other parts of the country proved more slippery. The Northeast, the Midwest, and West had never been explicit about school segregation. Their segregation was de facto, meaning there was no specific law to go after but rather a combination of policies that often did not mention race explicitly but still very effectively kept Black and White kids apart.

De facto segregation evaded lawmakers until *Keyes vs. School District No. 1, Denver,* a 1973 Supreme Court case that addressed residential segregation patterns, not just legal mandates. Black and Latinx parents filed suit against all Denver schools, and Justice William J. Brennan, who wrote the majority opinion on the case, introduced what would become a significant idea in the long battle for desegregation: intent. Though there were no official laws supporting segregation in Denver, Justice Brennan wrote: "The Board, through its actions over a period of years, intentionally created and maintained the segregated character of the core city schools."

In other words, the South, as brutal as its well-earned reputation is, said what it meant. The North and the West talked a big game about equality and then undermined it at every subtle turn.

The same is true in so many ways today. Researchers used public opinion data to identify the twelve most conservative and least conservative cities in America and then looked at the racial breakdown for school achievement data in each one. In places like Portland, Oregon, home of progressive mecca Powell's Books, in places like New York, where the Occupy movement was born, and, yes, in places like my own city of Oakland, where you can find a summer camp that will teach your kid to chant, "Hey, hey, ho, ho, the gender binary has got to go!," there is a significantly bigger gap between what Black and Brown kids achieve and what their White peers do. Progressive cities, on average, have achievement gaps in math and reading that are 15 and 13 percentage points higher, respectively, than conservative cities do.[27]

In Oakland, 63 percent of White kids are proficient in math, while 17 percent of Latinx kids and just 12 percent of Black kids are. When it comes to reading, things don't look much better: 71 percent of White kids in Oakland can read at grade level, while 24 percent of Latinx kids and 19 percent of Black kids can.

If you're a Black kid in America, you'd be better off learning in Tulsa, Jacksonville, or—and this one really gave me whiplash—my own conservative hometown of Colorado Springs than in Oakland, birthplace of the Black Panthers. De facto is alive and well, as it turns out. And it's got me and my upper-income White and Asian-American friends written all over it.

16

Tom and Mary, my cohousing neighbors, thought that Emerson looked "rough" in 2000. It was under construction at the time, so the kids ate lunch out on the blacktop. There was no art. The library was shut down. There were only one or two White kids in the whole school, they recall.

But Tom wanted to, he said, "get incarnational—in order for God to interact with us in a meaningful way, He became a child, in a particular place, in a particular time. To a poor family. He didn't have a lot of wealth or power. It wasn't like God had sent down some leaflets from Heaven. He came down, and He was there. So that incarnational thing is real. You have to be there," Tom explained.

My mind flashes on a concept attributed to the human rights attorney and racial justice advocate Bryan Stevenson that I've heard repeated often among Ivy League do-gooders. Stevenson reminds them that they need to *be of it* in order to make that happen—a secular version of what Tom is saying to me now. In his commencement addresses and interviews, Stevenson urges others: Whatever you do, "find ways to get proximate to people who are suffering."

Tom goes on: "I'm not sure anything in the end happens without the personal incarnational aspect in terms of deep change within us or the possibility of deep change for other people."

Tom got a job lined up at Emerson. He would help the school build up the reading program and coach teachers to get even the most idiosyncratic of little brains translating letters into sounds. He would be able to keep an eye on their sweet boy, Dave.

Mary doesn't mince words: "I regret it."

"Why?" I ask.

"I kind of feel like he was an experiment," she says.

Tom adds: "He literally was."

The phrasing hits me hard. When I've floated the idea of sending Maya to Emerson, friends and relatives have sometimes smiled politely and then said some version of "I admire your commitment to your values, but you don't want to turn your kid into an experiment."

It seems that next to "everyone has to do what is best for their kids," avoiding turning your own child into "an experiment" is the most popular reason White parents have for *not* choosing a majority-Black and/or -Brown school.

I'm weary of projecting my shit on Maya—which is why I let her toddle around our house in those god-awful plastic princess high heels while I am clear that I don't wear high heels because I find them uncomfortable. I've avoided putting her in too many T-shirts that profess my feminist values, as tempting as it is, for this same reason. I know her body is not a billboard for my values. She's her own person, even if she's just four years old.

On the other hand, what is parenting if not an eighteen-year experiment? Choosing a school might be a really big moment in the laboratory of a family, but there are many other moments that matter, too—what kind of house and neighborhood you live in, what kind of friends you surround yourselves with, what kind of extracurricular activities you do, what television you watch, what books you read, and what foods you eat. No one ever says, "Isn't that a little experimental?" about those decisions, big and small.

By the time I was Maya's age, I was already starting to ask my parents a lot of questions about the experiment they were running. *Why are there people without homes? Why do we have a home and they don't? Why are there people without food when we have a freezer full of Sam's Club chimichangas?* I don't remember any of their answers. What I do remember is a visceral sense that all was not what it seemed.

It created an existential snag in the matrix for me. It confused me. It curdled inside of me—this state of being a White kid given "the best" in a world of hypocrisy. The explanations don't add up, no matter how hard White parents try.*

One alternative, and this is what Tom and Mary did, is to throw your kid into the proverbial deep end and teach them about the truth of the world through experience.

It wasn't good. "He came to find me in my office that first day and just crawled into my lap and cried," Tom said.

"I think that was a bad choice," says Mary. Twenty years later, you can see the sadness pool up in her eyes.

"Why would you say it was a bad choice?" I ask.

"Because he was...the kids were too rough. They were just mean. And the teachers at the time weren't the best. Dave didn't feel safe. I mean, I only felt safe because Tom was there."

Tom chimes in: "No one from the surrounding neighborhood sent their kids there at the time. We were the only ones. You can imagine if, like, even five kids per grade level were from the neighborhood—and the parents tried to contribute what they could, volunteer in the classroom and all that—the whole school would be different. We'd lift everybody's boats."

"Yeah, that wasn't happening," Mary says. "It was just not good."

"Do you feel like it had long-term negative effects on Dave?"

"I do," she says, looking solemn.

"Yeah, so that's the regret," Tom says. "Because of his makeup, you know, his temperament. We understand it more now. But we didn't realize back then. If somebody is suffering, Dave feels that suffering. It was too much. We sort of asked too much of him."

I feel for them, for Dave. Then again, I'm suspicious of White parents' attachment to the shallow end. Too often, I'd guess, we don't give our kids enough credit for what they're capable of, or for their hunger for the truth of the world.

---

* Dr. Dena Simmons: "Fascinating that you explain this as a kind of suffering. It is in some ways, but some people might push back and wonder whether you see the privilege in this concept."

17

Who did we expect to jump into the deep end, to *do* integration? Black kids. Historically, we have asked them to leave their communities and comfort zones, board buses and subway trains, get in their parents' and grandparents' cars, maybe come on foot in rare cases, and enter school buildings where they are, best-case scenario, the obvious minority and, worst-case scenario, the obvious unwanted.

Think of that iconic image of impossibly tiny Ruby Bridges, walking down the elementary school steps, Mary Janes over perfectly white socks. She has a look of focus on her face, while White parents (outside the frame) lob all manner of disgust and projection her way.

Ruby Bridges was one of six children who passed a qualifying exam to attend a White school in New Orleans in the fall of 1960. On November 14, six-year-old Ruby Bridges walked onto the campus of William Frantz Elementary School. White moms around my age screamed racial slurs and chanted "Two-four-six-eight, we don't want to integrate!" White fathers, some of whom look like John in the pictures, threw glass bottles, eggs, and tomatoes at her.

After Ruby entered the school, flanked by U.S. Marshals, those White parents barged in and escorted their own children out. More than five hundred White children disenrolled from the school that day. Ruby attended class alone for nearly an entire year.

Eventually a few other White kids joined her for part of the day. Eventually the mobs grew tired. The White moms went home. The

White fathers turned their violent attention somewhere else. When the next school year rolled around, Ruby was no longer alone.

I slow down and let my conscience wrestle with the texture of this story, one I've skimmed many times before. The sound of breaking glass and rabid mothers. The smell of tomatoes, burst open on concrete. All those empty desks surrounding that one little girl. And amid it all, I keep thinking about Ruby's mom.

There is a video online of her talking about 1960. Her name is Lucille Bridges, and she is in a petal-pink ribbed mock turtleneck and matching cardigan, her glasses rectangular, her hair bobbed. She speaks calmly, deliberately.[28]

She simply wanted an education for her children that she, who picked three hundred pounds of cotton daily by the time she was fifteen, did not get, she explains. Abon, her husband, wasn't sure about sending Ruby to a White school. He, understandably, worried for her safety. He worried about all of their safety. But Lucille was insistent. In the end, she convinced him it was worth the danger. The superintendent summoned them before the first day of school and told them, "I hear you're praying people. You better pray, because things are about to get worse."

Things did get worse. Abon lost his job at a service station. Lucille was told her business was no longer good at the local grocery store. Ruby's grandparents were evicted from their farm, where they had lived for twenty-five years. They all received death threats. And yet, Ruby walked up those schoolhouse steps each and every day and sat at that desk. She had perfect attendance.

No doubt Lucille Bridges was told that she was "turning her kid into an experiment." But she persisted because she saw it as a generational journey, a fulfillment of her own and her parents' dreams of sitting at desks, a less precarious foundation.

I'm not Lucille, and Maya is no Ruby, but we're on a generational journey, too. I got the life of the mind but not the satisfaction of the spirit. I suffered no precariousness, but I suffered silence. I want to move myself and my kid further away from the divided life that feels central to being White and progressive in these United States and toward some sort of wholeness.

There's one other figure in the Ruby Bridges story who fascinates me: Barbara Henry. Barbara was the lone teacher who was willing to teach Ruby. She was White. It was her first year teaching at William Frantz Elementary School. She had grown up in Boston and attended Girls' Latin School, where she said she picked up her progressive values and her love of academics. She then spent some time in France, teaching on a military base. She fell in love, married, and returned to the United States—to New Orleans, where her husband's job took them. When the superintendent called to let her know she got the job, she asked if it was in one of the newly integrated schools. He said, "I'm not supposed to tell you, but it is. Does that make a difference?"

"Not at all," she replied.

Like a doctor who takes the Hippocratic Oath to heal whoever comes through the door, Barbara Henry believed in teaching any child who was placed in her classroom. Even if it was just one child. All year long. Even if she, too, had to weave her way through the mob of parents to get to the front door of the school.[*]

My grandmother was a schoolteacher before her children were born. She even traveled from her tiny farm town of Kearney, Nebraska, to the bustling city of Chicago to work at Hull House—one of the nation's first settlement homes for recent immigrants. Would she have done what Barbara Henry did? I want to believe she would have.

She also might have been one of the White moms screaming outside the school building.[†]

In 1960, my mom was twelve years old and attending an all-White school in Denver, Colorado. So my grandmother might not have opposed integration, but she certainly wasn't a force for desegregation either. Her temper ran cool. Sometimes disarmingly so.

But neutrality, in matters of justice, is the wrong side of history, too. You can be both very pleasant and very wrong.

---

[*]   Dr. Dena Simmons: "Are you turning Barbara into a white savior?"
[†]   Dr. Dena Simmons: "And how does this sit in your spirit?"

18

THE TWO CLOSEST ELEMENTARY schools to our house are Emerson and Piedmont Avenue, a bit farther afield but still bikeable. I look Piedmont Avenue up on GreatSchools.org and find out that it is a 2 out of 10. Is it twice as good as Emerson? Would getting my kid into a school that is ostensibly getting an F instead of an F- really be a comfort? I realize that I need to either buy into these scores and let them influence our decision or stop paying attention to them altogether.

Meanwhile, I'd love to finally cross the threshold of that cascading purple vine and experience Emerson for myself, then maybe stroll the halls of Piedmont Avenue and see what I can pick up.

I go to both schools' websites and hunt around for some sign of recent life. Most of the posts with any kind of data seem to have been written months and sometimes even years ago. My eye lands on typos, and my body recoils. *Maybe that's something I could help with if we end up at one of these schools,* I think. There is a calendar, but it's also out-of-date—populated with standard district information but with nothing pertaining to prospective families.

Finally I just pick up the phone and call. A harried-sounding receptionist at Emerson tells me when the tours are—weekdays, working hours, of course. No need to register, just come by the courtyard at nine a.m. Piedmont Avenue is the same—there's a tour coming up on a Wednesday, mid-morning.

I decide to check out Chabot's website, just for comparison's sake, and navigate with ease right to the tour calendar. You must register, and even with multiple tours a week for the next few months, everything is already booked. The scarcity activates the familiar feeling of scrambling to get a thing I didn't know I should have wanted. A flash of shame quickly follows it. *Am I a bad parent that I didn't even know this was happening? Is my kid going to get the dregs of everything because I'm too unorganized or out of the loop to get on the right lists at the right times? How did all these other parents know?* I wasn't planning on touring Chabot, but I put my name on a date in January. I am number 24 on the waitlist.

19

I DON'T KNOW WHY it should feel so significant to finally walk onto the blacktop of Emerson Elementary, but it does. Maybe it's because I've walked by this place so many times. Maybe it's because I, like that mom at the party, had wondered how I might help out at the school but saw no clear pathway in. It's always felt a bit impenetrable, like everyone inside was too busy doing their thing to welcome a stranger.

I wend my way around to the internal courtyard. There are nine parents, and all appear White except for one Black couple. We exchange small closemouthed smiles with kind eyes and then scurry back to the comfort of our cell phones. Eventually a White woman with buoyant energy emerges from what I'm guessing is the office and introduces herself as Ashley, a parent of two Emerson Cheetahs.

She leads us through some blue double doors, walking backward and chatting with the couple near the front. A true professional.

The hallway looks like any other school hallway to me. A few bulletin boards, some cute art, and lots of coats hanging on little identical hooks outside classroom doors. Some kids wander unaccompanied, and Ashley greets them by name and gives them a look that says, *Get to where you're supposed to be, I've got my eyes on you.* Ashley tells us she has a teaching credential and substitute-teaches at the school. "I know most of the kids," she adds. And then, raising her eyebrows mischievously, she says, "Especially the sneaky ones."

She asks who among us are sending kids to transitionary kindergarten, and who to kindergarten. Hands go up. One White mom pipes up, "I don't have a school-age child yet, but we are considering moving to this neighborhood. Our daughter is eight months old. We just wanted to get a feel for the school."

The maximizer is holding a little Moleskine in her hands, her pen poised to take notes. She's got a fleece vest on, the kind one expects to see at a liberal arts school in the Northeast somewhere. She reminds me of everything I haven't done to plan ahead. When Maya was eight months old, I had only eight-month-old questions—*Why is my baby the only one on the planet who doesn't like sweet potatoes? Is it bad if she crawls like an injured salamander?*

The first class Ashley takes us to is Ms. Walsh's. She pushes the door open gingerly, and we all shuffle in as quietly as possible. Ashley gives Ms. Walsh, a White woman who looks to be in her twenties wearing bright red lipstick, a pencil skirt, and heeled boots, a wink and a wave, and motions for us to clump together in a corner in the back of the class. About twenty kids, the vast majority of whom appear to be Black or Latinx, are sitting cross-legged on the carpet in front of the whiteboard, and Ms. Walsh is standing before them, teaching them about syllables. She's theatrical by nature. Her facial expressions enormous. Her voice booming. Some of the kids are listening. Some are wriggling and rocking and looking around, registering the ghostly apparition of grown-ups in the back of the room.

"Repeat after me: book," says Ms. Walsh.

"Book!" the kids shout back, a ragtag chorus.

Then she says the word again, but claps once at the same time: "Book!" The kids mimic her.

"So how many syllables are there?"

One little kid stretches his hand as high as it will go in the air, and all the rest shout, "One!"

"That's right. Way to go. Let's try a harder one. Repeat after me: elephant." Another kid inches away from the carpet and starts messing around in the corner of the room, pulling out little plastic tubs, rooting around for something. Ms. Walsh floats toward him while still teaching the lesson, puts her hand on his shoulder, and floats back toward the middle of the room. He follows like a loyal puppy, right by her side.

Meanwhile, the ragtag chorus hollers: "Elephant!"

"El-e-phant," she says again, this time tapping her chin three times with different fingers. The kids do the same.

"How many syllables is that, then?"

"Three," they shout.

"You guys are on it! Should we try one more? This time I'm going to need a special helper. Malcolm, do you think you can shout the word for me?"

The little kid by her side perks up and nods his head. She whispers in his ear. He stands in front of the class by her side and shouts, "Bicycle!"

They say it. They clap it. A few shout random facts about their own bikes, drowned out by the ragtag chorus. One kid lies on his back and churns his little legs like he's riding a bicycle. They triumphantly shout, "Three!"

I'm exhausted just watching. If this is the energy required to keep a couple dozen kindergarteners busy and learning for five minutes, I bow down to anyone willing to take it on. I like my room quiet and my cup of coffee hot while I silently wrestle words down on a page. I don't even like music playing. And the way she pulled that one kid back into the mix so subtly and without shaming him? Count me impressed.

Were the kids in perfect formation? Nah. Was it a little, as my friends like to say, "chaotic"? I guess? Yes?

In the scheme of things, chaos is not my biggest fear for my kid. She's pretty sensitive, it's true. She doesn't love big crowds. When I try to drag her onto the dance floor on a raucous Friday night at the Oakland Museum, she'd much rather stick with her dad and eat French fries. She only likes long-sleeved dresses of a particular brand—I think it's something to do with the way the texture of the cotton feels on her arms. But she's sturdy in other ways. And chaos is a part of life. If she's going to have to develop some skills to manage it, now is as good a time as any.

Next we're led to Mrs. Minor's even smaller TK classroom. It feels very crowded. There's a little reading nook in one corner with miniature faux-leather sofas that have seen better days, and a fish tank nearby. File cabinets are crammed next to a big shelving unit with a curtain covered in California poppies. A play kitchen is in another corner next to a few windows where the shades are drawn. I think, *John would hate that. No natural light.* There are three square tables large enough to seat eight kids at each, and there's a dingy carpet with the alphabet on it near the whiteboard at the front of the room.

The walls are covered in posters handwritten on big sheets of white butcher paper and kids' art. One poster explains the elements of a story in the shape of a flower: the petals read PROBLEM, PLOT, SOLUTION and CHARACTERS and SETTING. Another has GROWTH MINDSET written at the top, with a bunch of lightbulbs surrounding it and a few lines below: NEVER "GIVE" UP. ALWAYS "TRY" YOUR BEST. TAKE RISKS. NEVER LET YOUR "BEST" REST!" The punctuation drives me batty. The biggest bulletin board is reserved for pictures of Black inventors, like Garrett Morgan and Madam C. J. Walker.

"Welcome, welcome," says Mrs. Minor, a Black woman with a round face and big round glasses to match.[29] She's wearing a long, flowing skirt and a T-shirt with a super-colorful butterfly on it. Her long black hair is pulled back by a scarf. She goes on: "We were just wrapping up the morning with our SAM routine. Can someone tell these parents what SAM stands for?"

A little White girl's hand shoots up, and Mrs. Minor calls on her. In a tiny voice she says, "Stretch, affirm, and meditate."

"That's right, Olive, we are stretching, affirming, and meditating to get our day started off right, aren't we, TK community?"

I'm in love with her. Not Olive. She's cool. But Mrs. Minor. She seems totally in command of her craft, like someone with a passion for teaching, someone who grew up pretending to be a teacher to all her stuffed animals all day long. She's not rigid, but she's on it.

I realize that so much of school tours are about White parents looking to see themselves reflected in some way—their own values, their own dreams—in the school building. I'm not above that kind of primordial yearning. This is, after all, a place my kid might be all day every day.

We head out of the crowded classroom and back into the hallway, then down to the library. I glance around at the books carefully placed in plastic racks—*The Undefeated, The Last Stop on Market Street, Rad Girls Can*. There are also plenty of books about reptiles and superheroes, and construction, princesses, fairies, and friendships—the real crowd-pleasers, no matter how reluctant the grown-up reader may be. I've mostly made my peace with this. As long as Maya is into books, I'll brave the lazy antics of Papa Bear (grow up already, dude!) or the truly mind-numbing plots of PAW Patrol. This librarian has struck a sweet balance. Though she's nowhere to be seen.

"Our librarian isn't here today because she only works four days a week—a big step up from a few years ago, when we didn't even have a librarian!" explains Ashley. "Every class gets to come here once a week, and kids can check out books. She also does a lot of things to collaborate with our local public libraries like—"

A White dad interrupts: "Is there an art room?"

Right then, a White woman who looks to be about my age walks through the double doors that face out onto the courtyard. She's athletic-looking. Her hair is just below her ears and going gray, her jeans straight-cut, and she's wearing a T-shirt and sneakers—no nonsense. She smiles, but it's closemouthed.

She introduces herself as Principal Palin and asks: "What's on your mind?"

She's leaning on the librarian's desk, legs crossed at the ankles, folder in her arms, which are crossed across her chest. White dad persists: "Is there an art room and an art teacher?"

"No, we take an arts-integration approach here at Emerson because we don't currently have the funding for a dedicated art teacher. Nor the space, frankly."

"Is that something that could be changed?" he asks, a hint of incredulity detectable in his tone.

Ms. Palin smirks. She seems annoyed. "Sure," she says. "If the School Site Council, our governing body, decided to invest our allotted budget in that way. But then we'd have to cut somewhere else. We can move money around when we choose to. There's sort of never enough money, as you might imagine, so we have to prioritize. Anyone else?"

The mom with the baby at home pipes up, Moleskine at the ready: "Is there a second language taught here?"

"No, we have no formal second-language instruction," says the principal matter-of-factly, jutting out her chin a bit.

No art teacher, no art room, no Spanish teacher, no librarian on Fridays. The things Maya will miss out on are adding up in my head. Do other schools have these things? She loves art so much. Would I be depriving her of her biggest organic interest?

"But we do have a community very rich in foreign languages by virtue of our English-as-a-second-language learners," says Ashley, making unsatisfying lemonade.

"Yes, we have a great community here of recent immigrants, and we also have a nice relationship with the international high school a block away," says Ms. Palin. She's not exactly selling anyone on anything but is sort of reluctantly acknowledging that the school isn't made up of a bunch of oblivious English supremacists.

I've been half listening, half thinking of a question that would cut through the noise and get to the heart of what Principal Palin really thinks is important. Maybe disarm her a little. I find my hand in the air—like some kind of reflex. Ashley calls on me. I take a swing: "If you were a parent trying to decide what school to choose, what's a question you would be asking, or what's something you think it's important to look for?"

Ms. Palin squints her eyes and curls her lips inward, like she's just tasted something sour. "I guess I don't really know what you mean," she says.

Principal Palin doesn't like this line of questioning. She is not interested in being disarmed by a White parent who probably won't choose this school, her school, anyway. "Well, I just meant that there are so many factors to weigh here, and I wonder what you think is the most important as an educator yourself," I try.

"I think that's really different for every family," Principal Palin says, shaking her head almost sympathetically. That's it. No bones thrown. Her entire presentation—the body language, the facial expression, the spare answers—reveals just how uninterested she is in selling us on anything. I'm reminded of what the mom said at the birthday party: *They really didn't know what to do with me.*

It's not that they don't know what to do with us. It's that they don't want to deal with us.

Was my question as annoying as it seemed? It's pretty badass that the principal doesn't feel pressure to impress us. I'd like to be more like her—principled, direct, less concerned with making everyone else feel comfortable.

"Good luck with your search," Principal Palin says, finally giving us a wide smile before she makes a quiet exit through the other double doors, into the hallways of the school.

The grand finale is in the garden. It's past a portable classroom and a giant redwood tree. Four big tin tubs are filled with plant life—including kale, carrots, and onions—that looks neither unintentional nor rigidly organized. Parents' smiles, which grew a little tense during Principal Palin's refusal to tap-dance, loosen up again. Ashley beams. She has clearly saved the best for last. "This is our little garden program, led by the amazing Ms. Shadona," she says, motioning toward the Black woman emerging from a little shed with some buckets and shovels.

When asked to describe the program, Ms. Shadona says, "It's real hands-on. The kids get to come here and get their hands in the dirt, learn how things grow. We have to take turns with the classes because there's just one of me and a whole lot of them, but every kid gets a chance at some point during the year," she says.

She shares an anecdote related to the new magnifying equipment she's using to add a scientific component to the work the kids are doing in the garden: "They were giggling really hard when I said, 'You all can't see everything with your naked eye,' and they said, 'That's a bad word!'"

The little crowd laughs and smiles. And then she hits us with a real tearjerker: "When the kids are feeling down, there are a lot of things in the garden for them to come and see to lift their spirits. If I'm not feeling well, I like to walk out in the garden, and that changes everything. I take that motivation and bring it here."

Then she says, "There are some things in the garden that kids can see and adults can't see. Kids come in and say, 'Oh, my goodness, all the colors!' and adults pass by and say, 'It's so messy.' I like the kids to be able to see all the stages of growth, so I gotta keep it a little messy."

20

How well can you ever really know your kid?

What haunts me most in what Tom and Mary said about Dave's experience at Emerson is that it reminds me of that question I've been asking since the moment I looked into Maya's tiny little eyes.

I've never done anything as baffling or sacred as parenting a child. Maya rewrote my life as I knew it—no more sleeping in, no more devouring a novel in one endless sitting, no more rides to the airport without a pit in my stomach. But more important, she reversed one of the essential existential conundrums at the center of my life up until that point: Who is my mother? Will I ever really know her?

Now *I* was the mother, and I was looking at my daughter, delighting in her, sometimes becoming absolutely enraged in the face of her desires and refusals, and wondering: *Who the hell are you, girl? You came from me. I literally made your body inside of my body. And yet your soul is all yours. What is the nature of it? And what does that mean about how I should mother you?*

The older she got, the more real this question felt—mostly in the face of her own growing list of questions, which gave me a small window into the vastness of what was going on inside of her. When she wasn't even three years old, I was putting her to bed one night, and she asked me, in short succession: "What is romantic? How do you make black? Why do we lock our doors?"

And once, around that same time, I was biking her around the neighborhood, and she said, "Momma, the air smells like freedom."

"Did you hear that in a book?" I asked, stunned.

"No, I just know."

I write these things down haphazardly in a journal by my bed. These are actual questions, actual observations, of a person I birthed but now strain to know fully.

And once I had Stella, her little sister, who is a wildly different human being than Maya, the question became even more obvious. Maya is a bit of a black box. She's quieter than Stella, happy to lie on her bedroom carpet on her belly making art for hours in silence.

I can sense that emotions get trapped inside the complex plumbing of her psyche. Her tantrums, less and less frequent these days but still a very real possibility, have staying power. She can scream, red in the face, tears and snot streaking down her cheeks, for forty-five minutes. Which feels like four hours. Stella can sustain a sad face, or a mournful cry for, tops, four minutes—and she's in the supposed "terrible twos." Emotions just pass through her—strong but brief. With Maya, they go somewhere unknowable, inaccessible.

Which is all to say, if your approach to mothering a human, including choosing a school for her, should be based on the intimate knowing of that human, what happens when you know there is so much you don't know? Like every attuned parent, I can tell you exactly how Maya likes her pasta prepared or what her mood feels like when she needs a good tickle attack. I would venture to say I know her better than any other human on earth knows her. But it's still not all-encompassing. Which makes choices as big as where she'll spend so many hours of her days, at such a formative moment in her beautiful, unwritten life, feel really hard.

21

I walk about twenty minutes to Piedmont Avenue, the other public school close to us, for a tour. Like Emerson, it sits in a neighborhood filled with wealth, though one less hipster and more old-school hippie in flavor. On Piedmont Avenue you can find a whole store of yarn and another of beads, an optical shop perfect for an aging Jungian psychologist, and a sweet little movie theater that always skews independent. In cultural contrast, Piedmont Avenue is over half Black and 20 percent Latinx; 70 percent of students are on free or reduced lunch.

I enter via the heavy double doors and find myself in a big hallway, wider and shinier than Emerson's, the ceilings taller. It feels like older construction—a place built when schools were grander institutions. I can hear an assembly popping off nearby, kids shouting in reply to someone on a mic. I wander around the corner in search of the office and find it. I walk in and quietly wait while a middle-aged Black woman behind the front desk finishes a phone call. She looks up at me and says, "What can I do for you?"

"I believe there is a tour today?"

"Oh, is there?" she says, pushing some papers aside and looking at a paper calendar hung near her computer. "Well, look at that. There is. But we've got a lot going on today, and the person who usually gives them is part of all that. Do me a favor and come back another day, love, would you?"

"Oh, of course, no problem," I say, my irritation at the inconvenience softened by the unnecessary endearment.

"Great, thanks."

"Take care," I say, already backing out of the office.

It's sinking in: schools like Emerson, like Piedmont Avenue, feel unorganized to parents like me because they don't prioritize us or speak our language. I don't mean English; I mean Google Calendar, where we find time to "sync up" as quickly as possible, where we establish "strategies" and "deliverables," and move on with our always harried days.

We have come to equate respect with efficiency. But respect in multicultural city schools is about something else. I'm still learning what that something else is.

22

ONCE YOU'VE SEEN IT, you can't unsee it.

That's what one of John's friends told him about Park Day School, the "independent" school (a euphemism for private) just a few blocks from our house.

It's not, to be fair, all that easy to see—the school is behind a tall gate, topped with barbed wire and strategically surrounded by giant bushes. At one part of the fence, there is a break in the bushes, and one can make out about a dozen metal picnic tables surrounding a gazebo. Sometimes on my neighborhood walks with baby Maya, I would hear a chicken cluck or a group of children laughing from inside. Once, a new friend came to visit and told us that she could get us the code to the gate so that we could use the playground on the weekends (her sister's kids went there). But the code never came. Eventually she let us know that her sister said there was a crackdown on outsiders coming in.

I decide to go see the school by taking a tour. I am categorically against the idea of sending Maya to Park Day, but I want to see what we're *not* choosing. I want to understand what the kids inside all of those Priuses pulling up and through the metal gate each morning are actually doing once they are inside. I think I'm too much of a righteous asshole for the no doubt powerful force that is private-school marketing. But I'm not going to lie, I'm a little nervous walking in. Will the force be too strong to resist?

Coffee is offered. Beautiful brochures are handed out. The cover features a quotation by Tom Little, who, I will come to understand, is a major influencer in the "progressive education" movement and was a longtime Head of School at Park Day. It reads: "Progressive education prepares students for active participation in a democratic society, in the context of a child-centered environment, and with an enduring commitment to social justice."

Park Day School, I learn, was founded in 1976 at another location, and then it moved to this one (the website, of course, points out that it was once "a bustling Ohlone-Chochenyo village"). After watching the drone footage on the homepage for a while of kids running around the campus, complete with yurts, outdoor classrooms, and a plethora of towering palm trees, I finally find the financial information. It costs $29,000 for kindergarten, a fact that no one speaks of on the tour. Only 35 percent of students, schoolwide, receive any form of financial aid.

There are two words that I clock more than any other while walking around with this little scrum of nervous parents (all White or Asian-American): *social justice*. It is like the unofficial religion of the school.

Each classroom has its own way of worshipping. A timeline of rap music hangs high above a blackboard; DJ Kool Herc and Lauryn Hill seem to look down on circle time, where kids are discussing what they did that weekend (played Legos, skied in Tahoe, saw Grandma).

It's in the art room where I feel the force most. A bulletin board reads: IN ART CLASS, THE KINDERGARTEN STUDENTS VIEWED AND DISCUSSED ROMARE BEARDEN'S COLLAGE WORK. THEY LEARNED ABOUT THE HARLEM RENAISSANCE AND COMPLETED A COLLAGE DEPICTING THEIR IMAGES OF THEIR NEIGHBORHOODS WITH AS MANY DETAILS AS POSSIBLE.

I take a deep breath and try to resist. I imagine Maya sitting at one of these little tables, glue stick in hand, a magazine torn to shreds in front of her. She's a prolific artist already; piles of drawings and paintings cover our kitchen table. What if, instead of the philistine cartoon dogs and big-eyed cats she's learned to make from cheeseball YouTube videos, her artistic sensibility were shaped by weird and wonderful Bearden?

If the unofficial religion of Park Day is social justice, the ultimate deity is Martin Luther King Jr. One can't walk more than ten feet without seeing his face emblazoned somewhere—shining that beatific grin on all these terrifically loved, overwhelmingly White children. I start counting heads in the classrooms we visit. There are about fifteen, and what appears to be two or three non-White kids in each—a true-to-form example of what Nikole Hannah-Jones calls "curated diversity."

In an interview with *The Atlantic*'s Jeffrey Goldberg, Hannah-Jones asserts that White Americans are generally tolerant of about one in ten kids in a given class being Black. Any more than that, and they start to wonder about the safety and rigor of the school. In theory we value diversity, and in practice, we value whiteness. Research bears this out: when White parents see majority-Black kids on a campus, they think "bad school," and when they see majority-White kids, they think "good school," even without any actual information about the school, test scores, funding, and so on.[30]

The vast majority of White people simply don't *see* Black and Brown schools at all. In fact, some researchers have found that there is what they call a "bliss point" among White parents: if there aren't at least 26 percent White kids at a school, they don't even consider it a possibility.[31]

But that's not something any White parent in Oakland would own up to. The whiter our worlds get, especially in progressive parts of the country, the more desperate we become to reassure ourselves otherwise. The one or two Black kids in our kids' classroom, the MLK portraits and references everywhere, the passionate declaration of how much we care about social justice in the mission statement—all are evidence that we aren't, in fact, racist or elite.

Parents are sending their kids to schools like this so they can experience inquiry-based learning (which, don't get it twisted, seems amazing), but they're also buying a kind of moral identity. We want to believe that we can send our own kids to private or the highest-demand, Whitest public schools without harming other people's kids, that it's not a zero-sum game. The avidity with which we pursue reassurance that we are *not* the problem only confirms the truth: we are.

"Progressive schools" like Park Day appear to have been founded with the best of intentions. In the 1970s, as boomers came of age and recognized how much of our public-education system was geared toward conformity and building not creative citizens but dutiful worker bees, they busted out and reclaimed some very old and wonderful ideas about education. For the sake of context, this was also when White folks were fleeing Oakland; well-resourced, mostly segregated public schools in the hills, or private schools with poetic mission statements, would help keep them around.

John Dewey, philosopher and nineteenth-century educational reformer, is the intellectual godfather of the progressive school movement. He argued that education was not just about dumping knowledge down kids' throats; a school should be a place to learn how to, well, be a person. His dream was a robust democracy with schools as the training ground. Don't teach kids what to think, in other words, but *how* to think, and how to act in accordance with their own values, unique gifts, and pleasures.

In theory: Yes of course! But in practice: For whom?

The economic model of private schools cannot hold at scale. A robust democracy requires a demos, a place where equal actors join to express and debate shared values. The Park Day School educational experience, rich with resources and nurturing relationships, is available only to a lucky few scholarship kids in a profoundly poor city.

And for those lucky few, of course, the experience may be painfully dissonant. Imagine being the one Black kid who gets let in the gates while you watch a dozen of your neighbors, kids who look like you and who come from families that you know and go to church with, running toward the public school down the block. That, no matter how you dress it up, is an aristocracy.

Private schools have made a very lucrative art of persuading White parents otherwise, of soothing our consciences through talk of financial aid and "equity and inclusion." In this way, social justice has become the opium of progressives. We are reassured that teaching our kids systems-thinking is a noble substitute for extracting them, and our resources and attention, from that most fundamental of systems: public education.

When we enter the "innovation lab" at Park Day, the tour guide regales us with stories about the amazing things the kids have been making. Her favorite is clearly something called the "journey box," where second graders learn about forced migration and then pretend they have to leave their home countries and arrive in new ones. They not only build the wooden boxes but also fill them with the things they would most want to take with them. No doubt experiential learning is a great way to build moral muscles.

But then she tells us how fun it has been to let a class of Emerson Elementary students in once a week and give them access to the equipment. The prospective parents' heads nod, and one parent quietly says, "How cool." I am skeptical that any of them have made the connection—that a healthy percentage of Emerson students are kids from Guatemala and Yemen and God knows where else who have actually lived this lesson. The exercise of social justice in some way distracts these kids from the social and the just.

The tour ends in the interim headmaster's office. He's an older White guy, one of those congenial, frumpy fellows with pictures of his kids away at liberal arts colleges on the wall and an attraction to Buddhism and REI. A guy like my dad if my dad had been an educator. He gives us a warm smile and says, "Any questions? What did you notice?"

One White mom says, "I like that the kids really seem to get to move around with their own rhythm. They aren't forced to sit at desks all day."

The smile already plastered on his face grows even wider. "Yes!" he exclaims. "Yes! We are all about that. I was recently teaching a small seminar in here, and one of the boys lay down on the conference table, and I thought, 'Unorthodox, but let's go with it!'"

The touring parents laugh and shake their heads in amazement. I picture a White boy, spread-eagled on this conference table, and seethe. I close my notebook, quietly stand up, and leave the room. I speed-walk to the gate and feel a tremendous wave of relief wash over me when I find myself back on the outside.

23

SOMEHOW I GET BUMPED up the waitlist for the Chabot Elementary School tour. Even though we're not seriously considering it, I decide to go and risk seeing what I can't unsee, yet again.

The Chabot library has super-high ceilings, and it's packed with smiling, note-taking parents. The maximizers are all here: moms with the Rothy's flats and the heartache over trying to have it all. The guys who normally hop on Google and Facebook buses have stayed home for the day so they can join; *this* is important.

Everyone is hyped. Eager to please. Ready to be dazzled. A White mom gets everyone's attention and welcomes them to the school. "We are so excited to have you at Chabot!"

She's got blond, perfectly straightened hair and a travel coffee mug in hand. She tells us the logistics for the tour; we'll be splitting up because there are so many of us. Parent volunteers are here to take each smaller group around and show them everything they might be interested in seeing. Before we all break up and head out, they'd like one of their parent volunteers to say a few words.

A Black father in a button-down chambray shirt and black-frame glasses smiles and steps forward. "I just want to express welcome to *all* of you. Chabot is a really special place. It's a welcoming place. It's a place where people really value collaboration and diversity. We pride ourselves on our commitment to equity and innovation. But you don't need to hear it from me—you can see it for yourself! Get out there and enjoy. Ask questions. We're excited to have you here."

The undertone is clear. Chabot may look super-White, but we're not *all* White. Technically that's true; out of 562 students, there are 42 Black kids—probably many of them siblings. I wonder who the message is really for—the very few parents of color on this tour or the White parents? Both? Park Day clearly isn't the only school marketing social justice to progressive White parents this year.

The school building is huge. Classroom upon classroom, stairwells leading to more stairwells. The hallways are covered in well-organized bulletin boards featuring kids' work—comics about climate change, imitations of Mo Willems's popular Elephant and Piggie book series, studies in anatomy, and maps of the neighborhood, complete with Trader Joe's and Smitten Ice Cream (where you can get purely organic ingredients "fresh-churned in micro-batches" in ninety seconds flat).

We wind around and "dip"—as blond mom describes it over and over again—into classes full of buzzing, engaged kids. It doesn't feel chaotic to me. But is that because it feels so White? Or is it because there are at least two teachers in every classroom? Is my body just at rest because this is all, on some lizard-brain level, so familiar?

We stop in the lobby leading into the cafeteria for a moment, and someone asks, "I assume there is an active PTA here?"

The blond mom beams: "You betcha. You're looking at a bona fide member. We've got a great group—very active, very engaged. We put on one big fundraiser every year, our gala, and then lots of other little fundraisers throughout the year."

I realize the easy feeling that I have is not just familiarity; it's also something else—I'm being *cultivated*. Chabot wants me to feel at ease here now so that I will be generous here later on. We aren't just prospective parents; we are prospective donors. It was clearly thought out well in advance—the detailed emails, the careful orchestration of the small groups, the unabashed pride. Turns out, this place raises upward of $500,000 a year in PTA funds. They need parents like me, parents who can afford private school tuition but think of themselves as public school people.

"And what is the percentage of the students on free or reduced lunch here?" I ask.

Her eyes widen into saucers of shock. "Oh, I don't know that number. We wouldn't talk about that here."

"What do you mean?" I ask, dumbfounded.

"Well, we just wouldn't want to make anyone feel bad about that. We wouldn't talk about it."

She eagerly calls on someone else whose hand is raised. I don't hear what the prospective parent asks, because I am too busy trying to wrap my mind around what just happened. It's publicly available information. I could look it up on my phone right now if I wanted to.

Her reaction is equivalent to the color-blind ideology that I was fed as a kid in Colorado Springs. At Chabot, diversity is mentioned frequently—critical as it is to the marketing of social justice at the school—but class is still a bridge too far.

Later, when I get home, I look it up myself. Only 13.2 percent of the kids at Chabot qualify for free or reduced lunch in a district where overall 73.4 percent of kids do.

24

I START WRITING ABOUT my struggle to choose a school for Maya in my weekly column, which opens the floodgates of email from other equally anguished White parents trying to make the same decision. But it also opens the floodgates from a different kind of parent—one who has already opted out of the "good" school. I read their sometimes righteous, often humble screeds voraciously; it's like they are on the other side of a bright moral line that I am trying to will myself to cross.

And they are fine. They are better than fine.

A White mom from Indianapolis who has a child with special needs says that while "most schools don't like the fact that our kids bring extra work with accommodations," she found that the Title I school she chose for him welcomed him with open arms. It was something she found "surreal" after so many subtle disses on other tours. She writes: "These are schools that may not get the best test scores—they don't have the money that our schools in the suburbs have—but they promote an inclusive environment for all students, which is worth far more to us in the long run."

Similarly, a White mom whose kids are in the racial minority at their school in Seattle writes: "When one of my kids had to get pulled out of class regularly for speech therapy, I asked the counselor if he would get teased. She said, 'At this school? No. There is no normal here, so there's no teasing kids who are different; the kids are used to everybody being really different and unique.'"

Another White mom, who identifies as "an Evangelical from Oregon," writes, "There is currently this idea that you can desire the common good while also choosing what is best for only your own family. But this isn't true. Our decisions to pull out and divest of the public school system has led to unintentional segregation (and don't get me started on the intentional segregation! As a Christian, our history of both private schools and homeschooling becoming popular coincide with anti-segregation laws—not, as commonly believed, the decision to remove prayer from schools)."

It seems like the parents who write are overwhelmingly thrilled with the schools they've sent their kids to, but there are other losses. A White mom from Goshen, Indiana, feels like her community has abandoned her because of her choice: "Now we're over here, alienated by many of the people who should love us most, because we dared venture into 'enemy' territory. We sent our kids to a 'failing' elementary school where, they told us, there would be drugs, evolution, gay people, and gangs. It is the best thing that ever happened to us. I cringe to know how much a part of the problem I once was. I can only hope I continue to grow in ways that grind my old paradigms into dust."

A Mexican-American mom in the D.C. area who had just moved there from Nebraska was surprised that none of her new neighbors were even considering their local public school. At first she followed their lead, touring private schools, and she even looked into moving, but she finally decided she should at least tour the pariah of a school. She loved it and now sends her kid there, but she writes with brutal candor: "I think my very educated White neighbors are not afraid of their kids mingling with Brown or Black kids. I think they are afraid of poor kids and what 'baggage' they might bring. I was, too. I guess, maybe I still am! Our school, at the end of the day, has mostly kids from lower- to middle-class families, working families nonetheless. We don't have the really poor and troubled kids who might be in inner-city schools, and I ask myself, what would we do if that were the case?"

Her words—"troubled," "inner-city"—curdle my stomach. She's harboring a racist stereotype about kids who are growing up in families without enough money. I wouldn't use this language. Ever.

But is the trope in my own head really so different?

I would say I have concerns about toxic stress—the idea that stress floods little bodies and leads to real physical and emotional impacts. I might talk about epigenetics, the generational echo of trauma that literally exists within our very cells. I might talk about the vulnerability created by low-wage work or the lack of mental-health supports in low-resourced communities for addiction and abuse.

It's all substantiated by research. It's *real*—parental stress really does affect kids, many of them kids who go to majority-Black and -Brown schools. And theoretically, I'm locating the pathology in the structure, not in the individual.

Unfortunately, it all lands in the same place—on the Black kid of our imaginations. In this mom's head, this kid is "really poor and troubled." In mine, he likely has a lot of trauma to contend with and parents struggling to make ends meet, and they pay the cognitive tax that comes from that. As elevated as my version sounds, I know that it's not all that different from this mom's. If you asked us, What are White kids like? or What are middle-class kids like? We would say, Which kid? There is no White kid of our imagination. There is no generic middle-class kid.

And in this way, whether you are this Latinx mom in D.C. or me, a White mom in Oakland, Black kids—poor Black kids especially—still seem, and this feels very hard to force my fingers to write, less human. Less textured. Less known. Less real. They are subjects of a new report. Not kids with Pokémon collections, weird allergies, and quirky obsessions.

The flip side of this, of course, is also damaging. Our White kids, our middle-class kids, are so real to us that we don't see the patterns. Every decision we make for our own White child is an individual one. We're not acting as a class of people—White, elite, progressive, whatever; we're just us. We just want what's best for our particular kid. We just want a good fit. We just have this thing about dual-immersion education, because we studied abroad in Ecuador and it was really formative; it's not that we think we're above the kids at the local school with no foreign language. Or we just know our kid needs to be in a classroom with lots of movement and project-based learning; we're sure other kids—kids we don't know, who are largely Black and Brown—who attend the local school, with its traditional desks and its rigid curriculum, need that kind of structure, and that's great for them.

Even while not exactly admitting that whiteness, middle-class-ness, is a culture, we elevate it as the preferred norm. We raise our kids better. (Again, this is something no progressive White person would readily say out loud, even though it is what many of us truly think.) *We* read to our kids. *We* say thirty million more words to their spongelike brains. *We* provide stability. But by never fully admitting that *we* are part of a culture, we evade critique.

If we're going to wield generalizations against poor families, what about our own? *We* dominate, exploit, and dehumanize. *We* are shitty at apology and repair. *We* are repressed and masters of rationalization for our hoarding behavior. *We* drink more than Americans of any other racial background. *We* are the descendants of slaveholders and rapists and misogynists.

These are the paradigms we must "grind into dust," that whiteness and middle-class-ness are the preferred norm, beyond reproach. That other people's children are less real than our own. That they are vessels of pathology, deserving of pity, while ours are inherently good, deserving of "the best."

White progressives like me can talk a very big game—rich with randomized control trials—about how we see poor Black kids, but we don't *see* them, because we don't know them. We live among them, but not alongside them. Our kids don't learn or play with theirs. And that's because we have made deliberate choices to keep it that way.

Unless we choose differently.

25

I REALIZE THAT AN acquaintance—Dawn, also White, a journalist and poet and the mom of a November baby—is seriously considering Emerson. I met her one night while we were out with mutual friends, headed to a reading in the city. In my first memory of her, we're chatting on the BART train. She's hanging on to a pole, tall and lanky, with a beautiful full-lipped smile, talking about her work—she writes about food justice—and I notice the way she uses the phrase *White supremacy* with ease and speaks with an unapologetic anger about the state of things. I register it—*Dawn craves that elusive White moral life, too.*

When I hear that she's seriously considering Emerson for her son, Linden, we start texting more regularly. Unlike some of my other friendships, which have come to feel strained when it comes to this subject, ours has an almost first-week-of-camp feel to it. The texts flow happily and conspiratorially. Another person in the corner of the proverbial party talking about opportunity-hoarding and the achievement gap.

She and her husband, Jack—also tall and lanky, and standing in the corner at the party with me and Dawn—are choosing between Sankofa or Glenview, which they live very close to, in the Santa Fe neighborhood, and Emerson, which is a bit farther away. Jack, a museum preparator and exhibit designer with a brooding, artsy vibe, was the first to tell Dawn that he didn't want to do the typical White parent thing and strategize their way into the most highly rated school.

They had gotten close to some of the Black families in their neighborhood, watched many get displaced by gentrification, and grappled with their role as White neighbors in what had long been a working-class Black neighborhood. Jack had mentored a teenager from across the street, a brilliant kid who had been passed from each grade to the next despite not being functionally literate, so he had already seen the inequities of the district up close and personal before Linden entered the picture.

Both Dawn and Jack also had pretty formative experiences of being the White minority in spaces as kids. Dawn was a haole in Hawaii, where she was introduced in elementary school to the idea that her family was living on stolen land, and Jack attended a Black-majority elementary school in Massachusetts.

The most highly resourced, highly rated school nearby, Glenview, didn't feel great to Dawn when she visited: "The way their PTA ran the tour really turned me off," she told me. "They said, 'We raised $250,000 last year. Most of you are spending over a thousand dollars on day care every month. We hope that if your kid comes here, you will consider a donation of at least that size.' I totally get why they're doing it, but it was a very intense point of entry. I mean, I don't think it is a bad thing."

"Do you really not think it's a bad thing?" I ask.

"I feel conflicted about it," she says. "She took us to the art class-room, and we met the art teacher, and she explicitly said, 'We pay for this teacher's salary through PTA fundraising.' And so in that sense I don't think it's entirely a bad thing, because at least it's direct. They want everyone to know."

"It's transparent, for sure, but it's also exclusive," I say.

"Yeah, it is. It gave me a good sense of what the school was about, and maybe that was better than if I'd gone on a different kind of tour and then been sort of surprised by that culture at the school."

Dawn didn't hear anything about fundraising on the Emerson tour and liked the principal's vibe. At Sankofa, she met an interim principal and was unnerved that there was no official hire for next year. They were leaning toward Emerson because it felt like "middle ground"—not as highly resourced as Glenview but not as unstable as Sankofa.

Their rationale reminded me of just how relative this whole decision-making process is. Parents, at least the kind who go on tours, are using one hour, tops, in a school building to assess the place, and then comparing that assessment to the ones they form on the other tours they happen to go on. It's such an imperfect data set, no matter how you cut it.

If you decide that your goal isn't to get "the most" or "the best" for your individual kid, what should you pursue? In Dawn and Jack's case, it seems they have landed on a Goldilocks goal—not too little, not too much. Just right, as it were. Just enough and no more.

26

Dawn turns me on to a national organization she discovered called Integrated Schools—a network of White and/or privileged parents who are sending their kids to what they call "global majority" schools, meaning where White kids are the minority, aligned with the actual world. The language is a little too self-serious for my taste, but the website is refreshingly rudimentary, and the tone in the blog posts is filled with self-deprecating humor. I imagine many of the people who have written to me in response to my column are a part of this small, but growing, cadre of iconoclastic parents.

Courtney Everts Mykytyn, the founder of Integrated Schools, didn't set out to be the White parent that other White parents were nervous to be around. But when she moved to Highland Park, a majority Latinx neighborhood in Los Angeles, and realized that none of her White friends were considering sending their kids to neighborhood schools, she was stunned. Maybe it was her background in anthropology that gave her the ability to look at life—even her own, even her kids'—with a little distance.

Courtney did a deep dive into the research on integration and educational outcomes and started bringing this up at birthday parties and soccer games—*Hey, y'all, did you realize our White kids will do fine at these schools, and their presence can actually support the other kids to do better?* She sent her kids to the neighborhood school, and though doing so wasn't exactly easy, it was meaningful. She wanted people to know. She wanted people—White people—to know.

When I first spoke with her in 2018, Integrated Schools had been around for four years and already had chapters popping up across the U.S. She tells me that most folks arrive on her digital doorstep at one of two key points in their journey. Some, like me, seek the organization out when their kids are about to enter kindergarten and they are trying to choose where to send them. Another influx happens—and this is a pleasant surprise—when families have been at "global majority" schools for a few years and they want a community of other parents with whom they can discuss two main questions: "This is awesome. WTF were we so worried about?" and "How do I show up without being an asshole?"

Courtney's kids are twelve and fifteen, so she's shown up like an asshole plenty of times and lived to tell the tale.

"How many of these kinds of phone calls do you have in a week?" I ask her the first time we chat on the phone.

"Oh, like, three to five. A lot of people are really starting to think more about voluntarily integrating schools. It's kind of amazing, even as I reserve the right to be super-cynical about anything that White people express interest in," she says, busting out with a laugh.

"Fair enough," I say. "What do you hear as people's biggest reservations for sending their kids to integrating schools?"

"I don't want my kid to fall behind. That's one thing almost everyone says," Courtney answers without skipping a beat.

Worrying about whether your kid will fall behind is a powerful, if statistically improbable, fear for White privileged parents. But it makes some sense; fears are rarely rational. It's not so surprising that we can be irrational when it comes to our children; we are wired to want them to succeed. But are high test scores and grades really the ultimate expression of what we hope for these quirky, maddening, beautiful creatures who are our children? God, I hope not.

"So, why don't White kids fall behind?" I ask Courtney after discussing the research a bit.

"Social capital," she says, like a true academic. (She has a PhD in medical anthropology.)

White people have all kinds of resources—material and otherwise—to make sure our kids get opportunities to learn. One could argue that privileged parents basically all homeschool our kids. We fill the house with books. We limit screen time and/or steer our kids toward educational shows. We take them to museums, libraries, and cultural events. Privilege is hard to shake. Yet privileged people often behave as if public institutions that serve other people's kids will drain the privilege they've already invested in their children.

In fact, as Rucker C. Johnson argues, segregated public schools imperil our democracy in the long run. He writes: "Integration is like a surgery performed on a school system—it hurts, but it cures. Segregation (and white flight) is like a painkiller, providing instant relief for families looking to avoid diversity, but also plaguing them with long-term side effects."[32]

The most prevalent painkiller these days isn't straight-up segregation, which runs counter to how progressive parents want to see themselves, so much as curated diversity. White flight has turned into puddle jumping—you don't hide in the suburbs, you hide in a school just diverse enough to allow you to maintain your identity as a good progressive.

"The other thing I hear all the time is 'I don't want my kid to be unsafe,'" Courtney says. "Drives me crazy."

There is no more foundational responsibility as a parent than to keep your kid safe, and yet, as soon as she can crawl, you begin to realize that safety is relative. When this question is asked related to the school you send your kid to, it becomes interwoven with deeply racist notions of who causes violence and who suffers from its effects.

"What exactly does the White parent expressing this concern think might happen in a kindergarten classroom that would make his or her kid legitimately unsafe?" I ask Courtney. I'm imagining a bunch of four- and five-year-olds, flopping around on their carpet squares. They can be annoying as hell, sure, but dangerous? Seems far-fetched.

"Beats me," she says. "I think it's completely irrational. And racist, of course. I don't think those parents even know. They're just looking for rationales for talking themselves out of it."

I say, "The other big one I get from other parents, when this topic comes up, is a warning: don't turn Maya into an experiment. It's like they think I'm using her, like I've turned the choice of where she goes to school into the ultimate ally theater."

"And are you?" Courtney asks, surprising me.

"What do you mean?" I reply.

"I mean, that's a legit question. Not the experiment thing. That's a given. We're all experimenting. But the theater thing. I mean, part of this journey is getting vicious with yourself about your own shit. I can tell you, it's not for the faint of heart."

I don't *want* to be faint of heart. Does that count for something?

I take an audible breath and then say, "I mean, I don't want this to be a performative thing, but I get why it might look that way to people."

"Doesn't really matter how it looks to people," Courtney says. "Part of the journey is giving less shits about what White people think and more shits about how you actually impact the lives of Black and Brown families. But you don't have to get it now. You'll live into it."

We vow to meet up next time I'm in L.A. In the meantime, we begin a correspondence. She signs off every email with "OtherCourtney," as if she's the follower, even though we both know who the real mentor will be.

27

"IF A SCHOOL ISN'T good enough for your kid, why is it good enough for any kid?"

This is Susan, White mom from Oakland, paraphrasing Nikole Hannah-Jones, whose voice she heard on *Fresh Air* and couldn't get out of her head or heart thereafter.[33] She and I are sitting at the local Peet's at the border of our two neighborhoods, talking about the choice before both of our families.

I am leaning more and more toward Emerson. The conversations with Courtney, the emails I'm getting in response to my column, the reading I'm doing—all are strengthening my conviction. Dawn and Jack have put Emerson as their top choice. She tells me: "The minute before we pushed the button, I was, like, really? Are we really doing this? We're really not going to opt for the school that's two blocks away and more resourced?"

"I get that!" I say.

"Jack was way more like, 'Yep, we're doing it.' It was a process for me."

"What do you think allowed you to press the button?" I ask.

"I think it was a combination of me being a fairly mission-driven person and also just choosing to trust Jack and his values."

I feel like the bravest version of me is a "yes," and the other parts of me will just wither as the weeks go on if I neglect them enough. Besides, I'm pretty convinced that the only things I'm genuinely nervous about—*Will she be overwhelmed? Will her innate love of learning be protected? Will she get to do enough art?*—are just about school writ large, not about attending a majority-Black school.

Susan's bravest version of herself is, well, just herself. She has decided on Sankofa Academy for her incoming kindergartener. Sankofa is her zoned school, where 125 of the 187 kids are Black and 90 percent qualify for free or reduced lunch. I was introduced to her by Dawn, who lives in the same neighborhood.

Susan and her husband moved there fully aware that they were part of the growing wave of gentrification but hoping that they could live there in such a way that would set them apart from those with no respect for what came before. They tried to meet their Black neighbors—striking up conversations on the street, taking public transportation whenever possible, going to events at the school that were open to the public—but developing friendships with long-time residents was slow.

"There are so few integrated spaces," Susan explains. "Going to Sankofa also feels like a way for us to be meeting more families who don't look like us, that are in a different situation economically."

Susan is also brave, it seems, because she's Baha'i. Her faith is a steadying force for her in the midst of so much White fear. "Our purpose in this world is to develop our spiritual qualities," she explains. "And service to mankind is service to God."

This is not the first, nor will it be the last, time that I am envious of religious people during this journey. Being agnostic feels true to who I am, but it also leaves me feeling lost in an overly intellectual wilderness sometimes. The darker the day, the worse this feels.

"If I want my kids to truly be of service, they need to understand what's going on in this world. They need to be able to relate to all sorts of different people," Susan explains. "And so I feel like that's as important a part of their education as just the training of the mind. So many of the problems we see are from people getting a great education but not using it in a great way, using it in ways that enrich themselves or a small portion of their community."

To Susan's disappointment, it has felt easier to meet White families—who she knows are only a small portion of her community. They chat while pushing their kids in the baby swings, spot one another at the farmer's market later. They meet while inspecting some free toys set out on the curb. Most of these families, Susan learns, don't even consider Sankofa. The majority, it seems, send their kids to Chabot, Peralta, Glenview, or Kaiser, up in the hills.

She's attempted to push back but hasn't had much luck. "I've tried to just have conversations one-on-one with people," she explains. "I thought about organizing something bigger, but I didn't want word to get back to Sankofa that a group of White parents were meeting to, like, talk about whether Sankofa was good enough for their kids. Or White parents were trying to organize to, you know, go as a block to Sankofa and save it. I'm trying to avoid exactly that kind of colonial mindset."

But the playground banter continued to grate. She was so frustrated that White parents in her neighborhood acted as if Sankofa simply didn't exist, as if the real choices were all far afield. Eventually she decided that she would try to organize something with a wider frame to see if that would both make her White neighbors less defensive and also prevent the impression that she was trying to evangelize to get them to go to Sankofa. She posted on a neighborhood LISTSERV about a gathering at her home to discuss "school segregation and its role in perpetuating inequality, what this looks like in our own backyard, and what we see as our responsibility as parents of school-age kids."

Nobody came.

"I got a lot of notes saying, 'Thank you for continuing this conversation right now. It's really important.' But no one actually showed up," she says, her long face somehow looking even longer.

Susan, as it turns out, needn't have worried. She will get more White parents together than she ever could have imagined, or would have wanted, for that matter.

28

JOHN BRINGS THE MAIL in, as he always does, and throws it on the faux-granite counter in the middle of our kitchen. I grab the pile and sort it, absentmindedly tearing the envelope open from PG&E, our local utility company, and glance at our electrical bill for the month. As usual, it's preposterously low—about $15.

I flash on something our neighbor Tom said when I interviewed him and Mary. I was talking about how the parenting culture that I'm exposed to often makes me feel like I'm perpetually behind on a million little things. A constant low-grade anxiety pulses underneath my days about all the sign-ups I've missed. In response he said, "I think the truth is that you actually don't need to get it right all the time. You need to get it right in these watershed moments."

He described how, when they were building the community—super-stressed out and dripping with little kids at the time—he had a strong conviction that they should put solar panels on the roofs. Some people were frustrated with him; it sounded sort of out there, and it would be more expensive. None of them knew anyone with solar panels on their roofs—was this a fad? Money was so tight. They were already handling so many details of new construction on all these buildings. But he promised them it would pay off in the long run. He researched tirelessly and advocated gently but persistently.

Tom remembered: "I thought to myself, if we can figure out how to put the houses on the property so they're facing this way, then it allows all of these possibilities. It will be a continuing blessing to the community forever."

"Once these decisions are made, there are all these downstream effects from it," Tom said. "I think these moments, more than all the little things, are worth the extra time and energy. They have a momentum to them."

We talked about the cohousing community that we're a part of—how it is structured such that we can actually be pretty lazy, but there is, as Tom put it, "an inertia toward community." The common meals, the collective workdays on our land, the running into one another in the courtyard or while bent over a garden box of strawberries. We live together, so we build together. It's not painstaking; it's actually quite passive. If I lived in a typical home but craved community, I'd have to constantly think about what other things I could do in order to create that.

One might switch the question from "Where should I send my kid to school?" to "What kind of cultural inertia are we interested in being a part of?"

The tricky thing is that it's hard to know exactly what kind of inertia you're signing up for until you're already in the middle of its swirling, inevitable center. You have to have a hunch. You have to bet on that hunch.

In some ways, White parents who are considering being a part of integrating schools are being asked to bet on the hunch they know the least about. I know what the communities at Chabot or Peralta probably feel like. I'm already a part of them, in a sense, by virtue of being a White parent with a social circle that mirrors them demographically. I'm guessing it would be pretty familiar—talk of the newest beer garden to open, the strain of Silicon Valley commutes, and maybe even the latest protest march around Lake Merritt.

But it would also, I'm guessing, get under my skin. I don't want the cascading pressure or constant, albeit subtle, sense that all the parents are vying for the best stuff. I love my friends, but I don't always love our people. Most of all, I don't want to live with the hypocrisy of claiming to care about equity but abandoning the kids with the least resources in my own city from day one. I want *not* that.

This inquiry has painted me into a corner. It's not just that I would feel sheepish to tell my friends, my neighbors, Dawn, OtherCourtney if we sent Maya to one of the sought-after public schools after all this research and angst. I would feel that, but I could get over it if I knew I was doing the right thing for Maya. But I don't even believe that anymore. Not really. The burden of hypocrisy has grown bigger and bigger the longer I've looked at it, the more conversations I've had, and now it feels too big to put on her tiny shoulders.

We get the email a few days later—Maya got into Emerson. A simultaneous sense of probity and fear runs through me. It's not panic. It's like that moment you decide that you are brave enough to jump off a large rock into a river, and then you're relieved because you wanted to be the kind of person who would do that. You're still a little freaked out, but you like who you are. It's that kind of clean fear. And there's also something else in there: relief. The inquiry is over. Now we get to actually live into it.

PART II
ARRIVING

Disorientation is part of the American fabric.

—Ocean Vuong

29

Just about every night before I go to bed, I slip into my daughters' bedrooms for a moment and watch them sleep. The light from the hallway bathes their finally quiet bodies. I try to register the peace. There is so little peace in parenting otherwise. It's all picking up and preparation of bland, abandoned food, curdling worry about their aching ears, delight at their unselfconscious observations of the world and misspellings that are better spellings, and all the rest. But when they sleep, it's like all of that ceases, and I can register that they are, quite miraculously, alive at all, and that I am their mother, and that somehow it is sort of working out.

It's a chance to study their physicality. Stella's cheeks somehow seem even more plump in the dark of the night, a little flesh pillow on either side of her face that she can choose from when she finally crashes into sleep.

Tonight, the night before the first day of school, Maya's legs seem impossibly long.

I sit on the edge of her bunk and linger, tears welling up. There was a time when I couldn't imagine her figuring out how to do anything except nurse. She was a terrifying gift, and one I didn't quite know how to receive.

Now she is a person. A small person still lacking all sorts of knowledge and skills, but a person nonetheless. And tomorrow she will become a person who goes to school. And who will have all kinds of experiences that I will never know about. She will have friendships and frustrations and epiphanies, none of which will have much to do with me. And it's terrifying all over again, another gift I'm not exactly sure what to do with.

I imagine all the moms and dads and grandmas sitting on the edges of beds all over the dark city, marveling at the terror of their gangly babies.

30

A⟨T FIRST WE JUST⟩ mill around the playground, smiling first-day smiles at other kids and their parents. It's immediately clear who knows what they're doing and who is figuring it out for the first time. Eventually, a skinny Black guy in a Raiders cap, Coach Andre, blows a whistle, and the older kids take a knee on the blacktop.

The teachers are spread out across the playground, holding hand-written signs with their grades and names on them. We line up behind Mrs. Minor. She wears another long flowing skirt and a gray T-shirt with a big colorful butterfly on it and the words OAKLAND SCHOOLS ARE SANCTUARY SCHOOLS.

Principal Palin is dressed in a button-down shirt, a vest, and brown Oxfords. She stands in front of the amoeba of parents and kids slowly sorting ourselves into order and smiles and squints warmly while shouting into a microphone: "Good morning, Emerson community!"

"Good morning!" some of us shout back.

"I said, 'Good morning, Emerson families!'" she shouts again.

"GOOD MORNING!" This time we are louder, surer. Kids scream at the top of their lungs, mouths wide open to the sky.

"That's more like it. Welcome to all of our returning families and all of our new families. We are so excited to have you here. It's going to be a great year. We start every morning right at eight-thirty, and we really appreciate you being on time. Being at school every day and being here right on time are so important to our learning.

"I'd like our returning students to be especially loud and clear as we do our Cheetah Cheer for everyone. Ready?"

"YEAH!" the kids shout.

Principal Palin gets them started:

"I will be safe!"

The kids chant after her: "I will be safe!"

Palin: "I will be respectful!"

Kids: "I will be respectful!"

Palin: "I will be responsible!"

Kids: "I will be responsible!"

Palin: "If I work hard in school, I will win in life!"

Kids: "If I work hard in school, I will win in life!"

Palin: "I am a Cheetah Champion!"

Kids: "I am a Cheetah Champion!"

"All right, way to start things off right! Now please follow your teachers into your classrooms, and have a great day!" Principal Palin finishes. John and I exchange looks. This is ridiculously sweet and reassuring.

We follow Mrs. Minor—a shuffling, quiet line—through a side door. The hallway is filled with little hooks. Each hook has a kid's name next to it. Seeing Maya's name there is somehow a deep relief to me. This means that I didn't make some stupid administrative mistake and no one knew she was coming.

Maya forgoes breakfast, which appears to be some kind of sausage substance and egg in a biscuit packaged in sweaty plastic. Maya doesn't do eggs. She doesn't, in fact, do much that doesn't fall into the category of flavorless carb—bagel, tortilla, piece of organic whole wheat bread. Sometimes she holds up a cracker or a Cheerio and asks, "Does this have protein in it?" She knows that I lust after her rare consumption of protein. Since she's not going to eat breakfast, we sit down to read a book together.

I glance around and register the racial composition of the class. I've developed a special skill since becoming a mom: I can read an entire picture book out loud while making a mental note of the friends that I need to call back or a Target shopping list.

There are what looks to be about a dozen Black kids (some of whom are with English-speaking African-American parents, and some of whom seem to be with Amharic-speaking Ethiopian parents), and what looks to be about five Latinx kids, about as many White kids, and a couple of Middle Eastern kids.

When I tune back in, I realize that the book we are reading—*Mixed*—is an analogy for interracial tension. "Everyone lived in color harmony. Until... one afternoon, when a Red said, REDS are the BEST! The Yellows disagreed. NO! We're the BEST because we're the BRIGHTEST. The Blues were too cool to even respond." Don't want to ruin it for you, but the gist is this: yellow and blue end up falling in love and making a green baby. Soon everyone is fascinated and making babies. Miscegenation leads to desegregation.

The new city was full of color. It wasn't perfect. But it was home.

Mrs. Minor turns down the volume on music and announces that it is time for the grown-ups to say goodbye. A Black girl who I will later learn is named Zaya raises her hand. "Yes?" Mrs. Minor says.

"I like this school!" she shouts with a big grin on her face.

"Well, that's great," Mrs. Minor replies, chuckling a bit at Zaya's naked enthusiasm. Other kids also seem happy, smiling and jostling around the room, investigating all the new stuff they get to play with. Some are stoic, seemingly unfazed by the transition.

Maya is not one of these kids. I can feel her body seize up in my lap. I give her a big squeeze from behind and say, "Okay, Maya Moo, time to say goodbye. Can you give me and Daddy hugs?"

She pops up and John envelops her in a big hug, kissing her on the head. "Thanks for being best friends," he says. He says this every day. When she was really tiny, he actually called her Friendship. He has a thing for bizarre nicknames.

I squat down and get my hug, whispering in her ear, "I'm so proud of you, Moo. It's going to be great."

She clings. I pull back and see that her eyes are filled with panicked tears. "One last hug?" I urge.

We hug again, and then I pry her arms off my body and swiftly move toward the door. *Pull off the Band-Aid. Pull off the Band-Aid. Don't look back.* If you let even a glimpse of connection slip through your resolve, you are back at square one.

I linger in the hallway for a few minutes and then peek back in once I'm confident that her back is to me. She sits on the carpet with the other students, still wiping tears from her eyes. Only the White kids are crying.

31

E MERSON ELEMENTARY USED TO be filled with White kids. Here is a picture of the first class ever.

It's 1914. Woodrow Wilson is the president. Charlie Chaplin stars in his very first film. The U.S. government takes over the few radio stations that exist to communicate about the war, which begins in earnest just as summer ends for these kids.

I hold my hand over the bodies of the first row of kids so that I can study only their faces. Beyond being overwhelmingly White compared to today's average Emerson class, the kids look totally contemporary. Is there something about a five-year-old's face that transcends time? Those ruddy cheeks. Those varied expressions that seem to communicate exactly who each kid is at their very essence. The hair somehow never staying in the shape that a mother's comb hoped it would.

Construction of their brand-new school building—which cost the Oakland Unified School District $163,879—was finished in 1913. It had a central assembly hall and stage, with an east and west patio on either side, and lots and lots of classrooms on multiple floors. It must have seemed pretty grand at the time to these kids, many of them German and Italian immigrants.

Fast-forward forty-two years, and there's another archival photo of an Emerson class seated in their desks. It's 1956. Dwight D. Eisenhower is president. Elvis releases his first gold album. One hundred and one U.S. congressmen sign the Southern Manifesto in protest against *Brown vs. Board*. It reads, in part:

> This unwarranted exercise of power by the Court, contrary to the Constitution, is creating chaos and confusion in the States principally affected. It is destroying the amicable relations between the white and Negro races that have been created through 90 years of patient effort by the good people of both races. It has planted hatred and suspicion where there has been heretofore friendship and understanding.

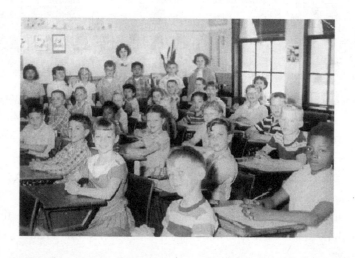

These kids are a little older and the picture is a little blurrier, but that Black boy in the front right shines through crystal clear—hands folded dutifully, shirt crisp and clean, eyes like accusations of an adult world. The White boy front and center, seems, likewise, like a symbol of the time—goofy and yet unbothered, confident in his place in the class-room. The White girl next to him radiates an easy pliancy, her bangs cut smart and straight, her dress cut big enough to grow into for a sensible year or two.

There are a couple of Black kids that year in that particular class. I track down the nephew of one of the students in the picture and he tells me that those kids were bused in from Oakland Army base, according to his late aunt. They're in the vast minority. But things are about to change. In that decade, the Black population of Oakland nearly doubled—from 47,000 in 1950 to 84,000 in 1960. By 1960, only the hill schools were majority White.

32

At 2:45 p.m., a gaggle of parents lingers around the same door where we dropped our kids off and waits for our turn to peek in and lock eyes with our little ones. The relief washes over Maya's face when she sees mine. She tears up but doesn't cry. Smiles bravely instead.

"You want to go get ice cream to celebrate?" I ask her.

She nods, still seemingly unable to say much of anything. I've brought her scooter and helmet, so we move briskly toward Curbside Creamery, where we usually go to grab a scoop on special occasions.

Dawn and Linden are already there when we arrive. Great minds. We settle into one of the red metal tables and try to get something, anything, out of our little ones about how the day went. "My tummy hurts," Maya says after a few minutes. "Can we go home?"

"Sure, honey."

"See you tomorrow," I say to Linden. "Congrats on a great first day!"

As soon as we are alone again, I can feel Maya's mood lightening. I think she must just be overwhelmed by it all. As she scoots, she volunteers, "It wasn't as bad as I thought it would be."

"That's great, sweetie," I say. I had no clue she thought it would be bad at all.

Later, while we are hanging in the courtyard in front of our house, she says, "I want to be a teacher when I grow up."

Maya continues: "One girl. With Brown skin. I think her name is Zaya." It's the first time she's ever mentioned the color of anyone's skin, other than that time she asked me why Stella was Asian when she was born. True story. Stella, who is now blond, looked surprisingly Asian right out of the womb, according to our Asian friends.

"She had a million beads in her hair. It was so pretty. Can I have hair like that, Momma?"

"Probably not."

"Why not?"

"It's sort of hard to explain," I say, searching my brain for the best way to define cultural appropriation to a four-year-old. Nothing comes.

"Mmm," Maya says. Confusion hangs in the air.

33

IT'S THE AFTERNOON OF day two of school, and we have our first parent-teacher conference with Mrs. Minor—just sort of a get-to-know-you thing. Though we're not really getting to know anyone all that much. John, Maya, and I sit down across a desk from Mrs. Minor and try to make small talk. "Are those your kids?" I ask, seeing a framed picture behind her of two toothy, adorable girls.

"Yes, these are my daughters."

"How old are they?"

"They're four and five."

"Oh, wow, do they go to Emerson?"

"No, they go to a Catholic school. It's the same one I went to growing up, so it's a bit of a family tradition," Mrs. Minor says.

"Oh, that's so nice. So you grew up in Oakland?" I ask.

"Born and raised," she says, and then quickly transitions: "So, it's wonderful to have Ms. Maya in class."

All three of us look at her expectantly, and then Maya looks down at her lap, wilting in the heat of all that attention. Mrs. Minor walks us through the goals of the year: building blocks for literacy and numbers, and lots of social-emotional skills.

"Do you have any questions for me?" she asks.

John immediately says, "How can we support you and the school?"

I cringe internally and shift in my seat. He sounds like such a White dude—formal right out of the gate, putting himself in the position of supporter rather than, God forbid, needing support.

Mrs. Minor seems taken a bit off guard. "Well, um, I don't know. That's nice of you to ask. I think they need volunteers at lunchtime—it's always such a zoo in there. And the PTA is always looking for new members."

"Anything *you* need?" he persists.

"I can always use more paper towels and hand sanitizer," she says with a smile.

"Consider it done," he says. I refrain from rolling my eyes.

Obviously, I, too, want to be helpful, but this is not exactly the first impression I was hoping to make. I've got all the same White savior impulses he does, but I try not to strut around like a superhero. Then again, maybe his version is just more honest?

We go get ice cream again and tell Maya that we're proud of her, like, 10 million times.

34

Iᴛ's ᴛʜᴇ sᴇᴄᴏɴᴅ ᴡᴇᴇᴋ of school, Wednesday. Morning time. I look up from the book that I'm reading Maya in the little library corner and smile warmly at Rosa's tiny grandmother, who has just walked in. *"Buenos dias,"* I say without thinking much about it. She lights up and asks, *"Habla Español?"*

"Solamente poco," I explain with a nervous smile on my face. *"Lo siento."*

A waterfall of Spanish falls out of her mouth. Something about a bag maybe? I am totally lost. It's embarrassing that I took Spanish for four years of high school and retained so little. When I got to college, I stupidly took Italian, and now everything is mixed up in my brain, and my confidence is shot in both languages. *"Uno momento,"* I say and try to access Google Translate on my cell phone, but I don't get service in the building.

"Momma, keep reading," Maya says, frustrated.

"Just a minute, Maya," I say.

"Anyone in here speak Spanish?" I shout over the music to the whole class of parents and kids. "Rosa's grandmother has a question."

Paul's mom, Jane—blond, tall, extremely gregarious—volunteers immediately. I will later learn that her husband is Afro-Latino, originally from Belize. She and Rosa's grandma chat for a bit while I try to follow along (mostly unsuccessfully).

"Mommmmm," Maya pleads, tugging on my shirt, "keep reading!"

I pull her body close into mine, as if smothering her will get her to shut up. By this time, Mrs. Minor has wandered over. Jane explains to us both, "Rosa lost her lunch box yesterday, and her grandmother is worried about it. She doesn't have another way to send her lunch."

"It's probably in the auditorium," Mrs. Minor says.

"I'll grab it," Jane says, enthusiastically rushing out of the classroom. I sit back down with Maya and realize she has tears filling her eyes.

"Oh, sorry, Moo. I was just trying to help our new friend. It's not a big deal," I say.

I always regret saying "It's not a big deal" to my kids as soon as it's slipped out of my mouth. Developmentally, I get that some things that are a big deal to them are very much, from a rational adult perspective, so not a big deal. Being served dinner on the pink plate. Getting a turn with the neighbor kid's plastic cell phone toy that beeps incessantly. Waiting three minutes to have your book read. I remember almost nothing that I've ever read in a parenting book except this nugget from *Positive Discipline:* tantrums are about either significance or belonging. All the little things are really about the big things.

Maya is not just storing tears in her eyes. She is letting them spill, and Mrs. Minor has just turned down the music, which means it's time for the parents to go. Reading time is over. "I'm sorry, Moo," I say. She cries harder.

Jane rushes back in, lunch box held high, triumphant look on her face. Eventually I am able to peel my child's body off mine and leave Maya on her assigned square of carpet, a deflated little heap of a human in her favorite star dress, smelling of lavender soap and hating her altruistic, monolingual mother. I had thought we had moved beyond the heart-wrenching drop-off season of transitional kindergarten. There had been no tears for a few mornings straight.

I don't blame her. But I also don't blame me. When we chose to send Maya to Emerson, it was, in some sense, a moment of not completely prioritizing her needs and preferences. I realize that's not a one-time thing but an ongoing one. As much as I hate making her cry, I like modeling that for her more.

35

MAYA AND I HAVE come up with a satisfying alternative to her request to have beads in her hair like the other girls in her class. "You can wear as many barrettes as you want," I tell her. "That's a lot like those little plastic beads."

We put five on each side, framing her face with sparks of red and pink and green and blue. I hold her up so she can look in the bathroom mirror, and she smiles proudly. Is there anything better than how damn satisfied a four-year-old girl is with her own reflection in a mirror?

During our morning time at school, we read a book with Zaya and Sally, two of her Ethiopian classmates. Zaya's mom, Liya, looks on approvingly; she's gorgeous—tall and curvy, high cheekbones—the kind of woman who might tell you she was once a model, and you would think, "Yeah, makes sense." She also appears to speak the most English out of the trio of Ethiopian moms who always hang out together.

When we're done, Liya says, "Maya, I love your hair today!" Zaya and Sally nod in agreement, and Zaya says loudly (Zaya speaks only loudly, while Sally hardly speaks at all), "Maya, it looks great."

Maya beams. "Look, it's a pattering!" she tells them. *Pattering* is a word she's made up. It means "pattern." When I go to the bathroom, I ask Kia, another Ethiopian mom, if she'll watch Stella, who has come along this morning. Kia speaks barely any English, but I've been able to learn that she moved to the U.S. only a few years ago and has two children—Aaron, who is a little boy in Maya's class, and a little girl about Stella's age and built just like her—two little cubs who stand side by side on stools at the fish tank and watch the guppies float along.

It feels nice to depend on someone other than Dawn, to break up my habitual pattering.

36

It's BACK-TO-SCHOOL night. Loud, chaotic, exciting. Long lines of families wait their turn in the open air of the central courtyard to load up flimsy paper plates with donated cheese pizza and Trader Joe's everything. The kale salad someone optimistically brought in a beautiful heavy clay bowl perches dangerously close to the edge of the table, mostly neglected. We brought carrots and hummus, also neglected.

We load up on some food and find a piece of concrete where we can eat. Dawn and Linden wander over with their pizza and sit with us. Dawn looks a little rattled. "You okay?" I ask.

"Yeah, there was a little drama in the line, but I'm fine." Later she will text me the story. One of the Black American moms got angry that, as she perceived it, a Black immigrant mom stepped in front of her in line, and said as much.

This isn't the first time I've heard this tension articulated. One morning when Liya and I were chatting at the miniature tables in Mrs. Minor's classroom, our long momma bodies folded into tiny seats, she said, "We love Maya. So nice. So quiet."

"Oh, thank you. You hear that, Maya? How kind," I say. I'm mostly thrilled (She likes us! She really likes us!) and yet a little turned off by the gendered nature of the compliment.

"Not like some of the girls here at Emerson. Some of those older girls on the yard have filthy mouths," she goes on.

"Really?" I say. "What do you mean?"

"They're not nice. Using bad words. Listening to bad music," she answers, her face in a grimace.

I cringe internally. *Respectability politics.*[1]

A politics of respectability limits expressive and authentic freedom for Black women or, in this case, Black girls. Are fifth graders cursing on the playground at Emerson a form of authentic expression or just kids testing their limits? Would these girls' own mothers see their "filthy mouths" as spirited or unacceptable?

It was the first time, but it won't be the last, that I realized Liya and I have very different values. While I find the Ethiopian moms easier to make friends with than the African-American moms, I also realize that our values are further apart. Perhaps this is no coincidence: Does Liya befriend me more easily, in part, because I'm White and she's invested in respectability as defined by a dominantly White culture? Does she see Zaya's friendship with Maya as a sort of intimacy with American "success," which is, ultimately, a White stereotype?

And what of my comparative ease with the Ethiopian moms? I'm not sure, honestly. Am I just following the lead of their open smiles and sisterly energy? Or am I sparking that energy with open vibes of my own, less worried about how I come off to them than I am about how I come off to the African-American moms?

Back in the thick of the chaos, the perky PTA president who gave the tour is selling raffle tickets at a small table in the center of everything. I whisper in John's ear, "Buy a lot of raffle tickets, but be subtle about it."

Finally free to do something, he nearly runs over to the table. There are also tables loaded with clothes and books for families to take if they need or want them—the kind of thing that I'm guessing doesn't happen at Chabot and certainly doesn't happen at Park Day. Maya and Linden abandon their pizza and go peruse the books. Stella follows them around like a puppy dog. Coach Andre comes striding through the crowd, hollering that it's time to get in the auditorium, so we throw away our detritus, grab the kids, and file in, looking for a bit of wall space where we can lean and listen.

John wanders in and stands next to me. All of a sudden I'm filled with dread. "How many raffle tickets did you buy?" I ask.

"Seventy-five dollars' worth. Very subtly," he says, mocking me. "And this T-shirt." He holds up a red T-shirt with the Emerson cheetah jumping across it.

"Shit, I just realized that it will not be very subtle if, because we bought so many tickets, we win every single raffle prize," I say. I don't know why this didn't occur to me earlier.

"Uh-oh, you're right. Though there were definitely other people buying tickets," he reassures me. Principal Palin takes the stage and welcomes everyone. She tells the parents gathered that we have good news at Emerson—a substantial improvement in our test scores and a 2 percent increase in attendance. I'm underwhelmed, but the crowd cheers.

A little Black girl near me is acting up, wriggling her body, laughing, and trying to get the attention of another kid. Her mom yanks her arm too hard for my taste and whispers some stern corrective in her ear.

Ms. Palin shifts pretty quickly from the seemingly mundane to the sacred: "I want to read a quotation by Toni Morrison to you. The teachers and I were thinking about it during our latest professional development time together:

> I tell my students, "When you get these jobs that you have been so brilliantly trained for, just remember that your real job is that if you are free, you need to free somebody else. If you have some power, then your job is to empower somebody else. This is not just a grab-bag candy game."
>
> This is the time for every artist in every genre to do what he or she does loudly and consistently. It doesn't matter to me what your position is. You've got to keep asserting the complexity and the originality of life, and the multiplicity of it, and the facets of it. This is about being a complex human being in the world, not about finding a villain. This is no time for anything else than the best that you've got.[2]

Then the principal pauses for just a moment, the air thick with the impact of what she's just said, all the wriggling bodies suddenly still. And then she says, "I want you to know that we take the power and privilege of teaching your children very seriously."

I tear up. A Latinx guy in front of me with a perfectly flat-billed black baseball hat and two long braids cheers loudly, clearly as touched as I am. His partner, a Black woman in scrubs, rubs his shoulder and shakes her head lovingly at his enthusiasm. Their two little girls sit nearby and laugh.

Principal Palin makes announcements about a range of programs and donations that are coming in (Clif Bar might buy us a real curtain for our auditorium stage! There is a dance program and a STEM program—all nonprofit-run). Twenty percent of Emerson students have an independent education plan (commonly referred to as an IEP); if your kid has an IEP, it means they have been identified as someone who learns differently in some important way and the school has a plan for how to meet their needs. She tells us: "Other schools come to our school to learn how to treat kids with various disabilities well."

She then introduces each teacher and tells us what grade they teach. As she announces each of their names, they come up to the stage and form a long line of unusual suspects—both young and old, Black and White, with perky ponytails and stately head wraps, all wearing Emerson gear of one kind or another. There are a couple of male classroom teachers in the mix—both Black—and two coaches—also Black—who are clearly beloved based on the volume of the cheering kids.

Finally it's raffle time. I hold my breath. There are gift certificates to locally owned bookstores (not us, please not us...not us, phew), swimming classes at the YMCA (not us, please not us...though we do need to teach these kids how to swim...not us, phew), and finally, the local hipster restaurant with giant loaves of artisanal bread and $15 herbal cocktails (not us, please, seriously, not this one please, not us...not us, phew).

I don't remember ever feeling so happy to lose.

37

It was, like, the most intense thing ever," she says, taking a sip of her latte and giving me a big, nervous smile.

I'm sitting on the back patio of said local hipster restaurant, interviewing Hannah, White mother of a biracial daughter named Amelia (father, Dan, is of Chinese-American descent).

About eight years ago, we wandered over to each other at the end of a conference, twin sparkling waters in hand at the cocktail hour, and started bonding about all the pregnant-lady taboos in our midst (wine, soft cheese, cold cuts, sushi). I was about to move to the Bay Area from Brooklyn, and she seemed like a fount of knowledge about everything maternity-related in the area. She had a round, welcoming face and the energy of a class treasurer (on it, smart, detail-oriented). She was a few months ahead of me on the journey—a sweet spot for having enough distance to be insightful, but not so much that she had the willful amnesia of my mother friends with older kids.

When we moved, she was one of the first people I reached out to. We'd take a waddling walk around Lake Merritt together occasionally and talk about the death of progressive media and how broken so much of philanthropy is. And babies, of course—the impending reality that we were about to have our lives rearranged.

I found that making friends, especially in the context of new motherhood, was fraught. On the one hand, I needed friends. Plain and simple. I had just moved across the country, pregnant. On the other hand, I didn't want to be like the girl who bonds with the least interesting person on her hall during the first few days of college out of desperation. I didn't want "mom friends"—women with whom I talked mostly about pregnancy and then babies, women whose whole lives got absorbed in sleep training and homemade baby food and resentment.

I wanted friends of a variety of racial backgrounds, some of whom weren't mothers at all, please. I wanted women, even and especially the White ones who were interested in racial politics and documentary film and great contemporary novels. If they were mothers, too, wonderful, but let that be one of many things we shared.

It seemed like I'd found just that combination in Hannah. I'd text her with questions about pregnancy but also questions about local politics. She gave me a giant blue Ikea bag full of baby clothes and a My Brest Friend—this monstrous pillow you are supposed to wrap around your body when you start nursing.

After our babies were born, we hung out less often, pulled into our respective caves of new motherhood, with all of its wonder and isolation. But we'd run into each other at the farmer's market or occasionally throw a blanket down on a lawn and give our now slightly older babies squeezie pouches to suck on. I started to get the sense that we were having very different experiences. Amelia wasn't sleeping. Hannah was exhausted. She and Dan had consulted a sleep consultant, and that hadn't been very helpful. We'd had our sleepless nights, no doubt, but were faring pretty well now that we'd let Maya cry it out.

That contrast was representative. Everything just seemed harder for Hannah and Amelia. And again, I by no means found motherhood easy. I had a million confusions and complaints. But the more we hung out, the less I felt like I knew what to say in the face of all of her suffering and stuck-ness. We didn't talk about media or philanthropy so much anymore. Were we "mom friends" after all? I wondered. I let the texts die off. We didn't hang out for years.

And then I ran into her at a local coffee shop a couple of weeks ago. We embraced warmly. I felt a real surge of gratitude for all the advice and onesies and welcome she'd offered me in my earliest days of being in the Bay Area. "Where is Amelia in school?" I asked.

"Park Day School," she said a little sheepishly. "Long story."

"I'd love to hear it," I say. "I'm working on a book about White parents and school integration."

And so we'd arranged to meet back up at this coffee shop. And I'd resolved beforehand to be empathic but also firm in asking her the hard questions, even if it felt uncomfortable.

After our text threads fizzled, Amelia had continued to be a hard baby. "She did not sleep through the night, not even one time, until she was four and a half," Hannah tells me. And then for emphasis: "Not even one time. Not even *one* time."

By the time kindergarten came around, Hannah described herself as "terrified." She talked to a friend who worked at the district. She read GreatSchools.org, which she was skeptical about, and the Berkeley Parents Network LISTSERV. She explains, "What I was picking up from the rumor mill was: there are good schools, and there are bad schools. Everybody knows which ones are the good schools; everybody knows which ones are the bad schools. And so you've got to get into a good school. But I was skeptical of that, too. Like, let me test that."

Her way of testing it? Fifteen tours.

And what was she looking for?

"I was looking for a felt sense of 'How would Amelia do here?' Everywhere felt too big and loud and overwhelming. Nothing felt quite, well, gentle, you know?"

Gentle. The word hangs in the air between us. I've got a husband and a daughter who have no official diagnoses, but from what I've read, seem like highly sensitive people. Maya gags at the smell of a maddeningly wide variety of foods. She's physically tentative (a late bloomer on the monkey bars) and already a perfectionist—her rainbows have been colored accurately since she was three. She's basically mute around strangers. She doesn't like loud parties. Gentle is her jam. I can imagine her really thriving with gentle.

But that's not what I chose for her—at least on a sensory level. Emerson is filled with loud noises and weird smells and kids having a hard time "regulating," as White people love to say. It's not uncommon for me to walk up to her classroom door after school to pick her up and have one of her classmates announce, "Maya puked at lunch again today." I nod my head knowingly. Not alarmed. Neither is the classmate. It's just sort of a status update.

Did I not give her gentle because I'm a less attuned mother? Or because her sensitivities aren't as severe as Amelia's? Did I not give her gentle because I slept more when she was a baby? Because she slept more when she was a baby? Does integration require White babies to sleep through the night so White parents can feel less terrified when they're choosing a school?

Initially Hannah was staunchly opposed to enrolling Amelia in a private school. Dan wanted them to at least consider it. He had sensitivities like Amelia and had thrived while in a smaller setting in high school (technically public, but a magnet program) in New Jersey.

An "ideological battle," as Hannah puts it, ensued. "It was so brutal. It's just, like, 'We don't do that.' I believe in the public school system. I've been an advocate for social justice causes my entire life. I believe that we need to invest in the public system in all the ways.

"I really think of it as a divestment. Right?" Hannah is on a roll: "Or I did at the time. I don't know if I still do. But we can't divest from the public system. Because when we don't go to the public school system, they don't get the money for our kid. Also, they don't get all of our talents. You know? We're pretty awesome. We can be good fundraisers and good PTA members."

I'm nodding my head. I'm sipping my coffee. She has me convinced, and yet I'm the one busting my butt to contribute to my kid's "bad" public school. She's the one with her kid at a school that costs $29,000 a year.

The whole family went to Dan's parents' house for Christmas, and Hannah had a plan. She would get Dan's dad, a lifetime public school teacher, in on the battle. Surely he would be on her side.

But it didn't work out that way. "If there's any way you can afford to send her to private school, you should do that," he said.

"Why did he say that?" I asked Hannah.

"He was actually critical of public schools. 'Public schools aren't out here to teach kids anything. They're just trying to teach them to work at Starbucks. They're just training kids to achieve some low rung in the capitalist system, training them to be cogs in the workforce,'" she explains. "That was a blow."

It wasn't the only one. She also had a pivotal conversation with a good friend, a Black guy with three kids just a little bit older than hers. They were out one night, shooting the shit about the decision she was facing, and he said, "You can't send your kid to public school."

Hannah laughs when she tells me this. Loudly. "And I was, like, 'Yeah, but I'm White. You go send your kids to private school and go get your Black excellence and do that. But, like, I don't know, shouldn't us middle-class White families just send our kids to public school?'"

"No," he answered, according to Hannah. "You have to separate your ideology from your parenting. It's not the same."

Between Dan, his dad, and her friend, she was persuaded to start touring private schools.

Once you've seen it, you can't unsee it.

Once you sense the gentle, you can't unfeel it. At this point, Amelia got a diagnosis: sensory-integration issues. Hannah describes it this way: "They're perceiving too much...and they can't process it yet. And so they're just in a constant state of anxiety."

Amelia's therapist didn't think Amelia could hack it at a public school and told Hannah as much. Park Day felt soothing. It felt, as Hannah puts it, like "a yoga retreat center." And it wasn't anything like the East Coast boarding school of her imagination. It wasn't "some elite place that elite people send their children to because they think their kids are better than everybody else, or because they have class bias or race bias against the public schools."

She goes on: "I came to understand that these schools call themselves progressive schools. And at first I scoffed at that. Ugh, these people and their marketing trying to make themselves sound like they're not private schools with their terminology."

Once again, yup. We're speaking the same language and yet still, somehow, landed in different stratospheres.

"But, I mean, the reason that they were founded, these schools, is not out of elitism but out of wanting something different from what the public system offers...a different sort of progressive pedagogy."

"So, how did you finally make the decision?" I ask.

Amelia got into five private schools—every one she applied to, in fact—plus their neighborhood public school, Glenview. Hannah had, at this point, at least a couple of different interactions with each of the five private schools beyond the tour, including one-on-one interviews and meet-and-greets at the private homes of current parents in the schools. The time and energy is adding up in my head like a mutant bar that just keeps growing and growing off the page of the graph—fifteen tours, plus additional research, applications, and social interactions with all of these private schools. Hannah confirms: "It occupied the majority of my brain space for nine months."

Ultimately, the deal breaker was an OUSD funding cut. Hannah went to a PTA meeting over at Glenview with a neighbor friend. They were discussing how they were going to tweak the budget given the cut. The principal impressed Hannah, as did the parents. "I left there feeling like, 'Okay, I can handle this. This is fine.'"

But then later, she went on yet another tour at Glenview, sort of a final gut check, and she asked the principal, "So, I know there's that budget cut. What's going to happen with the teaching assistants in kindergarten?"

And the principal answered honestly. She didn't know. The TAs might have to go. They weren't sure yet.

"I just couldn't put my kid in a classroom with twenty-five kids and no TA," Hannah explains. "I couldn't even imagine a scenario where she would be okay without an adult who could give her some personal attention."

The other thing that pushed her over the edge was that Dan got a $50,000 bonus at work, right as the decision deadline was looming. It seemed like a sign. Nearly two years of private school tuition, $7,000 more than the per capita income for *an entire year* for the average person living in Oakland, fell into their bank account, just like that. Hannah called it "miraculous."

It was getting late in the afternoon, and we would both soon need to go get our kids. I knew my time was running out, and I was still trying to make sense of the fact that she articulated my problem with private school better than I did, and yet her kid was going to one. I say: "So I hear you about the ways in which Park Day is different from an overtly elitist institution, but even if it isn't their intention to be elite, by virtue of the structure of it, it is an elite place."

"Absolutely," she says. "Absolutely."

"And so how do you think about that?"

"It continues to be a...like, a what? A place of cognitive dissonance in my life."

She explains that she made a deal with herself. If Amelia went to Park Day, she would spend a lot of time volunteering in the public school system.

But then she didn't.

"The truth is, to be honest, I just haven't done it. I haven't had time. Her school requires a lot of involvement."

They love the school. After crying a lot at first on drop-off and pickup, Amelia is now really happy. They like the people, even if they are richer and Whiter than they would like them to be. It seems like even the kids of color all have at least one White parent, she tells me. "We live in Oakland, and yet Amelia doesn't have this experience of the diversity of Oakland. And it's weird," Hannah says. "I feel like my own social circle is reducing its diversity. So that's a big loss."

She tells me about a birthday party they went to at a country club. The kids swam and ate grilled cheese, and the parents could order any drink they wanted from a waiter. She had two gin and tonics. She enjoyed herself, even as she continued to feel, somewhere in the back of her mind—growing quieter all the time—that "We don't do that." *We don't go to private school. We don't disinvest. We don't fall for the marketing. We aren't elite. We don't laugh at birthday parties at the country club.*

"I kept thinking, Dan and I, we have to talk to each other about this," Hannah says, and then laughs. "It's so weird that we're going to a birthday party at the country club, but Amelia's in the back seat, you know what I mean? It's just weird to talk about it. We can't really talk about it. So we just kind of pretend to her that it's supernormal."

"But does she ask about it?" I ask. "Does she wonder about the differences between her school and other schools?"

"She did actually ask us if all schools cost money."

"And what did you tell her?"

"I said, 'You go to a special school that does cost money. But luckily, most of the schools are free for people. And that's how it should be.'"

38

Most mornings Maya and I head out our front door, past the prolific persimmon tree, carefully avoiding the few red-orange orbs that have landed on the sidewalk before anyone has had a chance to pick them. We curve around the courtyard and out the back door, landing on 43rd Street, and head away from busy Telegraph Avenue.

Usually there's a lot of silence. I've learned to rest in it, to consider it a gift from my girl rather than some sign that we aren't really connecting. We pass a guy using someone else's hose while trying to shave. I try not to stare. Maya doesn't comment.

We pass the part of the sidewalk that buckled so severely that someone poured fresh cement into the gaps. As that fresh cement was drying, someone picked up a stick or used their finger to write LOOK UP. Every single morning, we both pause briefly and look up at the naked black branches of the tree overhead, the big soupy sky just beyond. If I forget, Maya reminds me.

We pass the lot that has been slowly but steadily transformed over a matter of weeks from a little run-down cottage into a two-story all-American dream home. The whole cottage was lifted to become the second floor, and then a first floor was built underneath it. Maya and I marveled at the construction workers' skills and speed. She wonders if the new family is going to get to move in by Christmas. I wonder how much they must have paid for the lot and such dramatic reconstruction. By late January it will be on the market for $1.4 million and have its own short film on the agent's website—apparently the new gold standard in Oakland real estate.

After a couple of blocks, we hang a left onto Webster Street and then walk past the back entrance to Park Day School. Then we walk just two more blocks to land at Emerson's back entrance, where cars are always piled up, their drivers trying to disgorge their little passengers before they maneuver on to their harried days.

It is at this moment—morning drop-off—when I am, perhaps, most aware of the class and cultural differences between our own family and those of some of the kids who Maya goes to school with. It's the cars. The loud bass bumping out, even at this early hour, the dented fenders, and the Uber stickers on the windshields. It's the kids sliding out of back seats where there is no car seat. It's the kinds of cars—not the narrow and predictable choices of White Oakland: Prius or Subaru, basically—but a wide variety of other makes, models, and colors. Some are clean and shiny—perhaps a prized possession, a statement piece. Some are held together by duct tape and a prayer.

As I'm reading more about the history of integration, I'm learning that transportation has often been at the center of the controversy. Likely you have the iconic imagery in your own head—a big yellow school bus, a crowd of rabid protesters surrounding it. In the 1970s and '80s, many cities, but particularly those in the theoretically more progressive Northeast, like Boston, got massive pushback from White parents when they attempted to desegregate their public schools.

Buses, of course, were just a means to an end, a way to get kids from here to there. But freaked-out and savvy White parents realized that they could frame their arguments in terms of "busing" and "neighborhood schools" to avoid using explicitly racist language. The media fell for it. The story—in the larger public's mind—became not that White parents were rejecting integration but that they didn't want their sweet, young kids driven far away. And it led to an attitude of resignation among the American public. *Look at the busing thing. Integration is just too hard.*

39

Jack, Linden's dad and Dawn's husband, has joined a school committee called the SSC. I have no idea what it stands for or what it does, but there must be a quorum or the meeting's resolutions don't legally count. He asks me if I can fill in for him on a Tuesday night, as he has to be somewhere else.

I wander into the library at six p.m. and see a box of donated pizza. I grab a slice, put it on a paper plate, and sit down at the table where a group of about six people is already gathering. I don't recognize anyone except for Principal Palin.

A White guy named Scott with a PC laptop open in front of him is apparently the SSC president. He's like a basset hound—big brown beard and droopy, sweet eyes. He starts the meeting by handing out an indecipherable agenda, and then proceeds to replace every other word with an acronym for the duration of the meeting. SIPSA. LCAP. SBAC. PD. PBIS. SIPPS.

I'm having a lot of trouble following the discussion. One thing is clear: our growth scores, as Principal Palin announced at back-to-school night, have gone up, and that's a very exciting thing to everyone. I try to take notes in my notebook, but it's like I'm writing down random words in a foreign language with no means of translating them. I consider asking for definitions, or just admitting to everyone that I am deeply confused, but I decide not to slow things down or reveal the level of my ignorance.

Later I text Jack: Um, I got to admit, I didn't really understand a word of that meeting. I've never heard so many acronyms.

Yeah, Scott is a little obtuse. He's a great guy, but he knows too much, he writes back.

I google the first acronym, SSC, and learn that it stands for School Site Council and that, as it turns out, it's supposed to be the central governing body of our communal life as a school. The SSC—made up of parents, teachers, staff, and even neighbors from the surrounding area—works with the principal to create the equivalent of a strategic plan for the school. It is supposed to define the collective values and goals and decide both how to measure the school's effectiveness in reaching those goals and how to spend money in alignment with them. Virtually all schools in California have an SSC.

As intimidating as I found the acronyms to be, I realize that this is where I need to be showing up. I put the SSC meetings in my calendar for the rest of the year.

40

I'M PUMPING OUR BLACK Xtracycle cargo bike up the hill and panting. Maya is perched on the back, gripping the silver bars, her purple helmet sparkling in the morning sunshine. We've just dropped Stella off at day care, and now we're racing to school, hoping not to be late.

I notice a Black girl a little farther ahead of me on the hill, biking hard. As I get closer, I realize it is the older sister of two Emerson kids. She's got the bigger one, a boy, perched on the front bar of her bike, and the littler one, a girl, clinging to her back. None of them have helmets on. As we ride alongside them, the boy says, "See, we need one of those kind of bikes!"

His big sister says, "Those are expensive, dummy."

She's right. We got ours used, but a new one, without the electric motor, is upwards of $2,500. With a motor, they're as much as $6,000. They are ubiquitous in Oakland now; the only vehicle you can drive more sanctimonious than your Prius or Tesla (both of which we own).

I turn and say, "I was amazed watching you get up that hill with those two! Do you want me to take one?"

"Really?" She's clearly surprised.

"Sure," I say. "I got room. I just dropped my other kid off."

We both pull over. I get off my bike, ask the little girl if I can pick her up (she nods yes), and then move her from her sister's bike to my own. I unsnap Stella's helmet from the bar where I've hung it and put that on her head, too.

We ride the rest of the way side by side, chatting a bit. The older sister is in seventh grade at a nearby middle school, and she drops her little siblings off first every morning. Usually they walk, but she was worried that they would be late today. When we get to Emerson, I unload the girls and realize that Maya already knows our fellow passenger. She's in kindergarten. I say to the older sister, "It must be a big help to your mom that you drop them off," and then immediately wonder if I should have said "caregiver." She shrugs, looking tired already, even though it's only 8:30 a.m., and bikes off.

I tie my little passenger's shoe when we get through the gate and say goodbye as she races off into the fray.

41

I spot her right away—blond hair, comfortable presence, that kind, almost cunning smile—it's OtherCourtney. She's standing in my hotel lobby, waiting for me. I approach and say, "I'm a hugger. That okay?"

"Are you kidding?" she says. "I'd be offended otherwise."

We embrace. This is our first time meeting up in person after lots of phone calls and emails. I'm a little nervous but mostly really excited. So many of my questions right now feel so idiosyncratic. *Should I be going to PTA meetings even though I don't bake or like to plan parties? How do you figure out if you're coming on too strong while making friends with parents of color?*

"I need a beer, you?" I ask.

"Yes, please. Unfortunately, we're in kind of a weird spot. We can do hotel bar or, like, California Pizza Kitchen," she says, scrunching up her face. "You've officially left hipster chic."

"Ha! That's fine. I grew up in the land of Cheesecake Factory and Olive Garden, so I can handle a little California Pizza Kitchen. Bring on the fried appetizers! As long as there's also beer."

We walk across the street, settle in, and immediately start talking about what she calls "the smog" of White-parent culture. (She likely got this from psychologist Beverly Daniel Tatum, who wrote that "cultural racism...is like a smog in the air...day in and day out, we are breathing it in.")

"You've got to counter the smog everywhere and anywhere," Courtney tells me. "It's insidious, so we have to be relentless. This is why I'm always talking about taking the fight to the playgrounds and the birthday parties."

"But how do you keep from sounding judgmental while doing it?"

"Why are you so worried about that? Aren't you making a judgment?"

"Well, yes. But I don't want to alienate people," I say.

"You don't want to alienate people, or you don't want to risk conflict?"

"I don't like conflict, you got me there. But isn't alienating people bad for the movement? We've got to call people in, not call them out, right?"

"Well, yes and no. White people—let's be honest, White moms especially—have to get less nice and more brave about saying uncomfortable things in pretty spaces. Our aversion to conflict is part of the problem. It leads us to prize White women's feelings over real change."

I take a big gulp of my beer. "Damn, okay . . ." I say slowly.

"Did I make you feel judged? Are you uncomfortable? Is it so terrible?"

I laugh out loud. I love this woman. "No, it's kind of awesome, actually. I love talking with someone who says it plain. I'm so tired of polite bullshit."

She smiles wide. "I'm not known for my tactfulness. Seriously, it's taken me a while to figure out how to talk about this stuff in a way that's clear but not shaming. I still get it wrong a lot."

I tell her a bit about what I've been experiencing in the first few months of school, and she nods and nods and laughs and laughs, and it's such a welcome relief. My eagerness and awkwardness with other parents, the flood of acronyms at the meetings, my confusion about how and when to offer our resources. She doesn't blow smoke up my ass. She also reassures me that my confusion is normal. She reminds me of the Integrated Schools mantra: "Show up, shush up, and stay put."

I can feel the way that her own experience, coupled with a growing national network of experiences, shrinks my own questions down to their right size. They're worthwhile, but they're not unique or even that important. The most important question—each and every time—is how I, how we, can continue to be a force for getting all kids the education they deserve.

OtherCourtney has a way of making my own questions and very specific context feel honored while simultaneously reminding me that it's not special, of encouraging me to do the inner work while keeping in mind that it's the least of the work to be done. I guess that's the art of a great organizer. I realize that I've never been "organized." Organizing is something that Black and Brown people do for one another, and, of course, White people do for Black and Brown people, but White people organizing other White people is a much rarer phenomenon outside of a labor union context.

Not that it hasn't been called for time and time again. The Black Power position paper published in 1966 by the Atlanta Project, an initiative within the Student Nonviolent Coordinating Committee (SNCC), argued that it was time for White people's role in the movement to shift: "White people who desire change in this country should go, where the problem (of racism) is most manifest. That problem is not in the Black community. The white people should go into white communities where the whites have created power for the express purpose of denying Blacks human dignity and self-determination."[3]

They went on: "There is no doubt in our minds that some whites are just as disgusted with this system as we are. But it is meaningless to talk about coalition if there is no one to align ourselves with, because of the lack of organization in the white communities."

42

Show up, shush up, and stay put. Show up, shush up, and stay put. Show up, shush up, and stay put. Show up, shush up, and stay put. Show up, shush up, and stay put. Show up, shush up, and stay put. Show up, shush up, and stay put. Show up, shush up, and stay put. Show up, shush up, and stay put. Show up, shush up, and stay put. Show up, shush up, and stay put. Show up, shush up, and stay put. Show up, shush up, and stay put.

43

We're back from winter break, and Maya is fired up as we walk home, talking about her day. "Me and Kofi are the leaders of Black History Month!"

If I had been drinking coffee, I would have spit it out. I give her a side-eye and say, "What do you mean?"

"It's in the auditorium. A showcase. It's a really big deal. We're still choosing between 'Man in the Mirror' or 'Greatest Love of All.'"

"That's awesome. Those are serious jams. But what do you mean that you're the leader?"

"Me and Kofi are."

"But what does that actually mean?"

She shrugs and then changes the subject: "Do we have any extra paper towels? Mrs. Minor says our parents need to bring them in. The school can't afford them."

We will spend the rest of the year regularly bringing in paper towels, soap, Kleenex, and other basics that our dysfunctional district apparently can't afford. We've been in OUSD for only five months, and its failings are popping up everywhere.

In conversations with other parents and then a damning grand jury report from Alameda County, I learn the extent of the dysfunction at OUSD. The report finds "repeated examples of mismanagement, favoritism, disregard for authority and poor controls."[4]

It goes on: "Policy and procedures are ignored causing one poor decision after another. Moreover, lack of accountability is rampant."

The report recommends: "OUSD can no longer afford to be philosophical. Restoring financial stability requires sacrifices throughout the organization. Stringent controls, adherence to contracting procedures, updated policies, and school consolidations are immediate priorities."

There's also the first rumblings of a teacher strike. They've happened in Arizona and Colorado and L.A. OtherCourtney writes on the Integrated Schools blog about her own experience joining the picket lines: "Some have called the teacher strike a middle class revolt . . . and in some ways I agree. Things had to get *this bad* in our district, classrooms had to get *this large* to mobilize action. Our schools had to get *this underfunded* that even the big-money parent orgs in the schools with much higher concentrations of privilege could not make up for the cuts. In the heady online discussion groups, I sensed a kind of awakened aghastness. Wait—not all schools have a nurse or librarian? What kind of public education is this?!?"[5]

Oakland is likely next. We sure as hell don't have a nurse at Emerson, and the librarian is a profoundly precarious line item each year.

It feels hard to make an argument that Oakland parents should be sending their kids to public schools, much less making the argument that White parents should be integrating those public schools, when the level of dysfunction at headquarters seems this profound. Then again, if White parents completely desert the public school system (already only 10 percent of Oakland public school kids are White), then the kids left behind will have even less chance of getting the quality education they deserve.

44

We walk down Rich Street, the prettiest little street in Temescal, toward our friends' house for brunch on a sunny Saturday. Maya's on her scooter, navigating the broken sidewalk skillfully. Stella is in our stroller, clutching a stuffed animal squid and watching the world go by. Our friends have asked us if we'll come and talk about our experience at Emerson, and school choice more generally, with a group of neighborhood parents who are all in the thick of it. We said sure and grabbed a bag of baby carrots from the fridge.

The air inside their home feels heavy. Four families are already milling about. Three of the four families have one East Asian–American parent and one White parent, and one family has two White parents. At first I have a hard time interpreting the palpable, weird energy in the room, until it suddenly occurs to me: this is just straight-up elite, freaked-out parent energy. This was energy that I, myself, had (at least to some extent) only a year ago.

The reason it's been hard to hold on to that feeling isn't just the typical shedding of short-term memory. The experience of being at Emerson is largely so incongruent with the fear that existed in my body before we actually sent Maya there that it seems preposterous. I excised it so fast because it had no relationship to the real thing.

I start to think about the best way to enter into the conversation. *This actually isn't that big a deal* is not going to work with this crew. Every parent has their own educational history, fears—conscious and unconscious—expectations, and kind of kid to contend with.

John speaks first: "So, why don't we just jump in by telling you a little bit about what it's been like for us at Emerson so far," he says. "We've been there about six months, and we're loving it!"

In every conversation John and I have ever had about schools, I have taken the initiative. I have no idea what is going on here.

"Maya's teacher is amazing—they're already learning foundational academic skills, plus doing all kinds of social-emotional learning stuff. Every morning they do what they call SAM—stretch, affirm, and meditate. There's a great gardening program. The principal is great."

I can see the "bougie pleasure centers"—as a more veteran White Emerson mom calls it—of the parents gathered firing up. Meditation! Gardening! Leadership!

I flash on a new fear: it almost sounds like John is evangelizing for Emerson, like we are trying to get more upper-income White and Asian-American parents there. Which is both true and not true. It would be great if a larger percentage of families in the neighborhood sent their kids to the school, building it up with their resources for all kids. Funding is allotted on a per-pupil basis. But it would be a disaster if the "wrong" families in the neighborhood showed up—that is, those with no consciousness about how they show up as privileged newcomers in a majority low-income school that has served many Black and Brown families for generations.

He's going on: "We had some worries going in, but all of them have proved unfounded. We love the school."

"Which is not to say that it's for everyone," I jump in. "It's just to say that some of the things that we were freaked out about from a distance have proven to be unfounded."

It would be an even more cataclysmic disaster if the school flipped—becoming majority White and Asian-American and displacing Black and Brown families who find it to be a hospitable place.

It doesn't take a lot to shift things when there are only three hundred kids total. Peralta, now considered one of the most desirable schools by White parents in Oakland, is a case in point. During the 2001–2002 school year, Peralta probably looked a lot like Emerson, with 14 percent

White kids. But then a "critical mass" of "like-minded" parents (what one researcher found to be the code words for White and/or privileged families in a neighborhood) decided to band together, enroll their kids, and improve the school.[6] Today, 53 percent of their student population is White. What the researcher found, in extensive interviews, was that many Black and Brown families left, no doubt because of the gentrification in the neighborhood, but also because some sensed they were no longer welcome in a culture that became more and more elite (polished PowerPoint presentations in the PTA meetings, professionalized fundraising, and so on). It would break my heart if we were part of a wave of White folks that destroyed the welcoming, informal culture at Emerson.

"We went on a tour of Emerson, and I found the kindergarten classroom to be a bit, how should I put this, chaotic," says one White mom. "Have you all, or has Maya, found it to be chaotic?"

I wince inside but try to stay neutral on the surface. "Maya is actually a pretty sensitive kid," I explain. "She doesn't like a lot of noise and responds strongly to a lot of different smells and that kind of thing, but she's coped just fine. And the way I see it, all kids have to get used to negotiating spaces like this at some point. I'd rather she figure out coping mechanisms now so she is more equipped and resilient for the long haul."

A White dad jumps in: "I'm not sure exactly how to describe this, but I felt like the parent who toured us around Emerson was almost apologetic, like kind of felt bad for letting us know all the things that the school doesn't have. What do you make of that?"

My blood is starting to not exactly boil but simmer a bit, but I keep a pleasant smile on my face. "That's interesting. I think it is probably less apologetic and more exasperated," I explain. "Imagine being at a school that most White parents in the neighborhood talk badly about. When White parents come on tours, it feels like they're picking the school apart, and then you sort of know they're going to reject it anyway. It doesn't make leading the tours that inspiring."

The parents nod sympathetically. Some look genuinely surprised.

Another White dad: "I'm worried that my kid will be bored at Emerson."

Bored? Now I'm the one who is genuinely surprised. "Why are you worried about that?" I ask, glancing over at his four-year-old, who is making a spitting noise with his mouth as he moves a Lego spaceship around the living room, stepping on a smaller kid in the process.

"I guess just because I was bored a lot in school," he answers.

"Ah, that's interesting. Yeah, I think all of us bring our own educational experiences to the table in these moments in ways we may not fully understand," I explain. "If you loved school, had a great experience, then it's easier to assume that the same might be possible for your kid. If you didn't love school, or even experienced some kind of educational trauma, then it's harder to feel like your kid will be okay wherever they end up.

"That was kind of true for John and me. I had a mostly positive school experience, but he didn't, so I had more openness initially to Emerson and other options that didn't feel as familiar."

"But from what I've seen," John pipes in, "the kids aren't bored."

"We really came to think of elementary school as much more of a social experience than an academic one. It's a time for her to learn how to be with other people—collaborate, solve problems, manage her own feelings when that gets tough. Our proudest moments so far at school have been when a teacher tells us that Maya supports other kids academically, like when she's been able to do something and realizes that they're struggling," I add.

"I was wondering about the grounds at Emerson," a Japanese-American mom says. "All that blacktop just doesn't seem safe. You think we could get a group of parents to help redesign it?"

"There are a lot of opportunities to get involved. That's one of the wonderful things about being at Emerson—you really feel like your presence can make a difference. I've heard that at Chabot, parents are jockeying to get to volunteer in the classroom because there are just so many parents who want to be there," I explain.

"Yeah, there were almost a hundred parents on the tour I went on at Chabot," a White mom chimes in.

"Yeah, same with Peralta, but I felt like the facilities there were inadequate for how many kids there were," the blacktop-weary mom adds.

"Part of going to Emerson is also about moving at the community's pace and in the direction that everyone is into," I explain. "I'm guessing lots of parents would be up for talking about replacing the blacktop, but it would be something to run by the rest of the school community."

We talk for about an hour while our kids run feral through the house. I feel a surge of compassion for these parents, remembering a bit of my own confusion at this moment, the sense of a weight you can't possibly carry because it is just so full of unknowns. But I also feel a lot of other things: exasperation with nervous people who rationally have so little to lose, defensiveness at having our kid's school picked apart and judged, and also a new confusion about our role here.

45

I'M DRIVING MAYA HOME from dance class and we start talking about how Monday is Martin Luther King Day and she doesn't have to go to school. "I know, Momma. I know who he is and everything. We've been talking about him at school," she says sagely.

"What did you learn about him?" I ask her.

"That he wanted his children to be able to go to the same schools, eat the same lunches, and drink from the same water fountains as other kids," she replies.

Not, I note, that he wrote: "First, I must confess that over the past few years I have been gravely disappointed with the White moderate. I have almost reached the regrettable conclusion that the Negro's great stumbling block in his stride toward freedom is not the White Citizen's Councilor or the Ku Klux Klanner, but the White moderate who is more devoted to 'order' than to justice; who prefers a negative peace which is the absence of tension to a positive peace which is the presence of justice."

Maybe they save that one for kindergarten.

In any case, we then have the most sustained conversation we've ever had about race and justice, mostly in the context of kids—where they get to go to school and what kinds of resources and teachers are at those schools. At one point she says, "There is a school near us with only White kids, and it's really nice."

"Where did you learn that?" I ask.

"Mrs. Minor told us. But our school has Black kids, too. That's better. It's more fun."

"Well, that's not totally accurate, Moo. That school near us isn't only White kids, but it's true it is mostly White kids," I say, but then can't help adding: "But I bet you're right. I bet your school is more fun."

46

I AM READING JENNIFER HARVEY's book *Raising White Kids* and I run across a passage that knocks the wind out of me:

> Philosopher Shannon Sullivan writes about the ways our ongoing habits and practices over time literally make up the physicality of our bodies—the feel, movements, perceptions. She explains this to point out the ways that White privilege does not just impact White people's way of thinking, but our ways of "bodying." Bodying, the physical correlate to thinking, is produced by the ongoing experience of being White in a White racial hierarchy. We end up bodying Whiteness because of the cumulative effect of what we do in spaces, how we are treated in and navigate spaces, what we do day in and day out—which creates habits, which creates environments, which "bodys" us again.[7]

An undeniable part of being in classrooms and hallways and meetings this year, especially with parents of color, has actually been being confused about what to do with my body. Is sitting "crisscross applesauce"—as the kids say—on the floor a White parent thing? Sure seems like it; the Black and Brown parents almost never do it. Is walking next to my kid while we snake our way into the building each morning overzealous? By count alone, it appears to be something that mostly White parents do.

And when I approach Black parents about something—anything: a birthday invite, a meeting, a homework assignment—do they feel the extra layer of racial consciousness that I'm carrying around with me? Do they find it reassuring—a subtle physical signal that I'm doing some inner work—or does it feel like one more thing to manage, like "White lady tears," but instead White lady awkwardness?

I'm pretty sure it's the latter. Harvey writes: "Even if we have all our ideas, beliefs, and thoughts correct, as White people, our bodies will give us away every time."[8]

Researchers recorded footage of White subjects with varying levels of racial bias—as measured by the psychological gold-standard Implicit Association Test—talking to Black subjects. They then showed that footage without sound to Black people, who could pinpoint the White subjects' level of racial bias based just on their body language. In other words, it takes a Black person twenty seconds to size up where a White person's head and heart are at with regard to race. And White people don't even have to say a word.[9]

Most White people were raised in such profoundly segregated worlds that the only thing our bodies know is the bodies of other White people. We've had a lifetime of practicing White bodying and almost no time being a body in multicultural, or even Black- or Brown-dominated, spaces.

And we don't have to. We can live out our entire lives as White bodies in predominantly White worlds and barely contemplate the difference.

People of color, on the other hand, are compelled to hone their racial-bias radar so exquisitely that they can tell what we're up to in twenty seconds. They, of course, can also grow up in deeply segregated worlds, but if they want to transcend these spaces for educational or economic reasons, they are forced to learn how to interact with White bodies—some hostile, even. And even if they never choose to leave their predominantly global-majority neighborhoods, White bodies enter their spaces, with guns and assumptions, curricula, and good intentions.

Sometimes at school I feel almost trapped in my White, awkward body. I long for more ease, to cease larding up my interactions with nervous expectation, to slip into the sweet relief of instincts. But my largely segregated childhood stripped me of the chance. They were never seeded. Never cultivated. Never blossomed. And here I am, trying to be a flower in someone else's garden. Harvey writes: "Only through conscious choices to desegregate our lives can we learn different ways of bodying."[10]

That's another thing I'm trying to give to Maya.

47

I KNOW IT'S NOT your favorite, but can we read *Fancy Nancy* tonight? Pretty pleeeeeaaaaasssseee," Maya begs at bedtime.

Ugh. I nod yes, reluctantly.

She picks *Fancy Nancy: Stellar Stargazer!* Nancy, her little sister, and her dad sit in chairs in the backyard. "My dad and I try to locate some constellations. They are groups of stars that make a picture like a connect-the-dot puzzle . . . " I read, yawning.

"The easiest constellation to find is the Big Dipper. A dipper is like a big spoon."

When it's finally done, I make sure her little purple Nalgene bottle is filled with ice water and she's got worse-for-wear Baby Bunny in her hands, and I give her a kiss on her forehead. She smells like bubble bath. I inhale deeply. "Good night, my sweet girl. Love you so much."

"Good night, Momma. Love you, too. Can you leave the door a little bit open?"

"Sure, sweetie." And I stop the door right before it closes all the way so a small, comforting shaft of light can shine through.

The next night, we go through the eternal return that is the bedtime routine again. Whenever I find myself in a deep rut of irritation, beleaguered by having to ask Maya for the third time to put on her pajamas or brush her teeth, I try to fast-forward in my mind ten years. I try to feel what it will feel like to have a teenager who shuts the door and doesn't come out, who never needs to be reminded to put on pajamas, who tells me things in little fits and starts that hurt my heart.

It's such an imaginative leap. It feels almost as hard to grasp as a female president or unicorns. Sometimes it helps. Sometimes it just adds to my irritation—she won't put on her pajamas, and I can't even feel grateful for my healthy child. What is wrong with me?

Fancy Nancy is blissfully absent tonight. Right as I'm about to pull the door shut, Maya says, "Mom, you know why I wanted you to read *Fancy Nancy* last night?"

"Why?"

"Because I wanted to check something. In class, Mrs. Minor taught us that the constellation is called the drinking gourd. Harriet Tubman used it to find her way to the north with the slaves that she saved. It was called the Underground Railroad."

I'm stunned.

"But, Mom..."

"Yeah?"

"There's no train. I mean Harriet Tubman didn't have an actual train. They just call it that. She walked a really long way with other Black people who were escaping slavery."

"Right."

"And I'm not sure why Fancy Nancy calls it the big dipper, and Harriet Tubman calls it the drinking gourd, but I'm pretty sure it's the same stars. People look at them when they're lost. Like a map in the sky."

My eyes are wet. There is something so overwhelmingly beautiful to me about my daughter's five-year-old brain connecting these dots. I was bored with the performative precociousness of Nancy, and Maya was working on her first ontological puzzle.

48

Zaya and Aaron come over for a play date. I pick them up after school along with Maya, and we walk the five blocks home together, holding hands across each street. We are all giddy with the novelty of it—the kids' limbs flip and flop around, Zaya's voice, always booming, is practically at a shout, and Maya is in hostess mode already, offering up all the things that they can play together (Legos, dress-up, UNO, waitress, doctor...).

When I unlock the door, all three rush in, bypass the kitchen, and head to the living room. Our house is small—about thirty-five feet from front to back—so it doesn't take long to see the whole thing. "Where's your TV?" Zaya asks immediately.

"We don't have one," I say. "We watch shows on our laptops."

She looks at me sympathetically, then rushes upstairs to catch up with Aaron and Maya, who are already destroying Maya's bedroom. They play happily for a while, and then Maya peeks down the stairwell: "We're hungry!"

"Great, come on down, and I'll get you guys a snack."

They tumble down the stairs and belly up to our table. I hand an apple, some string cheese, and a juice box to each of them. "What's this?" Zaya says, holding up the string cheese suspiciously.

"That's string cheese," Maya says. "Have you ever had it before?"

"No, never," Zaya says. She almost exclusively speaks on very shy Aaron's behalf.

"Oh, cool," I say, while unpeeling it for both of them. "It's great to try new things."

Maya shows Zaya the art of peeling a skinny string of cheese from the whole and dangling it into your mouth. "That's kind of gross," Zaya says.

"Yup," Maya says, as if that's a compliment.

Aaron tries a little bit and then leaves it on his plate. Pretty soon they are rushing outside to explore the courtyard. They find a big plastic bin full of balls, many neglected and deflated. A couple of our neighbors walk by, both named Tom, and we introduce them to Zaya and Aaron, who greet them politely.

Another neighbor gets home from work and walks by as the kids are playing a very dysfunctional game of Frisbee. He loves kids and is expecting his first. He meets them, being sure to clarify the pronunciation of Zaya's name, and then Aaron does one of his Fortnite dance moves for him. "Whoa, nice moves!" our neighbor hollers, and Aaron beams.

It's a sweet moment. And then I immediately feel a rush of worry. Does Aaron feel obligated to perform for us—the White adults—in some way? He's a quiet kid. Dance is sort of his language of connection, as I've witnessed in all kinds of settings, so maybe I'm overthinking it. Then again, maybe I'm not. There's a real power differential here. This is a strange place without a TV and with a bunch of White guys named Tom.

Liya comes soon after to pick the kids up. "Were they good?" she asks me, and then, before I can give her an answer, to the kids: "Zaya, Aaron—were you polite?"

"They were wonderful," I said. "Total pleasure. And they tried string cheese for the first time!"

"String cheese?"

"It's basically a little cylinder of cheese that you eat by peeling off strings." She looks at me strangely, and I hear, for the first time, how weird string cheese actually is. "They didn't like it, so one less thing to add to your grocery list."

"Have you decided where Maya is going to go to school next year?" Liya asks me.

"We're sticking with Emerson. What about you guys?"

"We're applying to the American Indian School. I really hope we get in. It's downtown. They have uniforms. They are much more strict. Discipline is the most important thing to me," she says.

I smile, searching frantically for something to say. I can't even pretend to relate to this. "Oh, interesting. I'll have to look up that school. I haven't heard about it. Was the education system in Ethiopia when you were growing up disciplined?"

"Yes, very," she says, nodding her head emphatically. "That's what I'm used to. I want Zaya to be doing her school work, to be respecting her elders, to be a good, good girl."

We both look over at Zaya, who is jumping wildly off our picnic table at just that moment, and share a laugh.

49

Maya's whole class is lined up outside the buzzing auditorium, each kid holding a book with a Black history theme in their squirmy little hands: *Henry's Freedom Box, The Story of Ruby Bridges, Follow the Drinking Gourd*. Getting them to stay in formation is a fool's errand, but that's my charge. Mrs. Minor is inside, approaching the mic with a fifth grader. She has led the planning for this entire day, not just her own class's performance.

The student nervously says: "Welcome to the Emerson Elementary Black history showcase."

The crowd of parents in folding chairs cheers supportively. She goes on: "This is a celebration of Black pride, culture, achievements, and contributions. This month we learned about Martin Luther King...and I always wondered, Are there any other kings in Black history?"

Mrs. Minor beams as she grabs the mic and says, "Great question!" Then she goes on to read a poem that she wrote herself (she sends me the text later):

> *When learning Black history we must acknowledge that it isn't just an American Story—*
> *The African Diaspora explains how Black people were taken from Africa, displaced and scattered all over the four corners of the earth!*
> *When we learn our heritage we see our glory—*
> *and GLOBALLY we see our worth!*
> *Our Contributions, inventions, leaders, and achievements are great.*

Not just a month but every day we should celebrate
We must research and learn that Black history IS world history!
2019 marks 400 years since we were taken from our home and brought to
*   this land . . .*
This is the history that needs to be taught so we all can understand!

When I later compliment Mrs. Minor on the moving introduction, she tells me that the teacher who was supposed to read it (also Black) didn't feel that it was appropriate to address slavery so directly with such young kids. Rather than remove the reference to slavery or soften it, Mrs. Minor decided to read it herself.

Who were we before 1619? We were told we were many things . . . but did
*   you know we had beautiful civilizations and ruled the Dark Ages . . .*
Yes Black is Beautiful and Brilliant and has gone through many stages.
Knowledge is what we need to succeed!
Knowledge is how we overcome adversity!
Knowledge is how we fight the power . . .
*   from TK to the University!*
With knowledge of self, we have Pride but, Education is the key!
*   and when we raise Educated, Proud Children they are free!*
Knowledge is power!!!

That's our cue. The little ones hold their books over their heads and march in, chanting, "Knowledge is power! Knowledge is power! Knowledge is power!"

They snake through the center of the auditorium, chanting their little hearts out until they are all on the stage and Mrs. Minor signals for them to stop. They lower their books and hold them against their chests. She looks like she is going to burst with pride.

They then sing Whitney Houston's "Greatest Love of All." Miles, one of four White boys in the class, keeps trying to grab the mic off the stand, so Mrs. Minor pulls it off herself and holds it in front of the kids. Maya smashes her cheek into Zaya's. All the kids are belting it out. Not a single nervous shuffle or closed mouth in sight. Maybe it's preparation. Maybe it's the unselfconsciousness of being five. Whatever it is, it's got me.

I decided long ago never to walk in anyone's shadows.
If I fail, if I succeed at least I'll live as I believe.

The kids are really hitting their stride now, some even adding in a fist raise for extra flair. I am openly weeping, and feeling a little sheepish about it, until I look over and see the same Latinx dad who got weepy with me after the Morrison quotation at back-to-school night with tears rolling down his cheeks, too.

50

MAYA LOVES RIDING THE BART train, swinging her legs, looking out the window, making wide eyes at us when it goes underground, as if we're traveling into another dimension. As we take the escalator up into the open air after our short trip to Downtown Oakland, I attempt to remind her that the adventure has a political significance: "So, all these people are gathering because they are trying to make clear that teachers haven't been getting paid or treated fairly, and schools don't have what they need to do a great job, and we want to change that."

The tension between the district and the teachers' union, the Oakland Education Association, is heating up, and there's a rally downtown.

"Who isn't being fair?" Maya asks.

"Well, that's a good question," I say, searching my brain for a five-year-old-size answer. "Have you ever heard us talk about the district?"

Blank stare.

"Well, it's sort of like Principal Palin is Mrs. Minor's boss, and the district is Principal Palin's boss. The district gets to decide how much money everyone makes, how much time off they have for vacations or when they're sick, all that stuff. And so the teachers are asking the district to be a fairer boss."

She nods unconvincingly and says, "Okay."

The rally is short and sweet. There are maybe five hundred people, giant, beautiful banners, and a few inspirational speakers, including the head of the union who breaks it down: OEA's three thousand members have been working without a contract since 2017, and they're sick of it. They want better pay (a 12 percent retroactive raise), less crowded classrooms, an improved counselor-to-student ratio (right now it is 1:600), more nurses, and so on.

He links their fight to so many that are happening across the country. Teachers are the canaries in the coal mine of economic inequality, and they're singing as loudly and clearly as they can. We can't say we value teachers and kids and then starve them of resources; we have to fund schools and pay teachers as if we actually understood the power of that investment.

The superintendent, a Black woman named Dr. Kyla Johnson-Trammell, pens an op-ed that argues that the teachers are right that things aren't as they should be but the union and the district have to find realistic common ground. She admits: "Our teacher retention issues are, in part, rooted in our financial issues, both underfunding and mismanagement."[11]

I'm beginning to hear patterns in the way people talk about the issues facing Oakland's schools—which I know mirrors how people talk about what is facing public schools across the nation. There are so many answers to Maya's question "Who isn't being fair?"

Pretty much everyone agrees that the way schools are funded isn't fair. In California, public schools receive funding from three sources: the state (58 percent), property taxes and other local sources (32 percent), and the federal government (9 percent).[12]

Most of the funding for K–12 education comes from the state; the Constitution essentially says that it is each individual state's responsibility to make sure that kids are getting a decent education. As a result, each state has different ways of determining how much money districts should get and where that money comes from. As you can imagine, this gets complicated fast, not to mention that it is vulnerable to political jockeying.

In Oakland, for example, one of the most profound influences on how much money schools get is Proposition 13. It basically froze property taxes for big corporations and landowners at their 1976 rates. This was part of a huge anti-tax revolt across the country, which led to Ronald Reagan's presidency (the first president I have any conscious memory of).

Over the next couple of decades, California went from being one of the states that invested the most in education to being one of the states that invested the least. Each year, California invests about $7,500 less per student than the average of the ten states that invest most generously in their public education systems. Over a kid's time in school, that's an investment gap of more than $100,000 per student.[13] For all the attention I've paid to how a kid's zip code can determine the educational quality they experience within a given city, there is much to be said about the huge differences state to state as well.

Prop 13 demands reform, but many people refer to it as the "third rail" of California politics. The corporate lobbyists in support of it have huge coffers to draw from to keep politicians on their side, and they confuse the average person about what the proposition really means and what kind of impact it has on the state's teachers and kids.

Rucker C. Johnson also looked at how funding affects equity. He and his team analyzed data on 15,353 people in 1,409 school districts in all fifty states. Unlike many researchers, they didn't look at test-score data, which has obvious limitations, but at longer-term measurements of equity, including number of years of education completed, earnings over time, and incidence of poverty. They found that just "a 25% increase in per-pupil spending throughout one's school years could eliminate the average attainment gaps between children from low-income and non-poor families."[14]

Meanwhile, there is no shortage of mismanagement at the district level. Oakland's educational financial crisis surged to prominence in 2003 when district officials requested a $100 million bailout, the largest public school loan in California history, in order to stay out of bankruptcy.

Since then, however, things haven't improved much. There's been a revolving door of superintendents who have overspent and misspent funding for years. As Dirk Tillotson, a local educational activist and blogger, writes: "This is the Titanic and some small course adjustment won't save us from another takeover—only bold and new ideas will—which unfortunately are in short supply—as the Board argues over seat cushion color on the deck chairs of a sinking ship."[15]

The union blames the expansion of charter schools in Oakland for much of the city's educational dysfunction. Minnesota passed the first charter school law in 1991, with California following right behind, in 1992. Charter schools, its proponents argued, would seed innovations that traditional public schools, known for their heavy bureaucracy and immovability, could adopt. There's a lot of disagreement about whether charter schools really do innovation better, and, further, whether the innovation transfers to traditional public schools at a meaningful scale. It's the kind of debate that sucks all the air out of so many rooms where people are discussing educational inequity.

But even setting those questions aside, the real damage, according to charter critics, is local and fiscal. Oakland is hit hard. According to OUSD, in the 2017-2018 school year, 16,070 of the district's 53,166 students attended charter schools. When parents pull their kids from public schools and enroll them in charters, the funding allotment for that kid disappears, too. Public schools with fewer kids have less funding and are left trying to make up the difference—which leads to an art teacher cut here, a custodian cut there, and soon public schools are looking and feeling shabbier than ever.

The wrath toward charter schools is potent among White progressives in Oakland and all over the country. They rage about the privatization of our schools, and the ways in which philanthropists and outsiders buy influence in cities they don't even live in by funding the campaigns of pro-charter school board members.

Black and Brown parents and activists tend to take a friendlier view of what charter schools have done for their kids—opening up another avenue for a quality education, providing more choice, sometimes even setting a higher standard to which traditional public schools must compare themselves.

Maya and Stella grow quiet and observant at the rally. It's a lot to take in. Plus, they're getting hungry.

We walk home, stopping by our favorite beer garden for pizza and lemonade. Maya takes a pause from slurping to say, "So, if there's a strike, I don't have to go to school?"

Her eyes are wide, the implications finally spinning out in her little brain in a thousand directions—hours of making art, building Lego creations, scooting around the neighborhood, and, best of all, watching *Daniel Tiger* and *Doc McStuffins* while I make work calls. "Yup, that's the plan," I say, smiling. "But it's not like a vacation. It's for a reason."

"Cool!" she says, the political gravity dwarfed by her fantasies of screen time.

51

At school the next morning, I mention to Mrs. Minor that we went to the rally, imagining she is probably part of the union fight. "How was it?" she asks, more neutral than I would expect from the woman who got a classroom of kids to chant "Knowledge is power" at the top of their little lungs.

"It was great," I said. "It was helpful to hear more about some of the issues and start to give Maya a sense of it all. Especially as the possibility of a strike looms..."

Silence.

"You think there will be a strike?" I ask.

"I really don't know. It seems that way," she says. Her tone is starting to make me wonder if she's not allowed to speak to me about any of this—union or district rules or something. But then again, we've gotten emails about it from the school. I'm so confused.

"I likely won't be striking if it happens," she says. "There's no telling how long it would last, and we're dependent on my income."

"Ah, I see. That makes a lot of sense. Totally," I say. It seems so shitty that she wouldn't be able to support the strike for financial reasons, when the whole point of the action is to help people feel less economically unstable.

"For what it's worth, I heard there's a fund being raised for teachers who can't forgo the pay so that they can still strike," I offer.

"Yeah, I heard about that. But it's a little uncertain. I'm not sure when you apply, and not everyone is guaranteed their full salary and all that," she says. "Anyway, I'm glad you're giving Maya these opportunities to learn what it means to be a part of an active community and be an engaged citizen. That's wonderful."

"Oh, thanks," I say. "After that Black History Month showcase, how could we not be fired up?"

She laughs. "Yes! That was the point. Fire people up. Our history is not history; these issues are still alive and well," she says, and wanders away to turn down the music, marking the official start of the day.

Sometimes when I'm talking to Mrs. Minor or one of the other parents in her class, a line of Ada Limón's poetry snakes through my brain: "I am a hearth of spiders these days: a nest of trying."

52

When I first found out that Maya was a girl, I was conflicted about my own elation. It wasn't that I wanted her to be a girl, or even that I always believed that she would be a girl, but it was the first piece of information I had about her. Having that one piece of information—I'm pretty sure it could have been her eye color (the most beautiful gray green in the universe) or the shape of her pinky toe (curled weirdly in like mine and my mom's)—made her feel more real. It made her feel more mine. And I was giddy with it.

What else was there to do to properly celebrate than eat doughnuts? So I headed to Golden Gate Donuts, the old-school place a few houses down from us where old Black dudes hang out and eat crullers and drink coffee out of Styrofoam cups and no White person ever buys a lottery ticket (or at least I've never seen it happen in seven years). I asked the very skinny, balding Cambodian guy behind the counter for one blueberry and one whole wheat sugar doughnut, the best ones in the whole place, determined by plenty of sampling. He smiled—his teeth crooked and his eyes crinkly—and said, "How are you today?"

"I'm good," I said, and then blurted out, "I just found out that I'm having a baby girl!"

"Wow!" he said. "Congratulations! What a blessing!" And then he started cramming little doughnut holes into the white paper bag—at least a dozen of them, which he didn't charge me for.

I would come to know this sweet man over time, and he would come to provide my girls with an obscene amount of those little doughnut holes. One of the old Black men and I would develop a little ritual, too. Whenever I popped in with baby Maya, this was our script:

Black man with the salt-and-pepper beard and the leather coat: "Oh, look, rubber-band wrists is here to get her latte!"

"Such a diva!" I'd say.

"I know she's running you ragged. It's hard work being her assistant!"

"Isn't that the truth?"

We'd exchange smiles. Sometimes he'd give Maya's pudgy hand a little shake, and then we'd get our doughnuts. Same conversation. Every single time. Never got old or lost its ability to make me feel the joy of that connection—a minuscule but refreshingly unfussy bond with someone who had clearly sat in these booths longer than I'd been in the neighborhood, maybe even longer than I'd been alive. It wasn't lost on me that my gentrifier status and my chubby White baby, sitting in her throne of a stroller, rolling in there for her doughnut, was part of the humor.

In any case, it's Friday morning, and Maya—no longer plausibly called "rubber-band wrists"—and I are picking out a dozen doughnuts to take down to the strike at school. Brian, the guy behind the counter, loads the pink cardboard box with a dozen and then some, and we tell him we're headed over there to feed the teachers on the picket line. My old friend says, "Good for them. They deserve better!"

"Got that right," I say, smiling at him.

"Where's the little one?" he asks.

"At day care," I say. "She'll be pissed when she hears we didn't get her a doughnut."

"You know she will!" he says, laughing and slapping the lottery ticket on the Formica in front of him. "You're gonna catch hell for that one!"

Maya and I head out and get on the cargo bike. She holds the big pink box in her lap as we bike the five blocks to the entrance of the school. When we arrive, I have to laugh out loud. There is a folding table set up in the grass with no fewer than six identical pink boxes filled with doughnuts, plus dozens of bagels and a few big carafes of coffee. About twenty-five people are gathered—teachers, parents, and their kids. Some are making signs. Some are standing around, chatting and eating doughnuts. About a dozen are marching in a circle while one of the teachers bangs on a drum.

Maya runs over to Linden and bounces around near him, asking if he wants a doughnut. He's there with his dad, Jack, who is at least a head taller than anyone else there, dutifully marching in a circle, knit hat and unassuming smile on. Jack is quiet but somehow never comes off as aloof. Dawn says he kills it with the Black ladies in the office, and I think, *Of course.* I'm starting to notice when a White person is comfortable in non-White spaces even before they say a word. And quite often, when I sense this quality, it turns out the White person went to an integrated elementary school.

I'm surprised to see a recent immigrant mom from Afghanistan in her *kameez* and Adidas sandals. She's got a kid in Maya's class and speaks no English. I wonder who, if anyone, explained the nature of this whole, very American-seeming spectacle—the over-caffeinated chanting (*Whose schools? Our schools! Whose schools? Our schools!*), the homemade signs, the absence of an actual audience. We smile at each other and say good morning.

I exchange smiles and a few pleasantries with other parents and teachers whom I recognize but don't know by name, then wander over to get some coffee. I overhear two White parents talking—"Can you believe it? Only one student and one teacher showed up to school."

"Who was the teacher?"

"Mrs. Minor."

"Huh, I wonder why she's not joining."

"Don't know. Maybe a financial choice. It's not like everyone can give up a week of pay."

Mrs. Minor remains inscrutable to me. I'm not sure if she's just keeping her professional distance. Or doesn't trust me because I'm White. Or maybe just finds me annoying or intrusive.

I try to get Maya to join the protest with me, and she eventually relents. We circle around for a few different chants. It's sweet to watch the teachers being so playful with one another. Mr. Limata, a Black first-grade teacher with short dreads and an effervescent smile, originally from

Zambia, is bouncing around, chatting it up with everyone. Ms. Mikhaela, a White technology teacher whom Maya clearly worships, swings her long, brown ponytail around while doing a TikTok dance with a couple of the Black girls in fifth grade. Ms. Grill, Emerson's union rep and a White third-grade teacher, is a bit more serious; she's got shit to do. People are clearly blowing up her cell phone.

Eventually Maya tugs on my arm. "Can we go now?"

But this is what democracy looks like! I think. But I reluctantly say, "Okay, we can go home."

53

WHILE I HAVE MAYA home from school, we do a lot of random stuff—make tall, wobbly skyscraper homes out of Legos, go to Blick and spend a long time lusting after art supplies, then bike home with sparkly duct tape rolls on our handlebars, and, of course, go to the library. We love the library. I start to notice the first glimmers of her interest in decoding words on a page while we are settled into our favorite chair at our favorite branch, reading a story about Georgia O'Keeffe.

"What's that word?" Maya asks me, pointing to *art* on the page.

"None other than your very favorite thing to do!" I say.

"Eat ice cream?" she says.

"Nah, just one tiny word. Something we do after we go to Blick," I say.

"Art!"

"That's right," I say, and point out the three letters and the sounds they make. Then she seems a little annoyed.

"Keep reading," she says.

I start to wonder: How *does* one learn to read?

It turns out that it is not as simple a question as one might expect. In fact, there are "reading wars" among different factions of educators about how one might answer that question.

The one in the 1990s was pretty legendary. One side might be thought of as the "leave well enough alone" camp: kindergarteners, surrounded by books, will gravitate toward subjects they care about and be self-motivated enough to decode the words and make meaning eventually. Teachers can follow the kids' lead. The other camp was less optimistic about the natural instincts of frenetic, runny-nosed five-year-olds. They felt instruction was good, not intrusive, and needed to include phonics and phonemic awareness.

Phonics is a teaching method that emphasizes letter sounds and the decoding of unfamiliar words on a page by using them. *Phonemic awareness* is a more general term, meaning awareness of the sounds in spoken words. Both, in my brain, feel sort of like the basic ingredients for cooking. You don't admire a chocolate cake enough to be able to intuit how to bake one; you have to learn about flour and sugar and butter. Letter names and sounds, on the page and spoken aloud, are like that—the beginnings of more sophisticated tastes and textured meaning.

Both camps were shouting from the rooftops. They both believed that the research was on their side. The debate got so contentious that the federal government had to step in. Congress asked that a panel be appointed, not to make recommendations on how to teach reading but to determine what it was that the research actually proved. The National Reading Panel, as it was known, concluded that some kids do learn to read naturally, à la the first camp's optimistic notion, but that many kids need explicit instruction on phonics and phonemic awareness in order to progress.

The peace treaty that ended the war was what is now referred to as "balanced literacy"—a mix of both approaches. According to a recent national survey, 72 percent of K-2 teachers say that they use "balanced literacy" to teach kids to read.[16]

The trouble with a compromise, of course, is that it often feels watered down. At this point, balanced literacy seems to mean a lot of things to a lot of different people. The phonics-and-phonemic-awareness instruction—which is most effective when it's integrated consistently by teachers who really get it—has been anemic in too many schools; K-2 teachers in the survey said they spent 39 percent of their reading instructional time on it. A lot of kids—especially Black and Brown kids, especially kids with dyslexia—have struggled and been passed from grade to grade, teacher to teacher, without the foundational skills. No milk. No butter. No sugar. No cake.

And so a new reading war is being waged—this time between the balanced literacy folks, who generally feel like reading has been taught in the right ways, just maybe not consistently enough, and the structured literacy camp, who argue—with good research to back them up—that prioritizing phonics and phonemic awareness is not just good pedagogy, but a matter of justice. Kids who aren't surrounded by language while growing up have even more to lose if schools neglect these basic building blocks.

These wars wage on as parents like me look expectantly at their kids, wondering when the marks on a page will finally have meaning. There's probably nothing I'm more excited about Maya learning how to do in all of life than read, but I'm trying not to put any expectations on her. I want her to associate reading with pure joy, not pressure. And I recognize that, in fact, she may not love books the way I do, and that has to be okay.

So much of parenting, I'm already learning, is about letting go of your own half-conscious, too tidy dreams for who your kid will be and getting interested in who they actually are.

54

T HE STRIKE LASTED FOR seven days.

On Sunday, March 3, unionized teachers voted to authorize a new contract—with an 11 percent increase in teachers' salaries over the next four years, plus a 3 percent bonus to account for losses during the strike. It also included a pledge to reduce class size, hold off on school closures for five months, and revisit a moratorium on new charter schools. It didn't meet all of the teachers' demands. Not even close. But in the end, enough of them were able to see it as a victory of sorts to vote to get back to the classroom.

The union reports that 97 percent of students were out of school, and tens of thousands were on the picket lines for that exciting, chaotic week. The solidarity school, a space where parents who had to work could drop their kids without hurting the strike, was surprisingly well coordinated, staffed by high school students, parents, and even a handful of charter school teachers who took sick days. Doughnuts were consumed. Signs were made. Chants were sung. Kids all over Oakland got a visceral, if vague, sense of something bigger than themselves. Maya, as expected, watched a lot of *Doc McStuffins*.

None of us had a clue that what felt pretty disruptive, albeit meaning-ful, was just a small taste of how our kids would spend many days in the years ahead.

55

THE CRAB FEED IS Emerson's annual fundraiser. It's a beloved tradition, usually occurring in February or March, when the PTA rents out a Masonic hall nearby—complete with creepy portraits of old White dudes in fake-gold frames and an elevator that smells like cigarette smoke. Ms. Champion, the beloved office matriarch, a Black woman who has worked at the school for decades, has a crab hook-up. Emerson moms strong-arm the local coffee shops and yoga studios into offering gift certificates and even a basketball signed by *the* Steph Curry for the silent auction. Someone, and God bless this someone, makes Jell-O shots.

Tickets are $50 a pop, or $450 for a table of eight, so we bought the latter, thinking we'd fill it with our friends, and maybe some of those parents from the nervous brunch.

We gather around our assigned table and start yucking it up, sipping a deep-red alcoholic punch, and tolerating a pretty terrible iceberg lettuce salad on paper plates. Waiters come around with baskets of garlic bread, little plates of shrimp, and eventually—the main event—big aluminum trays filled with crab. Near the kitchen is a table set up with a giant vat of melted butter that you can spoon into Dixie cups and take back to your table.

Ashley, the PTA president, gets up on the stage intermittently and makes announcements about the silent auction and the food. Ms. Grill, Emerson's union rep, gets up and thanks the parents and larger community for being so supportive during the strike. I look over and see a few tables with teachers. Mrs. Minor isn't there.

At one point, John leans over to me and whispers, "How much do they usually raise at this thing?"

"I have no idea," I say, giving him a don't-get-any-big-ideas look. He knows this look well. He gets a lot of big ideas.

I've never had crab before, so everyone starts teaching me how to eat it by breaking it open and dipping it in the butter. "It seems like a lot of work," I say. "But it's also pretty delicious. Although maybe just the butter is delicious? I can't really tell."

"As delicious as sea foam?" John asks, trotting out an inside joke between us.

"'Sea foam'? Do tell," says Malia, a close friend.

I tell a story about when John and I first started dating. He lived in San Francisco, and I lived in Brooklyn. I came to visit, and he rented a Mercedes (he didn't own a car), and we stayed in a beautiful modern-design home in wine country (that he had borrowed), and he took me to an astronomically expensive dinner. Up until that point in my life, I'd mostly dated guys with no money, so I was sort of catching up to this new development. Was I dating a rich guy? When the waiter brought out sea foam, I finally just asked him, "Okay, what the hell? Are you rich?"

He laughed so hard he nearly spit out his sea foam. "Rich? No! The opposite. I just spend every dime I make."

My jaw dropped. I grew up with a dad who squirreled away pretty much every penny he made from his bankruptcy-law practice, a field that he went into after suffering the trauma of answering the door for debt collectors. He took off his own braces with a pair of pliers because his parents ran out of money. Thrift was gospel in my house. "So you have *no* savings?"

"Savings? No, never thought about it," he said, totally earnest.

"Okay, no more sea foam," I said. "I don't really like it, but more important, you need to start saving money."

And thus began our decade-long dance of balancing one another out, financially speaking. John has done wonders in helping me understand that money is a tool—for pleasure, for comfort, for justice—and as such, some of it has to flow, not just sit like a safety blanket in a savings account.

And I have done wonders for him in teaching him that not spending every dime you make, if you have the margin, of course, is one of those things adults do. In case the car window gets smashed. Or the dishwasher breaks. Or, God forbid, someone gets really sick.

Our friends laugh knowingly. They've seen John's grand gestures— buying a bright orange 1975 VW bus off eBay; calling a restaurant when he finds out friends are dining there and paying their bill anonymously; always being the first to donate to any cause someone sends around. I had to talk him out of putting twenty bucks under Maya's pillow for her first lost tooth. "It's what *I* always wanted!" he said.

Another announcement: "Okay, guys, just have to let you know that the silent auction is coming to a close in just fifteen minutes! If you've got your eye on something, now is the time! We've got summer camps. We've got Roots soccer tickets. Now's the time! Bid 'em up. Last year we made nearly five thousand at the same event, and we want to blow that out of the water!"

I'm about to go back to the auction tables and bid another $5 here or there, when John leans over and whispers in my ear: "I think we should offer to match whatever is raised tonight."

My eyes become the size of saucers. "No," I say, under my breath. "Absolutely not."

"Why not?"

"Because. I don't want to seem showy. We're brand-new at the school."

"We can do it anonymously. I'll make clear we don't want anyone to know it was us."

"Babe, I just...I don't know...I really, really, really don't want this to turn into a thing. We should have talked about this earlier," I say.

"But we didn't. If she can announce that someone is going to anonymously match the total, it will motivate people to bid more. I've been at these things, babe. I've been that woman on the stage. Now is the time."

Folks around the table are tipsy, and John and I are being fairly quiet in the dull roar of the Masonic hall, but I can feel a few of my friends' eyes wandering over.

"It could be five thousand dollars," I say under my breath. "That's a lot of money!"

"Isn't that part of why we're sending Maya to this school? Isn't the whole point to share our resources? We have it. It's sitting in a bank. We can afford to share it."

"Fine," I spit at him. He's got me. He knew just the card to play. "But absolutely anonymously. I do *not* want this to be a thing."

"No thing. I got it," he says, already standing up and scanning the crowd for Ashley.

I make eye contact with Malia and roll my eyes. "Is this a sea foam moment?" she asks with a glint in her eye.

"You have no idea," I say.

Someone comes around with a tray of red and blue Jell-O shots. "Anyone?" she asks.

Malia says, "I've never actually had a Jell-O shot."

"Everyone is having a first tonight!" I shout, relieved by the distraction. "We'll take that whole tray. Everyone grab a Jell-O shot. This is Malia's first time. We have to make it great."

People reluctantly grab one and slurp it down. "Not bad," Malia says. And I love her more than I've ever loved her before.

John is striding back to our table. He gives me a wink and sits down as another announcement blares through the mic: "I've got a really important announcement, everyone! This just in: we've got a donor here, an anonymous donor, who has just pledged to match the total of whatever is raised tonight!"

The crowd cheers, and lots of eyebrows go up with intrigue. I try to avoid Malia's eye contact. I'm not even sure if she's looking at me, but I know I'll break if I see her pupils.

Panic fills my body. I take a big gulp of the terrible punch. And that's when I notice that the table next to us has a little dish delicately perched atop a metal stand with a tiny flame below. A Black mom whom I've exchanged only a few words with during morning drop-off is sitting there with what looks to be her family. Our eyes meet, and I ask, "What's that? We didn't get one of those."

"It's butter!" she answers, seemingly wondering if I'm pulling her leg. "For the crab!"

"We didn't get one," I say again.

"Girl, I brought this from home!" she shouts. "I come prepared."

"Wow!" I exclaim. "You're a professional."

"Damn straight," she says, beaming her big smile all over that echoing room. I stand up, pull my chair over to their table, and start shooting the shit.

"You're Amber's mom, right?"

"Yes, and remind me of your son's name. Linden, right?"

"Nah, that's Dawn. She's over there. My name is Courtney, and my daughter's name is Maya."

"Oh, right! Maya, that cute one with the bunny always stuck in the neck of her dress."

"That would be the one," I say, laughing.

Two moms talking about our kids (she's got four; Amber and her big sister, who also goes to Emerson, are the second wave), talking about the best way to prepare and enjoy crab (with hot butter, of course!). Just talking. And I feel so warm and full of love. This is a genuine community event—people laughing and talking, butter dripping down our chins, small donations coming in from hardworking people who all, together, love our kids and want the best for them.

My reverie is interrupted when she says, "So, how about that anonymous donor! Who do you think it could be?"

My stomach flips. "I don't know," I say. "It's exciting. Whatever helps the kids is great."

I slowly stand up then. "It was so good talking to you," I say.

"You, too," she says warmly.

"And now I know for next year: BYOR. Bring your own ramekin," I say.

"You got that right!" she says, cracking up. "BYOR!"

I pull my chair back to our table and rejoin our group. Did she have a hunch it was me? I have no idea. But I do know that this donation is confusing as hell. On the one hand, I know John is absolutely right. The point of enrolling at Emerson, beyond the pleasure of being part of this racially diverse, crab-dipping community rich in Oakland history, was sharing our resources.

On the other hand, how and when to share them is no small quandary. Was it right to make the donation anonymous, or did that inadvertently make it a spectacle? Would it have been better to just write a check on our way out? But then they couldn't have leveraged it, to John's point, to try to get more money out of the crowd.

But *should* this crowd be leveraged? What is each person's real capacity here to donate? Should this even be a fundraiser? Would it be better if it were just a party and no one felt any pressure to give above and beyond their meal ticket? It's a *public* school, after all.

Then again, small donations mean a lot—to the giver and the receiver. Our $5,000 might be someone else's $50, and I don't want to begrudge anyone the feeling that they've done something generous for the school. It can be patronizing to *not* give people the chance to contribute.

The final announcement of the night: Ashley is back up on the stage. "Attention, attention people. Our night is coming to an end."

The crowd groans.

"I know, I know, it's been so fun. But I have a really exciting announcement to make. We're still tallying everything up, but it looks like—between ticket sales, our silent auction, and our anonymous match—we've raised over three thousand dollars this year!"

The crowd cheers. I squeeze John's thigh under the table while he claps enthusiastically. "Not. A. Thing," he says in my ear. "I was the epitome of subtle."

56

I'm PSYCHED TO HAVE escaped the tangle of little limbs and Honey Nut Cheerios that is my house on a Sunday morning and made it to a yoga class. When I walk in, I see that my friend is already there. I give her a hug, unroll my mat, and plop down next to her.

"How are you?" I ask.

"A little hungover at the moment. We had our annual school gala last night, and I think I had a few too many glasses of wine."

Her kid goes to a nearby private school. Twenty-four thousand a year.

"That'll happen. How was it?"

"Good—we raised, I think, a hundred and thirty grand."

"Wow! That's crazy," I say.

"Okay, class, let's do this," the instructor says, weaving her way to the front of the packed room. I cat and cow my tired-ass body unmindfully and chafe at those six figures.

One of the unanticipated effects of being part of the Emerson community, for me, is feeling sort of sideswiped by casual comments. Things that would barely have made me pause before, and likely only in an analytical way, now give me stomachaches.

One of the great losses that comes from privilege is having a range of experience so narrow that it makes you emotionally bullish. Or as Cathy Park Hong describes it in her beautiful book *Minor Feelings,* "Innocence is both a privilege and a cognitive handicap, a sheltered unknowingness."[17]

Stupidity born of insulation can make others feel unconsidered, unknown. Because you don't, in fact, know. You have never had to know.

And the thing about knowing—not in a bookish way but in a lived way—is that it's edifying. It's not just that it makes you kinder, more aware of how a number like that might land, though it does do that; it's that it makes you more connected. It right-sizes your problems and pleasures, it makes you pissed off *with* your community rather than on behalf of yourself. There's a relief in knowing. The relief sits next to the sting.

57

Even though Mrs. Minor and I have little exchanges that feel legible and sometimes even intimate, she remains like a text I can't read.

The late literary critic Barbara Johnson talked a lot about "the art of rereading." She saw it not just as a necessary practice of a critical thinker but also as a political act: "A single reading is composed of the already-read, that what we can see in a text the first time is already in us, not in it."[18]

At first reading, I saw in Mrs. Minor what was already in me—a love of children, a belief in the power of education, a commitment to fight for justice. I reveled in the unearned familiarity of it.

But Johnson argues that we must keep reading and rereading to get beyond the "already-read text"—our stereotypes and frames and biases about what the book is trying to tell us. "When we read a text once," she wrote, "we can see in it only what we have already learned to see before."

I realize how little I really understand of who she is and what she thinks, how and why she makes decisions. Why did she support the strike—in theory—but still cross the picket line? Why doesn't she celebrate Halloween, the cutest holiday of them all? Why is there a glimmer of solidarity between us but also a sense of distrust that is still so palpable?

Johnson promises that if you read enough, you begin to see the true complexity of the text. You see, not what you have already learned but what has been unknowable up until that point, what she calls "a difference within," rather than between.

My disorientation when trying to read and reread Mrs. Minor is productive. It means I'm moving beyond my own biases and assumptions—the version of her composed of my own symbols and sentiments. The differences between us, the differences *within her,* are something about which I'm still illiterate. And what else would I expect? There are so many dynamics between us—teacher and parent, Black and White, Oakland-born-and-raised and newcomer. The fact that we keep trying to gently, respectfully read each other at all takes real stamina.

58

I T's THE LAST PTA meeting of the year. The library is surprisingly full, pulsing with end-of-year giddiness. Ashley passes the baton to the new president, Elizabeth—another White mom, less cheerleader and more camp counselor, energetically and aesthetically speaking. Elizabeth has long red hair, untrendy glasses, and speaks in a painstakingly careful way about everything, no matter how big or small.

When I interview her about how she ended up at Emerson, she says, "Golly, it was just heart-wrenchingly awful to have to deal with school choice; it was maybe one of the worst things that has happened for my mental health in my life."

She went on to explain that she is a Quaker and so deeply wanted to make a choice that was in alignment with her religious values. When she asked folks at her meetinghouse about the local Quaker day schools, a tradition she was used to from her upbringing back East, they said, "We don't believe in private schools. We believe that sending our kids to public schools is the best way to contribute to our society."

She heard from some friends that Emerson was a sweet place, but others told her that it was full of kids who were traumatized. A parent had been shot. A family was living in a car. She wondered, *Do I have it in me to confront that kind of trauma, or help my child confront that kind of trauma? Because that's not something that I'm used to.*

She decided they would try it. If they needed to switch schools, they would. But they didn't switch, and in fact, Elizabeth has dug in deep.

She's omnipresent at the school—the kind of mom who seems to be everywhere at all times.

Principal Palin stands up to give her updates—largely small budget adjustments, plus new information about the high school softball field that the district is going to build on our unusually large playground. Then she drops a real bomb: "We also have a few teachers that are moving on next year."

She names a couple of people I don't recognize and then says, "Mrs. Minor will not be coming back either." The room gasps. "She's a big loss, so if anyone knows someone great to fill her slot, send them my way."

59

Thirteen Ways of Looking at a School

a neighborhood institution

a training ground for future workers

"good/bad/failing/rough"

a common good

a place where small humans learn how to be friends with other small humans (and sometimes big humans learn to be friends with other big humans)

a place where tiny bubbles are filled in by anxious hands

a 1 out of 10

a litmus test for your fitness as a parent

a dance—Coach blows the whistle at 8:30 a.m. on the dot and three hundred kids take a knee on the blacktop

a social experiment

a vehicle for recess

a community

the best last chance we have of realizing democracy

PART III
CLASHING

The assumptions are, if I'm around, you either need
to help me or you need to get away from me. What
if my presence is really just the presence of another
American who wants this country to be something
that actually works for all of us?

—Claudia Rankine

60

I PARK IN FRONT of the pumpkin stucco house with a sign on the lawn advertising the name of the school and the number to call. I grab a pile of board books that I snuck from my daughters' bookshelves (all featuring Black characters) and head to the front door, pausing on the porch to text that I'm there rather than ringing the doorbell.

Mrs. Minor opens the door slowly and smiles wide: "Thanks for texting! You knew not to wake the babies!"

"I was hoping not to. Thanks so much for having me," I answer, giving her a hug.

The Learning Forest, her new preschool, is on a dead-end residential street in East Oakland, a predominantly Mexican and Black neighborhood. It's fifteen minutes on the highway from my house (which is West Oakland–adjacent) but a reality away. A kid born here is twenty-one times more likely to be born in poverty and three times less likely to read at grade level than a kid born in a neighborhood like mine. Adults in East Oakland live four fewer years on average.[1] Imagine all one might see and taste and love in four years. The ultimate inequity: time.

Mrs. Minor's got her large, round wire-frame glasses on and is wearing a long, flowing white skirt, a T-shirt with her school name and logo on it, a floral headscarf, and big hoop earrings with white tassels hanging from them. Around her waist is a lime green African print fanny pack.

She gives me a brief tour of the four rooms that make up her school. They're filled with bright colors and her trademark sayings. A big map of the world has a sign under it that reads LEARN GEOGRAPHY / LOVE OUR WORLD / KNOWLEDGE IS POWER. Bookshelves are in every room, featuring books like *I Got the Rhythm* and *The Colors of Us*. There is a plastic bin filled with West African musical instruments—a miniature *djembe* and *shekere,* among others. All the dolls are Black. Even the sign urging parents to help keep the school a "germ-free zone" features Black cartoon characters vigorously washing their hands.

This is Mrs. Minor's queendom. It's an unapologetically Black space created with tremendous attention to detail. I'm moved to see her disentangled from the bureaucracy of a district school and world-building this way.

"This is amazing!" I tell her in an enthusiastic whisper.

"Thank you!" she replies. "I inherited some money from my grandmother when she passed, so I put a lot of it into this. I've been working on it for a while."

We peek in at the children sleeping in a little room—side by side, their little bodies barely detectable in the dim light. A soft lullaby plays. The sweet smell of napping children makes me tear up a little bit. I know that relief so well.

We settle down in the kitchen, and Mrs. Minor pulls out an article she's printed and highlighted about how integration has failed to raise test scores among Black and Brown kids in Berkeley. I'm surprised. I didn't imagine her laying groundwork like this, though that reveals my own blinders; why would she feel safe going into a conversation with a White mom, much less a journalist, without doing some preparation? She smiles at me and launches in: "So, you texted that you're wondering about White parents integrating schools, but did you really mean gentrifying them?"

Lullaby record scratch.

"Well, that, too," I say. "I mean, well, tell me what you're thinking when you ask that?" I'm fumbling around. I can feel my face getting hot.

What follows is a flood of stories. About Mrs. Minor's childhood in Oakland, growing up in the flatlands, a place where you can't get a house these days for less than $1 million but where she once lived surrounded by exclusively Black working-class families and a rich sense of history.

Little Artemis Minor attended Catholic school, where she felt the powerful force of her teachers' expectations. It was an almost exclusively Black space—filled with Black teachers who believed that every child was the face of God and could excel. When she switched to Berkeley High for one year, she felt that her teachers—even the Black ones—didn't give a shit what she learned (the White teachers most certainly didn't). She sat in the back of her geometry class, spitting sunflower seeds and rolling her eyes. Not learning a damn thing. Twenty years later, a teacher herself, she's outraged that a Black teacher let that happen.

She sees this same "tyranny of low expectations" among parents and teachers who let White guilt rot into pity. They take it easy on Black kids when they should be "loving on them *and then* insisting they get the work done, whether they slept in a car last night or not."

She finally tells me her truth about the teacher's strike: little more than a performance, a way for mostly White teachers to feel woke while Black and Brown kids fall even further behind. I'm relieved to have the enigma solved. The strike was, as Mrs. Minor sees it, a big distraction from learning, and the kids who are most hurt by that distraction are those who were already behind.

I genuinely believe that the strike's aim, led by a multiracial group of educators, at least here locally, wasn't misguided. In the long run, teachers are only going to be able to serve students if they, themselves, feel supported. They need a living wage, good benefits, and the respect they deserve. I don't push back. I'm here to listen. Maybe we'll have that conversation another time.

Mrs. Minor saved her true vengeance, however, for the apathy she witnessed during Black History Month. The assembly, of course, was Mrs. Minor's pride and joy. "I had one teacher tell me that she already talked about Black history in January, so she wasn't going to revisit it in February. Are you kidding me? Do I talk about St. Patrick's Day in December? You don't get to just pick a date according to your own schedule!"

Mrs. Minor is fed up with White educators who think they're doing Black kids a favor by spoiling them with love but not teaching them to read at grade level. She's fed up with Oakland progressives who pat themselves on the back for joining the equity committees at their lily-White schools and donate the dregs of their PTA funds to the "poor schools."

Mrs. Minor has shed her politic self like a crusty old chrysalis and is now pure, shining truth—angry and beautiful and seemingly unafraid to tell me exactly what she has seen and heard. Every once in a while she apologizes for the tirade, but I encourage her, "No, please, go on." Eventually a groggy toddler stumbles into the kitchen, squinting in the bright kitchen light, dragging a blanket behind him. The kids are waking up.

I didn't even know if Mrs. Minor would be open to talking; now she's opened the floodgates. My insides are reverberating. Is this what fragility feels like? Off-center. Porous. Overwhelmed. I hope I'm not physically shaking.

"Can I just ask you a question before I get out of your hair?" I ask. "What would you do if you were me? I mean, if you were a White parent in Oakland, would you send your kid to Emerson?" As the words are coming out of my mouth, I can already see that they annoy her.

She is quiet, searching, I presume, for something sort of polite to say. She lands on "I can't answer that. I'm not you. I can't give you a simple answer. I don't think there is one."

The silence hangs in the air and then finally breaks: "But we can keep talking about it."

61

It's the middle of summer, and the district has released a plan for reducing the number of schools in Oakland. They call it the Blueprint for Quality Schools.

The official name isn't fooling parents, who mostly seem to regard it with suspicion and no small amount of panic.

The district claims that this is an attempt to finally correct for the fiscal recklessness of the early aughts; the board approved a small-schools policy in 2000, and a decade (and half dozen superintendents) later, there were forty new schools. The thinking back then, not just in Oakland but throughout the nation, was that smaller schools serve kids, especially those who have been marginalized, more effectively. But it didn't work. According to the *Oakland Tribune*, "The Oakland school district was transformed, at least on the surface. But many of its problems—low test scores, high dropout rates, staff turnover—remain."[2]

Small schools weren't the Holy Grail. And they are expensive, in a district that is already starving for resources. As the superintendent puts it: "The fact that Oakland has more schools per student than any other large California school district prevents us from using our scarce resources efficiently, and makes it more difficult to retain excellent teachers and maintain high-quality schools."[3]

Reducing schools is like getting toothpaste back into the tube. And when White and/or privileged parents are involved, it gets particularly ugly.

In this case, Peralta and Kaiser—schools with great test scores, tight-knit parent communities, and low percentages of kids on free or reduced lunch—are each "being threatened" with the prospect of merging with Sankofa—where the test scores are dismal, there isn't even a PTA, and the vast majority of kids qualify for free or reduced lunch.

Peralta is majority White, and Kaiser is more multiracial but still 35.8 percent White in a district that—overall—is only 10 percent White.

I didn't tour Kaiser, but I heard a lot about it over time because a number of families who are in the Emerson catchment go there instead. I began to think of Kaiser as a sort of escape hatch for White progressive families in our neighborhood. There was enough racial diversity at Kaiser that White parents could reassure themselves that they weren't driving up to the hills because they were trying to avoid Black kids. In fact, on the contrary, they emphatically *loved* the school's racial diversity—"it looks like Oakland," Kaiser parent after Kaiser parent told me proudly. Except that it didn't live like Oakland; the year I looked at schools in Oakland for Maya, only a quarter of kids at Kaiser qualified for free or reduced lunch (in a district where three-quarters do).

So, in a sense, these White progressive families were able to maintain their anti-racist cred in their own minds by choosing a specific kind of diversity that felt safe, and that kept the test scores up and the poorest kids out (there is no viable public transportation up to the school). And choose they did. The vast majority—89 percent—of the kids who go to Kaiser don't live in the surrounding neighborhood.

Peralta is geographically close to Sankofa and busting at the seams, with 324 kids on its small, sweet grounds (80 percent of whom live in the surrounding coveted neighborhood), while Sankofa is under-enrolled, with 132 kids, and roomy, with a massive green space. When the district attempted to merge Peralta and Sankofa in the past, all hell broke loose, including the bringing of lawsuits.

Yvette Renteria, the deputy chief of innovation for OUSD, has come to Peralta to discuss all of this. She fires up her PowerPoint and launches in, explaining that the district is now in a time crunch—they've got two months to decide how to "right size" the number of schools—and they are trying to involve parents and educators in the process. Emerson is safe for now; we're under-enrolled (in part because of all the families that live in our neighborhood but strategize their way into Kaiser and Peralta) but not by a huge amount, and we're also the only school in Temescal.

It's the summer, so that's challenging. The Peralta principal is in Bali, so that's challenging. (*Not for the principal,* I think to myself. *Good for her.*) The PowerPoint slide passively begs the crowd: CHALLENGE IDEAS. RESPECT PEOPLE.

A White blond woman in skinny jeans, a T-shirt with—you guessed it—an artfully drawn bird on it, and a blazer asks Yvette, "Did you do a meeting like this at Sankofa? What did they say?"

"We did," says Yvette. "We only got a few parents to come out, but they seemed to be open to a merger on their campus."

"But why were there only a few families there?" the blonde asks incredulously. "Do they just not care?" The crowd shifts in their seats; she has betrayed the White custom of refraining from judgment, in public at least, of Black parents.

A White guy in a business suit (unusual for Oakland) punches up instead of down: "Where's Chabot in all of this? Why are they being protected in a way that we aren't?" The crowd murmurs, seemingly with approval. He's fluffed up now: "This is ridiculous!"

Chabot is the one other school in the surrounding area that is more White and privileged than Peralta. But Chabot is two miles away and has 580 kids enrolled. They are not part of the plan. It is either Peralta or Kaiser that will be forced to merge with Sankofa.

"There is a two hundred percent demand for Peralta," Yvette says, leaning in like it's a big compliment, and then hits them with the consequence: "And you all are bursting at the seams. I don't have to tell you that."

One brave mom waits until the very end to speak. When she opens her mouth, it is like a treatise comes pouring out: "The reason we have underperforming schools is because of the legacy of racist and classist disinvestment in urban areas, and we're proposing transactional fixes to deep structural problems. We're working with the master's tools to break down the master's house."

At this invocation of Audre Lorde, a healthy number of the parents clap and even snap like old beatniks. The brave mom continues speaking: "That being said, I think that what this conversation is really about is redistribution, so when I think about the value of why a scenario like that third one [a merger between Sankofa and Peralta] is important to consider, it's that I'm a well-resourced person, and I'm part of a well-resourced community, and I want to think about how we extend those resources out to people who don't have the same material conditions. And that's why I'm interested in having more conversations with other people here about scenario three. I'm not opposed to it."

No clapping. No snapping.

Later I will learn that the speaker is Aleah, an Iranian-American public health organizer. When I interview her, I begin by telling her how much I appreciated what she had to say at the meeting. "Before you put me on a pedestal, let me tell you: Sankofa is our zoned school, and we opted out of it," she says. "We got off the waitlist at Peralta and we went."

"Did you struggle with that decision?" I ask.

"It's the hardest political decision I've ever made in my life," she said.

Later, the Peralta PTA will do an internal survey to see what the parents' and teachers' appetite is for merging with Sankofa. After sending out 500 emails to all families—incoming, outgoing, and current—305 people responded (84 percent of them White). Sixty-four percent disagreed or strongly disagreed with the idea of merging with Sankofa; 40 percent said it was likely or extremely likely that they would leave Peralta if the plan were implemented. Half of the teachers said they would be likely to leave, too.

62

"No one talks about how Black people continue to resist the idea of integration," says Dr. Noliwe Rooks, the director of American Studies at Cornell University.

I'm chatting on the phone with her after my first visit with Mrs. Minor. As part of Dr. Rooks's tour with her most recent book, *Cutting School: Privatization, Segregation, and the End of Public Education,* she met with small groups of Black people in church basements and living rooms all over the nation. She would start by saying, "So, we know desegregation works," which seemed like an uncontroversial statement.

And then she would inevitably get pushback—not from academics like Professor Rooks, but from community organizers and working-class parents who would raise their eyebrows and skeptically ask, "Do we know that? That's not what *my* momma experienced."

And then these parents and grandparents would tell Dr. Rooks stories about the beautiful Black schools all over the South in the 1930s and '40s, schools filled with top-notch Black educators (many wildly overqualified to be teaching in elementary and secondary schools, but barred from more prestigious institutions).

Schools like Dunbar High School in Washington, D.C., one of the first public high schools for Black students in the United States. In its heyday in the 1930s, '40s, and early '50s, Dunbar was so good that Black parents would move to Washington so that their kids could attend. Unlike many other vocationally focused schools for Black teenagers at the time, Dunbar had a faculty of brilliant Black college graduates, some of whom even had PhDs and all of whom were paid as well as their White counterparts. The excellence spread. By the 1950s, 80 percent of Dunbar graduates went on to college; at the time, only 13 percent of Black Americans overall even had a high school diploma, and only 2 percent had a college degree.

Central High School in Louisville, Kentucky, another excellent Black school, had poor facilities, but the teachers were competent, the parents involved, the academics rigorous, and the extracurricular activities abundant. According to a former student and teacher, Thelma Cayne Tilford-Weathers, who spent forty-four years at the school, it was "respected and loved by thousands of students who have passed through her doors," including a young Cassius Clay (who would become Muhammad Ali).[4]

Some Black schools, which were largely depicted as places to be pitied by White educational reformers of the time, were in fact places to be protected according to those who learned and taught and fell in love and goofed off and got in trouble and otherwise triumphed in those hallowed halls.

Many schools that were experienced as havens by Black people all over the nation were ultimately deeply damaged by short-lived, ill-conceived integration efforts following *Brown vs. Board*. Today, Central High School is back to being majority Black, but only 45 percent of those students are reading at grade level. Dunbar High School is now 95 percent Black, but only 6 percent of its students read at grade level. Eighty-six percent graduate, but only 3 percent have SAT scores that indicate that they are college-ready.[5]

White resistance to integration was hard to miss leading up to and following the *Brown* decision. White mothers, "segregation's constant gardeners," were everywhere. They created petitions, amassing signatures by stirring White neighbors' fears of the degradation of the education their White children would get, the federal takeover of local schools, and any number of other red herrings (communism! chaos! rape!).[6]

"I mean, it makes sense," Dr. Rooks tells me. "If White people are this hateful, why would we send our babies to them?"

This is not to say that the promise of integration wasn't seductive in some critical ways. Unlike Central and Dunbar, many Black schools were starved for resources, overcrowded, and failing their students. Jim Crow ate away at even the noble efforts of Black communities to get educated. No matter what parents and educators did—staggering kids' attendance in order to deal with overcrowding and the lack of school books, teaching after their own long hours in other jobs, donating what little money they had to supplement inadequate funding in order to keep schools up and running—they couldn't give their kids what they knew they deserved.

Many Black educators and parents were open to integration, but they also weren't naive. Dr. Rooks explains, "Many of the educators who supported integration were hoping it would begin with teachers and administrators switching schools. Let the adults get on the same page and then start moving the kids in both directions."

But that's not what happened. The burden of desegregation fell on Black kids and Black families. They were the ones who had to travel long distances—literally and socially—for the chance at a high-resourced education, even if it meant displacement. Black kids were subject to White loathing, even from their own teachers—what law professor Patricia Williams called "spirit murder": "disregard for others whose lives qualitatively depend on our regard."[7]

Black kids were the ones who endured, despite pushback on the part of White Americans and no small amount of warranted, if underacknowledged, ambivalence and fear on the part of Black Americans.

"There's always been a strain of Black people, one of whom, I discovered, was my own grandfather, who resisted integration," Dr. Rooks explains. "The thinking was, they're not going to love our children, and without love, you can't teach."

63

CAN WE LOVE ONE another's children? Can we love one another's children? Can we love one another's children? Can we love one another's children? Can we love one another's children? Can we love one another's children? Can we love one another's children? Can we love one another's children? Can we love one another's children? Can we love one another's children? Can we love one another's children? Can we love one another's children?

64

SCHOOL IS BACK IN session. Maya is a legit kindergartener. Her teacher is that energetic White woman named Ms. Walsh, whose classroom we visited on the tour. When she struts onto the blacktop on the first morning to retrieve her line of students, I count six of the two dozen who are White. The other kindergarten class line looks markedly different—there is only one White kid—Linden—in the whole crew; their teacher is a Black woman. I'm guessing Principal Palin, understanding the power for a kid in having a teacher with a similar racial background, has deliberately split the rolls this way.

Of the neighborhood families who attended that nervous brunch, only one has sent their child to Emerson (and she'll be gone soon, too—off to Whiter, wealthier Peralta Elementary).

No matter. We are no longer new to Emerson. We are *of* Emerson. And we love it. We joke around with Coach Andre on the way in and exchange warm greetings with moms, dads, and aunties.

The parents seem collectively relieved that school is back in session, but the kids haven't shaken off the summer wildness. A soccer ball flies into the plywood backstop. Coach yells compliments and corrections to a crew of Black fifth graders, including a few girls, I'm happy to note, playing basketball.

That's when I see her.

Smooth black ponytail. High heels. A-line skirt with flowers. Cloying smile, petite frame. Porcelain White skin. I immediately imagine her marching down a school hallway, handing out flyers advertising her desire to be homecoming queen.

What she's doing, or appears to be doing, is collecting the name and email address of every parent milling around the playground. They are responding warmly enough to her intrusions, though this is highly off-brand for our school, which is the kind of place where friendships are formed one tired, genial chat at a time or a text here, a text there.

This person is not going to be happy with just showing up. I can sense her ambition one hundred feet away.

65

Wow, LOOK AT ME and my privilege, you know, proudly in a nice house, you know, in Temescal or what have you. I really sincerely care about people of color, and I see what's going on in our nation and in our communities. So, *boom,* I decide to put my kids in this, what maybe should be classified as a 'Black school' or a 'flatland school' or whatever you want to call it, to make a difference, right? To show my kid something different, and to support the school because that's my local school, right?"

Mrs. Minor is trying her best to answer my question. Which was: "What would you do if you were in my shoes?"

It's naptime again. We're at the kitchen table, which still smells of skirt steak and garlic noodles—the home-cooked lunch.

Mrs. Minor goes on: "Integration is something I never, a thirty-five-year-old woman, grown up in Oakland, I *never* looked at. *Integration* or *segregation*—we didn't use those words as I was growing up. There was a Black school here and a White school somewhere up in the hills."

Mrs. Minor had a front-row seat to what happened in the flatlands in the 1990s and 2000s: "All of a sudden, you get an influx of White people coming into your neighborhood, North Oakland. You know, I saw the change when I was in high school. And then I got the term: 'gentrification.'"

She stretches the word *gentrification* out like she's teaching it to me: "It's like, oh, *that's* what's happened to my neighborhood, yeah. And all of a sudden, those old warehouses that were just nothing for years as I grew up are now housing Cal Berkeley students. And now the park that I grew up going to, they used to call it Pepsi-Cola Park, is a charter school.

"So it definitely just tells you, flat out, when people of Caucasian descent move in, things change. And you could say for the better. But what's 'for the better'?"

I can feel my brain and heart short-circuit the way they often do when gentrification comes up—particularly if a person of color is saying it. Like a lot of progressives, if I'm making an argument with someone I consider White and clueless, I sometimes catch myself wielding the word like a weapon against unfeeling economic elitism.

But when I'm the one being implicated, I feel it shut me down, and a swell of guilt and helplessness rises up. Systemic complexity and my own complicity in it are overwhelming. It is no coincidence that my family and I showed up just as soon as $6 oat-milk lattes became available within walking distance.

So many Black families at Emerson have been displaced, yet they continue to loyally drive their kids, or grandkids, back to the old neighborhood to attend school. Which is no longer the old neighborhood. Because of me. As Eve L. Ewing, author of *Ghosts in the Schoolyard,* so beautifully puts it: "The troubling history of racism in housing and schooling as paired institutions in the community—at once parallel and circling one another like the strands of a double helix."[8]

There might be some net good created by sending my kid to the local school rather than strategizing my way into the White, better-performing one. But the fact that I can walk there and maybe even want a cookie for my courage is a really impoverished way of understanding my impact on the community where I live.

"Things are just unfair in so many ways," says Mrs. Minor, the energy in her voice cranking up. "It's education. It's the neighborhood. Historically, that's how it's been. Now the question is: How can we make things more equal?"

I realize that Mrs. Minor is sort of interviewing herself. ~~And I'm here for it. Better her than me.~~[*]

---

[*]   Dr. Dena Simmons: "I do not think you need to say this. It feels very colonial or taking-advantage-of."

"But Black kids need to grow up in a way where they're taught to be excited about being Black. If that's not promoted from the beginning, then are we really blending cultures? Are we really getting to know each other?"

Her gaze wanders over to the corner of the kitchen where one of her littlest students, who put up a valiant nap rebellion, has finally fallen asleep in a high chair, his little neck draped over one shoulder. We share an affectionate laugh. "He's like, 'This conversation is putting me to sleep,'" I joke.

"I know! Ahma, what are you talking about? All these words! Those aren't the words I'm learning," Mrs. Minor says. Ahma is what Mrs. Minor prefers her students call her these days; it means "mother" in a variety of languages.

She goes right back to her point. "When you're taking a downtrodden people who do not understand their culture and are living by the skin of their teeth, so to speak, and then you're just, you know, throwing them together with rich White kids and thinking that's going to help... well, no, because the bigger picture is who they are. It's supporting their families. It's not just giving them sharpened pencils or even a salad bar, for that matter. There's a deeper hurt there."

Mrs. Minor's priority isn't teaching my child, who will get taught anyway, who gets messages every single day that she comes from and is bound for excellence. Her priority is healing the deeper hurt.

Mrs. Minor goes on: "A school like Emerson, as beautiful as it is... I mean, you know, the actual campus itself, it's amazing. There's so much potential, right? And then, I mean, there were times when I literally would see... or, like, I don't want to say it like that, but, like... some of the kids are just so, I mean, from families that are so poor, so just, just... oh, my God, it's just, like, awful conditions."

Mrs. Minor is uncharacteristically tongue-tied. It's like she doesn't want to reduce children and families struggling with poverty to their economic reality, especially in front of this White mom. And yet she also needs to paint an accurate picture of the extremes that made her so weary that they eventually drove her out of the public school system and here to build her own little sanctuary where Black toddlers are called king and queen and no one ever wonders about their worth. She's even pulled her own daughters from their Catholic school and started homeschooling them so that Black excellence could be at the center of their educational experience.

"I mean, I told you before, like living in a car.... A teacher should not have to have kids that live in the, you know, eight-hundred-thousand-dollar house around the corner, and another that lives in a car. In one classroom. *What?* That feels like a crazy world, right?"

66

OAKLAND UNIFIED SCHOOL DISTRICT BOARD
MEETING, AUGUST 28, 2019
TOTAL TIME: 5 HOURS, 52 MINUTES, 28 SECONDS

T HE SCHOOL BOARD MEETS to hear public comment on the proposed merger of Sankofa and Kaiser. Peralta mostly faded from the district's plan in the weeks following that initial meeting; there is speculation that powerful Peralta parents had the ear of district leaders or board members, or perhaps the district was just so determined to reclaim the real estate on the hill that Peralta was a less desirable option. The school board are seven elected officials, plus two high school student directors, all people of color with the exception of a single White woman.

I'm curious to hear how these school communities will talk about themselves and each other, what it can teach me about how we show up. The meeting starts at six p.m.

Different speakers approach the mic and spend one minute hurling an ideological frame, past wounds, and, quite often, personal insults at the school board and others in the room, then march back to their seats, hearts presumably pounding. During their own official discussion period, the directors sometimes address what has been brought up in public comment, but only insofar as they follow up on a particular question and then quickly weave it into what appears to be their own preconceived position on the matter at hand.[9]

Oakland is not unique in this regard. School board meetings all over the country look and sound much like this, according to the many parents and educators I've asked. I begin to think of it as a Greek chorus—a strange combination of actors, singing the pain of our fractured cities. The chorus speaks what the main characters—the vast majority of our city's families who never come to these meetings, never wait until the wee hours of the morning on a school night for sixty seconds on a mic—experience and believe.

I begin to listen as if the public comment period is an act of unearthing the city's true confusion and hurt, its unexamined racism, its generational wounding. Their words, their anger, poured over me and through me.

White mother: [18:26] For my child and many others just like them, this could be life or death. The suicide attempt rate is over forty percent in these kids. The district knows this. [Openly weeping.] They know that Kaiser is a long-established gender-queer school that has inclusionary systems already in place and it's the only one that has it. They know that uprooting this community can be an actual death sentence, and they also know most of the parents won't go to the media...because they don't want to [screaming now] out their children!...Shame on you for putting us in this position. We haven't failed the families of Sankofa!...You have![10]

Black father: [37:00] How are the children? "How are the children?" is a common greeting among the Maasai people. They believe that if the children are well, all are well. How are OUSD's children? How are you—the superintendent, the staff, and elected officials—feeling about our children? How are Sankofa's children? How are Kaiser's children?

East Asian–American mother: [48:20] The thing that I don't understand through all of this is that you're closing an excellent school, a good school in Oakland. I mean, how many good schools do you have? Aren't there other schools you could close?[11] We're doing well. You can't guarantee that we're going to be as successful somewhere else. One of the reasons why we're so successful is because of this community dedicating thousands of volunteer hours and tons of money.[12]

White father: [57:18] Have no illusions. You're killing something beautiful. These hearings are less like meetings and more like memorials. And this time those of us in green and yellow shirts on our backs are the family. We've been consoling each other for months because we saw the cancer coming. It came through a series of meetings in which we were given the news like patients, not partners, like accepted casualties in the perimeter of a blast. You think I'm overreacting? You think Kaiser isn't special?[13]

South Asian–American mother: [1:00:55] Hi, my name is Saru Jayaraman, and I'm a parent...at Kaiser. I also run a national social justice organization and have been fighting for social justice around the country. I'm currently under investigation by the Trump administration because of the fights I've been engaged in for social justice around the country. I fight for people in Mississippi. I fight for people in Pennsylvania. I fight for people in Michigan.

But I live in Oakland because I thought that this community reflected the values that I wanted my family to grow up in. I thought this community valued integration, social justice, progressive interracial values.... In my own home community, you are reflecting the values of Betsy DeVos and Donald Trump, the values of property, and wealth, and capitalism over social justice.

[Her allotted time is up and the mic goes silent. She continues to yell into it, inaudible to all but the closest in the crowd, and then walks away.]

Black student: [2:11:54] My name is Isiah, and I am in third grade and . . . at Sankofa and . . . [long pause] . . . I like my school a lot.

Susan: [2:29:55] Good evening, my daughter is a first grader at Sankofa. It's our neighborhood school, and it was our first-choice school. . . . Sankofa students have thrived when they've had stability and resources. These past few years, Sankofa has had neither of those things.

Speaking of instability, the neighborhood around Sankofa is changing fast. The new residents, like me, are by and large White, and, judging by the sale prices of homes we walk past on our way to school, they are very affluent.

It would be an insult to this community and all that they have built to push them out of this beautiful building just as so many families are now being priced out of the neighborhood.

Black mother: [2:55:03] My name is Lakisha Young. I'm the executive director of the Oakland REACH [a local organization that organizes on behalf of Black families]. You're heard from many of our parents in this meeting. You've heard from people who have given their lives and their children's lives to a system that has failed them. A system that, frankly, has been screwing them for generations.

You heard last meeting from April, who went to school her whole life in Oakland public schools and didn't read her first book until she was thirty-eight. . . . If you can imagine having children, trying to build a life, and you have not gotten a decent education—you don't want to live that life, okay?

Our parents grew up in schools that didn't meet their needs. . . . Now they're stuck in the same schools that are not meeting their kids' needs. Parents are turning out because their story will not be their children's stories. We are willing to totally disrupt our lives for the chance of something better. . . . The wait is over. The time is now.

Crowd begins call and response. One woman yells: "Time is..."
Crowd yells: "now!"

School board directors' comments:

Jumoke Hinton Hodge (Black woman): [3:23:52] To all the integrationists...there's a school at Emerson that has seats.... If people want to talk that game when it comes to protecting themselves or sounding politically correct, go right on ahead, but if you want to do something about integration...if that's a philosophy [people in the audience screaming over her]...I'm sorry, I don't think I opened my mouth when you were speaking, so don't disrespect. [The crowd quiets down to a dull roar.]

I want to say to our colleagues: let's do our job. There are people standing up saying the time is now. We don't have time for people to get comfortable. We paused this once already.... There are children that need us right now to make decisions.

James Harris (Black man): [3:30:20] I guess as folks from Kaiser go home...you're coming from a special place. I would ask you to think about what would it mean to share that experience with people that have not had that special experience? [The crowd screams over him.]...It's a question—again, I'm presenting this for you to think about as a community. [Continued screaming.] You can take it or leave it. I'm not here to argue with you.... We are too far away from what it's going to feel like for a fourth grader, because we are in our adult feelings.

67

I'M SITTING IN THE corner of the library on the carpet. I've agreed to volunteer at Emerson on Monday afternoons during the one hour that Ms. Walsh's kindergarten class comes each week. I help Jennifer Vetter, the librarian, reshelve books. She even lets me use the scanner to check books out to kids—the fulfillment of a nerdy childhood dream.

Ms. Vetter is a White woman with a passion for getting culturally relevant books in kids' hands. This doesn't just mean she curates books carefully, but she stands by her conviction that kids should feel agency over choosing the books *they* are most interested in. When well-intentioned donors suggest distributing books randomly to kids, she steers them in another direction; for her, developing kids' innate literary love *and* discernment are the most lasting gifts.

In 2015, the Emerson library was barely open: a pair of volunteers handled checking books in and out one day per week, and classes visited on a rotating schedule once every two or three weeks. Only 873 books circulated that fall semester. Ms. Vetter was hired in 2016 and quickly began building up the collection and getting circulation flowing again. During the fall of 2019, nearly eight thousand books circulated among Emerson students.

In 2016, Ms. Vetter had a budget for acquiring books, but since then, there hasn't been enough funding to do so. Undaunted, she has applied for grants and used district and community donations to build up the collection by selecting and adding more than two thousand new books: fiction, nonfiction, early readers, picture books, and graphic novels. She has also created collections of bilingual Spanish-English and Arabic-English books.

Maya is in my lap, practically melting into me, as we listen to Ms. Vetter read. I notice that Maya's wearing her sparkly boots again with no socks. Her feet are going to stink. A more attentive parent would be on top of getting her to put on socks in the morning.

Darius, a Black boy, moves a few feet over so he can sit next to us, as he often does. I give his back a tender little rub to let him know that I see him. His nails seem too long and his hair has gotten fuzzy. It must have been a long time since he got his hair braided. *Is everything okay?* I wonder, then catch myself in the double standard: if my kid's feet stink, it's just a matter of prioritization, but if Darius's nails are too long, something has to be wrong?

White kids come to school with holes in their pants, shirts on backward, hair a mess, and it's largely seen as quirky and innocent; if kids of color do the same, it raises eyebrows.

Steven, a Black boy, shows me his brand-new high-top sneakers—cherry-red, shiny, laces untied. "Wow, those are awesome," I tell him.

"My dad got them for me," he says, the pride spreading across his face.

68

E<small>LIZABETH</small>, <small>THE PRESIDENT OF</small> the PTA, is worried that planting a tree on school grounds is White supremacist. She asks me about it on the playground one day, and I am flummoxed. *Huh? Black people like trees, too!*

Then she sends an email to me and OtherCourtney to follow up.

Hi Courtney & Courtney,

Do either of you have any sources you can send me addressing the link between school beautification and gentrification?

We have some new White parents at Emerson who would like to start a beautification committee. I believe those promoting this idea are promoting White-normed beautification. As a White lady, this is all I know, too, but I am concerned that what I call beautification (more trees) means more safety concerns (tree climbing), mess (leaves), and maintenance for our school and district staff, and I know there will be pushback around this from those who maintain the school yard currently. Our blacktop playground is anathema to me, but that's part of being at the school we're at and not colonizing it. I think.

I'd love your feedback.

Thank you,

Elizabeth

OtherCourtney has a way of untangling the most complex of knots, always getting to the simplicity on the other side with a few lighthearted, straight sentences. She replies:

Hi Elizabeth (and hi Courtney!),

You're definitely right that the "beautification" piece is one we see a lot w/ White folks in integrating schools (what is "beauty," eh!?). This is definitely something that should be run through the PTA. Perhaps the Black and Brown parents DO feel that a beautification committee is worth spending time and energy on? Do PTA parents agree that it is more worthy than other things that the PTA could be doing? If so, start the committee! I'd also suggest that there be something in place that urges/requires committees to be representative of the school. If, for example, the beautification folks are all White, then perhaps it isn't actually of value and the committee should hit pause. . . . And that could work for any idea that could be considered colonization. Does that make sense?

Warmly,

c

It reminds me of Brené Brown's wise mantra: "I'm not here to be right. I'm here to get it right." I notice this instinct in myself and other White parents: when we get caught up in wanting to be right, we start looking for a reading, an outside expert, a protocol on being anti-racist, rather than just asking the parents of color who we are in community with, *What do you think? How does this feel to you?* We twist ourselves up in email threads when the source is right in front of us.

Sometimes the work is hard. But sometimes we need to try easier.

69

BRIAN STANLEY FOLDS HIS tall body into a seat across from me, takes off his flat cap, and sips his coffee. He's a Black dad whose two sons go to Kaiser, and this is our first time meeting; he's very easy to talk to, warm, engaging, liberal with his laughter. When I ask him about his family's experience of choosing a school, he first begins by telling me about the family that they share a duplex with. "They are basically family," he explains, "and got into Hoover, our neighborhood school."

Hoover is a 1 out of 10 on GreatSchools.org, with 82 percent Black and Brown students, the vast majority of whom are not reading at grade level. Brian told his neighbors, also a Black family: "You're not sending my nephew to Hoover. The babies can't read over there. You're going to go down to the enrollment office. If we have to go every day, that's what you're going to do, but you're going to get your kid someplace else.

"They basically went down every day for a couple of weeks and got him into Peralta, because that's the way the system really works," Brian explains.

He's quick to add: "Look, families like mine benefit from racist policy, too. The district has had open enrollment forever, and families like my own have always used that privilege to leave schools in certain neighborhoods to go to schools like Kaiser. And the kids who do not have the chance don't do that.

"We all know this, and we do it anyway because our highest ethical duty is always to our own kids, which means I'm not sending my baby to a school where I don't feel like they're going to get the education that

I know they need to get to try to have a shot in a society that's designed to beat them up."

When it was time for Brian's first kid to enroll, his wife, a Montessori teacher, took the lead. They toured a few schools, including Kaiser. Brian's first impression? "You know...it's an elementary school. I have a doctorate in education, so, you know, unless I see some foolishness, it's like, okay, it's a hills school. Music, cool. Good, good, good. Kids learning-ish. Teachers teaching-ish. Got it."

Kaiser had impressive stats; its Black and Brown kids scored substantially better on standardized tests than kids at almost any other elementary school in the district. It was also run by a Black male principal—a great role model for their sons.

Theirs has been a good experience, but they've had some concerns along the way, particularly as the Black population has dwindled. When they first enrolled their kid, the school was 30 percent Black, and today it is 20 percent, a drop that at a school of only 250 kids is significant. But their son has been happy and "devours books—like, eats 'em for breakfast." He's had plenty of friends and lots of inspiring teachers. They enrolled their younger son, and Brian's wife has even become the PTA president.

Brian grew up in Oakland, going to Oakland public schools, and has worked in education his entire career. When the possible merger was announced, he wasn't resistant. He saw it as the district finally doing hard things to heal decades of racist policy making and financial mismanagement.

He published a searing piece on *Medium* arguing as much: "Some in the Kaiser community greeted this recommendation with resistance so intense, it trickled down to my kids. Last spring, I was shocked when my boys came home from Kaiser repeating some of the fears they heard on the schoolyard. I reminded them that 'Those families at Sankofa are just like us. Those kids are just like you. And never let anyone convince you that someone, especially someone that looks like you, is somehow less than you.'"[14]

Some teachers and parents in the Kaiser community have responded to the proposed merger by hunkering down and plotting a path of personal preservation, an understandable instinct when something you love is threatened.

Brian seems to have done the opposite; he's depersonalized and taken a more telescopic view of time. He explains: "Kaiser exists, in spite of all the wonderful intentions of the brilliant people that go to and work in it, as a product of decades upon decades of racist policy. But we can't seem to have that conversation honestly. If we can't use our knowledge of how we got here to figure out where we should go next, then we're not going to get any better."

OUSD threatened to close Kaiser previously but eventually backed off. Brian gets fired up when he remembers: "I mean, when they tried to close the school last time, everyone thought, 'We won because of our advocacy.' You didn't win because of your advocacy," he says, looking incredulous. "You won because the last superintendent got death threats slipped under his door, and his children were harassed, and he decided, 'This is some bullshit, I'm leaving.' That's what actually happened. You didn't win because of your brilliant plan to bring people up to scream at the school board meeting. Give me a break."

"That last school board meeting *was* pretty brutal," I say.

His face falls, and he says, "Oh, girl, I'm sorry. Did you at least have a glass of wine? The best way to watch school board meetings is to watch on livestream at home with a really nice bottle and a charcuterie board."

We both laugh. "I'll remember that for next time," I say.

We break down some of the arguments that Kaiser parents made for why the school can't close—particularly the notion that it would be unsafe for gender-nonconforming kids: "The previous principal was a dynamic queer woman," Brian says. "She was phenomenal, and making that place safe for kids just like her was her life's work. I'm horrified by some of the things those parents were projecting onto the Sankofa community. Based on what evidence?"

Talking to Brian confirms what I felt while at the school board meeting—that White parents have this galling way of leaning into our fears. We do it when we choose schools—honoring our own individual nightmares about safety and test scores and artificial sweeteners above collective dreams of equity and justice. We do it when our neighborhoods shift—resisting affordable housing because of some imagined threat to our local vibe. As essayist Eula Biss writes: "What will we do with our fear? This strikes me as a central question of both citizenship and motherhood."

White people feel entitled to our fears. We nurture them alone at night in our beds and together, huddled around PowerPoints. And White parental panic festers in a state of historic amnesia. All the more ironic because *sankofa*—in the Twi language of Ghana—literally means "Go back to the past and bring forward that which is useful."

The less that White and privileged parents see our choices as contextual, that is, situated in a particular place with a rich history, the more likely we are to tunnel and hoard. We aren't thinking about the city or the district or even our neighborhood—who and what has been here, how they've fared because of past policy. We are thinking about Monday morning and our own emotional comfort.

Americans who have been the least besieged by horrible shit are the most fearful that horrible shit is going to happen to them. Not only are we quick to play victim or drum up elaborate conspiracies, but, as the school board meeting demonstrated, we sometimes step into this role zealously. The few Sankofa families who were present at the meeting sat mostly quiet and observant, speaking into the mic politely, their kids reading carefully from written statements, while the huge crew of Kaiser families literally made a scene—shouting into the mic past their allotted time, breaking into tears, their kids chastising the school board members as if they were evil stepparents in a fairy tale.

In a couple of weeks, the final vote will be counted.

70

THE BABIES CAN'T READ. The babies can't read. The babies can't read. The babies can't read. The babies can't read. The babies can't read. The babies can't read. The babies can't read. The babies can't read. The babies can't read. The babies can't read. The babies can't read. The babies can't read.

71

Ms. Vetter pulls out my favorite children's book of all time—*Extra Yarn*, by Mac Barnett and Jon Klassen. Maya squeals, knowing how much I love it: "This is my mom's favorite book!" she tells Darius in a whisper-shout.

It's about a little girl who starts knitting colorful scarves and sweaters and hats for her family and her pets and her neighbors—who have previously been relegated to a world of black and white. The yarn never runs out. Eventually, an archduke catches wind of the girl with the big heart and infinite resource and tries to buy it from her, but she refuses. It can't be bought. So the archduke's henchmen steal the box in the middle of the night. When the archduke opens the box, the yarn is gone. He throws the box into the ocean, and it floats back across the sea to the girl's town, where she finds it.

The yarn, in all its infinite glory, is intact, ready for more creative altruism.

"So, what do you think?" Ms. Vetter asks the kids. "Why wasn't the yarn in the box when the archduke opened it?"

The kids writhe around, confused, but several hands shoot up, as they always do. One kid blurts out: "Because the magic doesn't work for him. He's a bad guy. He wants it all for himself."

Another kid adds: "The magic only works if you're willing to share it."

72

OAKLAND UNIFIED SCHOOL DISTRICT BOARD
MEETING, SEPTEMBER 11, 2019
TOTAL TIME: 7 HOURS, 16 MINUTES, 39 SECONDS

The meeting where the merger will be decided on.

Black mother: [3:42:30] Good evening, I'm LaKeisha
Young. . . . You've heard over the past few weeks from a lot of our
parents, and you've heard a lot about these parents who have been
born and raised in Oakland, how much they've sacrificed over fifty-
plus years, how much they've struggled, how long they've waited
to try to get a quality education for their kids. We can't ask them
or their kids to wait five more years for change. They've waited
long enough.

It needs to be about what is right. Focus on where and how we
can expand quality, not in the long term but in the short term. Our
families have been waiting their whole lives for this.

Black mother: [3:50:48] If you want to merge us with Kaiser,
we're very open to it. I'm the only blind person that is at Sankofa.
It's not a bad thing, but me as a parent, I walk my kids to school,

plus my niece and nephew. It is a good place. It is near. And I
don't have to worry about anything happening to my kids. People
watch over them.... Merge with Kaiser, great. Merge with Peralta,
fine.... We need to think about the children.

A big group of teachers, mostly White, gather around the mic. They
each approach to say a few sentences:

[3:52:09] We the faculty and staff of Kaiser school stand united
against any closure or merger in OUSD.... Oakland does not have
too many schools. Oakland has too many charter schools. They draw
students and dollars away from the traditional public schools.... We
will not participate in any planning process or transition team
around this move...
 In solidarity, the Kaiser school faculty.

White father with his son by his side: [4:04:21] I'm the proud
dad of three Kaiser kids. I'm also a physician in the community. I
want to talk to you today about trauma.... I have three children,
and they have all been deeply traumatized by the threat of moving.
To where doesn't matter.
 You can't fracture a community and remove a child from a place
to another place like you're selling a chicken sandwich at a different
Chick-fil-A down the road. My kid is not a chicken sandwich.
None of these kids are chicken sandwiches!

White student: [4:14:03] I want to spread my friend's message
who is currently on vacation in another country. She has been at
Kaiser with me and our whole class since kindergarten. She has
made it clear that that is her home.

A White girl who has already spoken this evening comes back up
to the mic.

Director Eng: Speakers can only speak once, so have you guys spoken already?

White student: Yes, but I have a lot more to say. [Heard from the audience: Go Mila! Grab that microphone Mila!]

Director Eng: Have you spoken yet? Is there anybody that hasn't spoken yet?

Same White student: Okay, my name is Mila, and I still have a lot more to say.

Director Eng: Thank you. It's really not fair—

Same White student: I can speak if I want... you cannot shut me up. [Crowd laughs.] Okay, my name is Mila, and I'm here to ask you some questions. Why do you guys think you can close Kaiser down?[15]

Board comments:

Student Director Mica Smith-Dahl: [5:16:13] I would like to say that I am speaking as a child of West Oakland, a child of color, and a child with a learning disability. Kaiser is a predominantly wealthy school with middle-class people. And Sankofa is low income predominantly.... It's a sad truth, but with White families brings equity, and that's because people tend to listen to White families. That's why we have disparities at Black schools like Sankofa...

Student Director Denilson Garibo: [5:17:55] I really understand the problems mergers have, but I also don't want Sankofa to close. Sankofa has so much to offer, just as well as Kaiser.... About 46 percent of Kaiser students are coming from the... neighborhood. Only ten percent of families live in the Kaiser neighborhood. If we have this opportunity to provide a school that is closer to low-income families, why don't we go for it?

Director Eng: [5:19:20] What I heard last night in meeting with the Sankofa families was a deep desire for action by this board today.... Even though this option was not my preferred option, I did feel very compelled by what I heard from families about the urgency of making a decision tonight that would help to propel a vision forward.

Director Eng calls for the last round of public comments. Wednesday has become Thursday. It is almost one in the morning. About a dozen people get the last word; at least eight of them are White dads who have already spoken—an astonishing number given the wide variety of people whose lives will be affected by this decision. Their delivery differs, but their message is clear—slow down, don't shut down Kaiser, you are traumatizing our children.

Director Hinton Hodge: I'd like to call the question.

Director Eng: Are there any other board comments or questions at this time?

The directors all shake their heads no. They look utterly exhausted, demoralized, misunderstood.

A White man screams off mic: "If they make a no vote, that doesn't matter! If they make a yes vote, that doesn't matter! They have no power! We have the power!"

Director Eng: At this time, we are going to vote on this item.

A big crowd of parents, mostly White, stands up in the front of the room, next to the stairs that lead up to the dais where the school board members are seated.

Parliamentarian: [5:56:18] Student Director Garibo?

Sixteen tense silent seconds go by; it seems like an eternity.

Student Director Garibo: I'm going to abstain. [The audience yells, "Thank you!"]

Parliamentarian: Student Director Smith-Dahl?

Student Director Smith-Dahl: I'm going to abstain.

Parliamentarian: Director Hinton Hodge?

Hinton Hodge: Yes. [The audience boos loudly.]

Parliamentarian: Director Torres?

Torres: No. [The audience cheers loudly.]

Parliamentarian: Director Gonzales?

Gonzales: No. [More cheering.]

Parliamentarian: Director Harris?

Harris: Yes. [Boos. Hissing.]

Parliamentarian: Director Yee?

Yee: Yes. [A kid shrieks "No!"]

Parliamentarian: Vice President London?

London: Yes. [The crowd boos even more loudly.]

It's 3 to 2 now, with both student directors abstaining. If Director Eng votes no, it will be a tie—meaning another delay for the Sankofa families. If Director Eng votes yes, Kaiser's previous school site, in the hills, will be closed, and Sankofa and Kaiser will merge in the flatlands, on Sankofa's campus. An unprecedented, one might even say historic, moment for Oakland public schools.

73

Thirteen Ways of Looking at the Proposed Merger

an opportunity for two schools—a wealthier, more academically
    excellent one and a low-resourced, academically struggling
    one—to pool their respective resources
an inadequate Band-Aid on a long-festering wound
an attempt to finally do a hard thing that must be done instead of
    delaying discomfort
a way to right-size the school system and balance the budget
a counter to gentrification and White resource hoarding
the desecration of a special community
a step toward privatizing our public schools
a step toward integrating our public schools
a rare counterexample to the district's past and present preoccupation
    with keeping White middle-class people in the district, though
    they constantly threaten to flee
hasty
overdue
a trauma
a repair

74

Parliamentarian: President Eng?

Director Eng: Yes.

Parliamentarian: The motion is adopted.

There are a few moments of what seem like shock, and then the hissing and booing starts in earnest. A woman's voice rises above the rest: "Do you hear the children crying? Do you hear them?"

A small White boy starts ascending the stairs toward the school board members, screaming at the top of his lungs, shrieking, really: "You idiots! You can't do this! You're traumatizing us!"

Director Eng: We will now take a recess.

75

THE SCHOOL SITE COUNCIL meeting, which is usually a pretty casual environment—pizza box open with a couple of cold donated slices, a grease-stained sign-in sheet—is thick with tension. Principal Palin is a no-show. She's got pneumonia. Blair, the homecoming queen I spotted on the playground, is livid, explaining that she canceled a business trip to make sure she could attend this meeting. (Those of us around the table share a surprised look when she says this; we will come to learn that this is trademark self-serious Blair.)

All hell breaks loose when Blair, acronyms blazing, tries to get the parents around the table to discuss the low test scores and approach to literacy in Principal Palin's absence (Blair brought print-outs). She is a passionate believer in "structured literacy"—with a heavy emphasis on the *structure* part. Every letter has a picture, name, and sound; teachers must drill these into kids' minds over and over again so that they learn how to then blend those sounds together to make words. Not only is this her pedagogical preference, but she's the CEO of an edtech nonprofit that specializes in curriculum that is focused on it (among other things).

The test scores *are* abysmal (thus the 1 out of 10 on GreatSchools.org). Last year, for example, only 6 of 76 Black kids and 3 of 19 Latinx kids met the standard on the state reading test. Data for White kids isn't even available because there are so few of them.

Elizabeth, the PTA president, jumps in to defend Emerson. She gives a mini-lecture on how complex poverty is and how test scores map directly onto socioeconomic status. While Blair is self-serious, Elizabeth can be condescending—"You can't undo four hundred years of trauma!" she shouts.

They're both, in a sense, right. The test scores are low and indicate that too many kids at Emerson aren't leaving with the academic skills they need to thrive. But it's not just a matter of curricula; educational researchers have found that "out-of-school factors account for a significantly greater share of a student's academic achievement and attainment than do in-school factors"—up to 80 percent.[16]

This is why there is an argument for looking not at the scores in isolation but for growth over time. Emerson's cumulative growth score—a measure that even test skeptics find intriguing—was truly impressive in the 2017–2018 school year: a whopping 82 percent. It dipped again last year after some significant teacher turnover in the upper grades.

At the meeting, things got personal fast. Blair accuses Elizabeth of not caring. How could she justify these low test scores when they were disproportionately affecting Black and Brown kids, the very children that Elizabeth professed to care about supporting? Elizabeth recommends that Blair read some Nikole Hannah-Jones and Jack Schneider. And send her kid to a charter school if she wants a place that focuses primarily on test scores. The SSC chair closes the meeting. The agenda will languish another week, which means, from Blair's perspective, the kids will suffer because of our politically correct bullshit.

A lot of thoughts are running through my mind as I head home, but perhaps the most dominant is this: there wasn't one Black or Brown parent in that meeting. We—the White parents—can participate in philosophical fisticuffs all day long, but we will be no smarter about how the majority of parents at our school feel about test scores, approaches to literacy, or anything else until they are in the room.

As I'm harassing the girls to brush their teeth and wedging their little feet into footie pajamas, my mind keeps returning to Blair. It's important to take a clear-eyed look at how our school is doing by our kids, but that doesn't mean heaping all the blame on the teachers and the principal.

If this isn't a "go get your girl" moment, I don't know what is. Should I recommend a less alienating approach to a fellow White woman? It's not just that I'm historically conflict-averse (something I'm working on), but also that I don't really want to hang out with her. I was never best friends with the captain of the cheerleading team or the valedictorian; I was best friends with the taciturn skater from art class and the smart girl who edited the newspaper and knew where all the best parties were on the weekends.

But I text Blair anyway: The meeting this evening was a little contentious. Want to meet up for coffee and talk sometime this week?

She writes back within seconds: Yes, that would be wonderful. Where and when?

We meet up a few days later at Julie's, the epitome of gentrification in our neighborhood—big glass jars of bone broth (eighteen bucks for a quart) sit in a cooler next to the register.

After exchanging some niceties about how our girls appear to like each other, I launch in: "So, I gather from your comments that you know a lot about education. Tell me more about your background."

She tells me about growing up in a wealthy, largely White town near here, and never thinking once about racism or inequality. She tells me about showing up as a Teach for America fellow in a classroom in the Bronx right out of college with zero context for what the families were experiencing. She tells me a lot about her heartbreak for those kids. (*Heartbreak,* I will come to understand, is her default. She uses the word over and over again.)

She tells me a little bit about her ineptitude and lack of preparation, but then quickly pivots to the *Dangerous Minds* version of her story, in which she decides one tearful night that she is going to teach these kids to read come hell or high water, and ends up becoming a "masterful" teacher.

She was an assistant principal at a charter school for a while, but it was too taxing. She knew she needed to lower her stress, get a change of scenery and pace, so she and her husband moved to Oakland. She's got a new company she's running and a cotton candy pink travel mug with CEO emblazoned on it to prove it.

She tells me that she enrolled Sofia, her daughter, at Emerson without taking a tour. My brain can't square this information at all with the woman sitting in front of me. She's got her blazer on, ponytail tight and high, notebook in front of her, pen at the ready even though I haven't said a word in an hour.

She talks about how appalled she is by the test scores at Emerson. She cries when she talks about the state of the bathrooms. She has discovered that Sofia is "gifted." She doesn't want to make her "a social justice martyr."

I decide to finally interrupt: "That must be really hard. Maya isn't gifted, so I don't have to think about that."

I love this little experiment with White parents. If you say your kid isn't gifted, it's like you've shit on the avocado toast in the middle of the table.

"Oh, I mean—I hate that word *gifted*," she course-corrects, though she just used the word without any sign of discomfort a minute earlier. "I just mean that if you put Sofia in a first-grade classroom, she would do fine."

"She's advanced," I say.

"Yes, advanced. That's it," Blair says, seemingly relieved.

"Maya's not," I say matter-of-factly, shitting on the toast again. A look of confusion and panic crosses Blair's face very quickly.

"She's doing fine," I reassure her. "I'm not worried about her academically. We're there because we want to be part of the Emerson community."

"Yes," Blair says. "Exactly. At the end of the day, I just want every child to have a beautiful, clean school with a joyfully rigorous classroom and a loving teacher."

I can't argue with that. This kind of clarity is where I find Blair intriguing. What is she telling the Emerson community that we don't want to hear?

She's been a classroom teacher, an assistant principal, a coach to teachers and principals, and is now leading an edtech company. In some ways that sets her up to be a massive boon to the community. But it also feeds her arrogance and makes her seem, to some, suspicious. Does she have some personal stake in influencing what curriculum Emerson buys or how the teachers are trained? (This might sound far-fetched to someone who has never been around educators, but trust me, there are myriad examples of people getting rich off of the backs of poor school districts via consulting fees and overhyped curricula or technology.)

Blair goes on to explain the "broken windows theory," as applied to schools; if the bulletin boards are in disarray, if there is litter on the playground, if the landscaping around the school appears haphazard or neglected, then you can bet that the teaching is substandard, the behavior out of control, and the test scores low.

What might sound sort of intuitive is actually racially charged and rich in sociological dispute. Philip Zimbardo (yes, the same guy who made Stanford undergrads prison inmates and guards) did an experiment back in 1969 in which he left one unmarked car in a predominantly poor, crime-ridden section of New York City, and another in a higher-income neighborhood of Palo Alto, California. It took all of ten minutes for the one in New York to get vandalized, but the one in Palo Alto was left alone for over a week. Then Zimbardo took a sledgehammer to it, and learned, as people walking by tore it apart, that Californians had just as much capacity for vandalism as poor New Yorkers.

Seeing that something or some place is already in disrepair encourages more destruction. That was the seed for the broken windows theory, a concept named by criminologists George L. Kelling and James Q. Wilson in *The Atlantic* well over a decade after Zimbardo took a sledgehammer to that car.[17]

Kelling and Wilson proposed that police departments should think more about cleaning up streets and going after petty crimes, like jumping turnstiles or loitering, than solving major crimes if they want to improve whole communities. Fair enough—in theory. Except in practice, the broken windows turn out to be Black and Brown people—criminalized for the smallest of infractions—while White people, under the radar of biased police officers, continue to break laws willy-nilly without repercussions.[18]

Taking this controversial theory and applying it to a school filled with

Black and Brown kids is not exactly a neutral posture. But I'm taking deep breaths, trying to hear her out.

Blair thought Emerson was great the first couple of weeks she was there: the Monday-morning routine, the smiling adults on the playground, the spiffy bulletin boards. But after two weeks, she started to see everything sliding into disrepair, and no one seemed to care. Principal Palin expressed no outrage or urgency. She didn't apologize to Blair, even after she pointed out how filthy the bathrooms were.

"Can I offer a perspective on what I think is going on?" I ask.

"Yes," Blair says, her eyes hungry, her hand poised over her notebook to take exacting notes.

"You've only been at the school for a couple of months. So, for a lot of people, your feedback feels like a lot, very fast. I sat in meetings for months, just trying to learn: Who are the people who have been here for a while? There are families at Emerson who have been attending for generations. What do they think?

"That's not your style, but it's hard for people. They're used to a gentler approach. I know your criticism comes from a good place."

She's nodding, but with a cringing smile. The idea of slowing down seems painful to her.

"I hope this is coming off as compassionate," I say. "I mean it to be."

"No, it is. I appreciate it. For me, every day that we lose is another day when kids aren't learning to read," she says. "But I totally know what you mean. So, what do I do?"

I encourage her to apologize to the School Site Council, to reaffirm that she cares about the kids and that's the bottom line, and to acknowledge that she knows she can sometimes come on too strong. I urge her to take a listening posture more often. She has a lot of expertise, but there are all kinds of expertise. She takes notes. She nods a lot.

We part ways with a smile and a quick hug. I feel like her big sister somehow. I get her. I was her, or maybe just parts of her, in my twenties—sure that all problems had solutions, passionate and urgent, heartbroken and helpful. I was never that arrogant, thank goodness, or that unaware of the larger political contexts in which I was operating, but I definitely had that toxic White girl mix of indefatigability and fragility.

But I'm left unsettled. Is my slow approach to this school community a sign of maturity or complicity?

76

T HE CLIP IS ON all the local television stations and websites. People scream "What the fuck!" at the police while simultaneously recording the chaos on their cell phones. Police officers hold their billy clubs horizontally and slam back against parents and teachers who bum-rush the stage. The force is indefensible. Soft bodies go flying. A White guy tries to keep playing his banjo as the police manhandle him. Saru Jayaraman, the Kaiser parent who referenced being investigated by Trump, continues chanting while being arrested, her arms twisted behind her back by police officers at the top of the stage.

What I watch over and over again is this: a quiet mother-daughter interaction right before the clash.

Eighteen minutes into the beginning of the October 23, 2019, OUSD school board meeting, Stracey Gordon, a Black mother whose kids go to Kaiser, comes to the mic, wearing an OAKLAND NOT FOR SALE T-shirt. A dozen other people (mostly White and Asian-American) flank her on all sides. They are wearing the quickly produced merch of the resistance that has been formed from the disgruntled parents and teachers at Kaiser. The little girl standing next to Stracey, who looks to be her daughter, is wearing a headband with pink cat ears.

Saru is standing to Stracey's left side in a black T-shirt that says SAVE OAKLAND SCHOOLS. With her right hand she grips the barrier that has been put up on both sides of the podium and holds a folded white piece of material in her left hand, presumably a banner waiting to be unfurled. Her own small daughter stands by her side. With a strangely serene smile on her face, Saru nods her head as Stracey speaks, laying out the "Oakland Not for Sale" demands: a moratorium on all school closures, no more school-to-prison pipeline, an end to the board's coziness with charter schools, and an increase in financial transparency and genuine community engagement.

As Stracey is shouting about "charter management companies," her allotted time winding down, Saru's daughter reaches for Saru's arm. It seems like she is trying to make room for herself between the podium and her mom (her father, a Black activist and local advocate for justice, isn't at the podium). Saru gently pushes her away. Mouths *no*. Her daughter looks confused, maybe even a little hurt. She raises her eyebrows. An East Asian–American woman behind Saru guides the young girl over to the other side of the speaker, as if to give Saru space. The girl whispers in the ear of the other little girl—the one with the cat headband.

Stracey shouts the climax of her speech into the mic: "We will continue to disrupt these meetings, and there will be no more business as usual until these demands are met! No school closures!"

The dozen flanking her join her in the final scream: "Oakland is not for sale!"

Saru grips the barrier harder and hurdles it with her right foot. She is wearing sneakers, ready for action. The police rush in.

There's something about the brief disconnection between mother and daughter, the wounded look on the daughter's face (so familiar to me), that fascinates me.

Is this leap over the barrier brave?

It is physically brave, no question. I'm taken with how serene Saru looks. I wonder if she's undergone some kind of training, as so many did during the civil rights movement, for facing physical violence with equanimity. I look at notes from a tactical nonviolence training session in 1963.[19]

When "going limp," there are specific styles. They sound like dance moves: the Buddha style, the Flabby-limp style, the Walking limp-collapse, and Going rough.

There is a section on what is and isn't police brutality: "To fuzz the most heinous crime is 'contempt of cop.'"

The training teaches protesters not to provoke brutality, but when faced with it, to surrender so as not to get hurt. Saru definitely jumps into "the fuzz." It's no doubt a provocation. She won't jump again for a long time. Her ACL, MCL, and meniscus in her knee are torn in the confrontation. She will walk around on crutches for months and brave reconstructive surgery.

But is the leap over the barrier morally brave? Is it just? I'm not sure.

In Eve L. Ewing's *Ghosts in the Schoolyard,* about a historically Black school that was closed in Chicago and the resistance to that closure, she writes: "In losing a school one loses a version of oneself—a self understood to be a member of a community, living and learning in relation to other community members."

The Kaiser community prided itself on being a progressive, multiracial space where all kids thrived. The district's proposal, and the Sankofa community's reaction (essentially, *Sure, come on over, let's work together*), forced their hand. Were they "progressive" enough to expand and enfold, to be inconvenienced and challenged for the possibility of a broader, poorer, Blacker community?

The answer for Sankofa was yes. A community of families, the vast majority of whom have been profoundly impacted by anti-Black racism, cared enough about the possibility of building a better school that served more children that they said yes to welcoming the stranger. Even as the stranger, who often looked like their oppressors, screamed their disgust. The parents at Sankofa were willing to compromise on their dream of Black excellence for a dream of multiracial community.

The answer for much of Kaiser was no. They dressed their no in larger political ideologies. They pointed the finger at school board members and billionaire-backed charters. It's not that the influence of these actors isn't a worthwhile line of questioning; all of it is worth wrestling over. But in this moment, concerning this merger, it also served as a distraction from the pain of realizing that many Kaiser parents were not as willing to share resources or risk discomfort as they thought they were. They recoiled against letting go of one dream in favor of another that they had far less control over.

The Kaiser parents and teachers who said no, now dubbed "Oakland Not for Sale," turned their grief into anger, and now their anger into righteous indignation. Rather than seeing themselves as part of a history within a city where Black kids have been systematically starved of the resources and quality of education they deserve and joining common cause with those kids, their moms and dads, and their aunties and uncles, Kaiser parents seemed lost in a fog of their own grand political notions. They saw no forest. Only trees.

One Kaiser mom, who was open to the merger but silent during most school board meetings for fear of reprisal from the rest of her community, told me a powerful story. A school psychologist was seeing a Kaiser student who claimed to be traumatized by the proposed merger. After some opening conversation, the psychologist realized that the kid didn't actually understand where Sankofa was. Once she explained, the student's eyes grew wide as saucers, and he said, "Wait, Sankofa is that place where I go play basketball on the weekends? I *love* that place!"

77

I walk in right under the wire for the School Site Council meeting to begin. There are more people in the room than I've ever seen for a meeting. Usually it's just the requisite number of staff and teachers to satisfy the district rules for a quorum. Tonight the whole library is packed. A group of teachers sit around a table. None of them are required to be there. Clearly they've come to send a signal to Blair: *You fuck with any of us, you fuck with all of us.*

There are a bunch of parents standing around whom I've never seen at one of these meetings. Blair's recruits.

It's as if our typically bureaucratic-to-the-point-of-boring School Site Council meetings have been transformed into *West Side Story.*

Blair is standing in the back in workout clothes with a low-slung side ponytail, taking notes on a legal pad nestled into a leather portfolio.

The meeting is called to order, and a district representative walks us through a badly designed PowerPoint slide deck about the obligations and structure of the School Site Council committee at each Oakland public school. We're supposed to create a school site plan. We are also supposed to help the staff decide how to spend our "Title I and Title IV categorical expenditures," by which she means money.

It's important that the SSC "stay in your lane," the district rep says multiple times. "Title I money and its expenditure is your lane. Complaining that the salad bar is too cold? Outside your lane." The salad bar. Right. As if. But I do wonder if she's been warned about the recent upheaval at our usually docile SSC.

Principal Palin takes the meeting back and announces that today is an overdue nominating meeting. I don't plan on running for anything, I quickly decide in my head.

Even after attending a whole year of meetings, I still feel like I'm just starting to follow the conversations.

"Okay, we'll start with president," Principal Palin says. "Any nominations?"

"I nominate myself," Blair chirps from the back of the room.

"Okay, got it," says Principal Palin. "Any seconds?"

"I second," says a parent that I've never met wearing thick hipster glasses and a hoodie.

"Got it, thank you. Any other nominations?"

My mind is still processing that Blair has just nominated herself to run this committee when Ms. Grill pipes up: "I nominate Courtney."

"Wow, thanks," I say, genuinely shocked.

"I second," Jack jumps in.

"Any other nominees?" Principal Palin asks. Crickets.

Uh-oh. This wasn't the plan. Show up and shush up was the plan.

"Okay, so I think we'll have you both say a little something about yourselves so others can have a sense of who they're voting for. Courtney, you want to start?"

"Uh, okay," I say, standing up and turning around to face the room. "Hi, guys. I'm not sure what to say, honestly. I'm a good listener. I'm a journalist, so I like researching things, which seems like it might come in handy here. I have a lot to learn, but I care about this school and the kids a lot. I am particularly committed to making sure that kids of color, not just my own kid, thrive here. Anything else?" I ask, looking at Principal Palin.

"No, that's great, thanks, Courtney." Everyone claps kindly, and I sit down.

"Blair?"

Blair approaches the front of the room and says, "Thank you very much. Well, first I want to start out by saying that I worry I didn't make the best first impression, and I'm sorry if I offended anyone. I care a lot about kids and educational excellence and I'm not always good at controlling my passions when it comes to them."

I think this is her version of the apology I recommended, but it sure doesn't sound like much of one. Once again, she's managed to put other teachers and parents on the defensive. Is our passion too "controllable" in comparison to hers? It's a question I genuinely hold. Her presence has made me question my own passivity in the face of all of this academic disparity—should I have made more of a stink about the test scores last year?

"I nominate myself to be the president, because I'm good at being a boss," she says, smiling her most winning smile.

I laugh out loud, assuming it's a self-effacing joke, but then realize that she is dead serious. No one, not even the parents she has recruited to vote for her, is laughing. In fact, the teachers—the whole lot of them—are mean-mugging her.

Blair goes on to recite her résumé—the schools she's worked at, the consulting and coaching she's done, the company she started, the press coverage she's received. She's even written her own children's book. She names the publisher.

I quickly flash on all the impressive shit in my bio. None of it is currency here. It's not that it doesn't matter, insofar as those are experiences that I can bring to the table. But, and this is a huge but, my ability to put those experiences to use for the kids here is only as good as my ability to befriend and collaborate with other parents and teachers. Her misread of the room, of what has value here and how, is political suicide.

We vote by secret ballot, all writing down the president of our choice on a little piece of paper and then passing them up to Principal Palin, who quickly records the tally. "And our next School Site Council president is...Courtney Martin," she says, smiling. The teachers clap enthusiastically. "Thanks, guys!" I say to them, then turn to Jack and flash my deer-in-the-headlights eyes.

There are two other official leadership positions—vice president and secretary. Blair nominates herself for both. She loses to Jeremy, a young White guy from the neighborhood who is a former math teacher, for vice president; he's dutifully showed up to every meeting, weighed in carefully and politely. When I found out he didn't have a kid at the school, my jaw dropped to the floor. If more people like him existed—people without kids who were benevolently interested in contributing to equity in public schools—so much would be different.

In the age-old custom of wriggling out of the thankless job of note-taking, the two other people nominated for secretary both decline the nomination, so Blair runs unopposed. And wins.

By the time I get home that night, I already have an email from Blair, introducing me to Kareem Weaver, a "former educator and neighbor who cares," and, as it turns out, was one of the new faces at the meeting last night. I do a little digging and realize he is also the local education rep of the NAACP. Not just "a neighbor who cares." Blair and the NAACP are aligned. I'm still trying to wrap my head around that one as I fall asleep.

She texts me at 6:20 a.m. the next morning: Have you ever seen a Title I school that is crushing it? Would you like to? (Might involve an overnight cross-country trip.)

I flash on the image of riding next to Blair on an airplane. I'm watching some depressing art film and eating all the free snacks, no matter how unappetizing; she's speed-reading a book about being a girl boss, with a giant pink highlighter at the ready, some pre-cut veggies by her side. This cross-country trip fills me with social terror.

Also I am banned from helping in class. I am heartbroken. ☹

What is happening at that school is not OK, Courtney.

78

S ofia, Blair's daughter, comes over to play. She and Maya are upstairs playing dress-up. "My mom doesn't like high heels," says Maya.

Sofia, incredulous: "Why?"

"Because she says you can't walk twenty blocks in them. You could fall," Maya says.

She's not off. I told Maya that I personally don't like wearing high heels because I like to feel like, no matter what comes, I could walk twenty blocks if I needed to. A New York thing. A 9/11 thing. I don't know.

Sofia replies, pride in her little voice: "My mom never falls."

79

BRIAN STANLEY AND I are back at our spot—afternoon light streaming through the big, exquisitely clean glass walls of the office tower. We're talking about the emergence of the Oakland Not for Sale movement—the shutting down of school board meeting after school board meeting, the clash with the police, the constant drama.

"We have to close schools," he answers emphatically. "My argument is pure dollars and cents. The small-schools movement was cute. It seemed like a good idea, but, y'all, read a balance sheet! It's twice the cost with half the resources. We cannot deal with a constant threat of fiscal insolvency year after year. It's devastating."

"But getting back to Oakland Not for Sale's position," I nudge.

"Look, people tend to sprint away from complexity. They don't understand, and they get scared. The stakes are high, and the shit feels real. It's like, 'This is too much. I'm going to go with the easy story because I can handle it.'"

"And what's the easy story here?" I ask.

"The easy story here is that the bastards downtown stole all the money. And OUSD does not help itself, to be clear. The endless cycles in administrative restructuring and, quite frankly, incompetence and sloppiness don't help."

"I've wondered if it's more of an organizing technique, like good organizers always have a villain," I say.

"It could be," Brian says. "And damn if the school board isn't playing the villain. Sending the police in there was a bad idea. You all just fell for the trap! It was the Sarlacc pit! It was waiting for you, and you were walking through the desert, and there were signs that said SARLACC PIT, DON'T GO INTO HERE. Now you're being digested over a thousand years."

Indeed. Saru and other members of the Oakland Not for Sale movement are suing the district for assault and civil rights violations.

80

W<small>ILLIAMS</small> C<small>HAPEL</small> B<small>APTIST</small> C<small>HURCH</small>—"The Church That Stays in God's Will and Not in His Way." 9:45 a.m. on a sunny Saturday.

We're in the windowless basement, but the mood is bright. There's a generous spread of scrambled eggs, grits, and fruit in big aluminum trays and carafes of weak coffee in the back. I grab some, head to a seat in the middle, pull out my notebook, and take a look around. There are about fifty people here for a meeting on a new literacy campaign being spearheaded by the Oakland REACH and the NAACP. The guys are almost all in suits, and the women in some version of their own Sunday best. I count only four White people other than me. One of them is Blair. She's sitting in the front row in a white turtleneck sweater, chewing gum, and nodding her head vigorously as people speak at the podium.

School board member Jumoke Hinton Hodge is up next. She's wearing an African-print shirt, peplum cut, and her signature black square glasses: "Giving thanks to God and my amazing ancestors. I'm so blessed to be here. I've had the opportunity to serve on the school board for eleven years and a few months, and I have about three hundred days left...so use me."

Jumoke explains: "Why I'm so happy about this campaign around literacy—one is that it is a conversation about our children, but what is very real is that it's a conversation about our families. We have mamas and we have babas that are also not literate.

"This is no hating on Oakland, but we've got a lot of answering to do for this school district for a number of years," she goes on. "Some of us, we're going to make it. We made it. We did all right. But there are still too many folks that did not get what they deserved inside of here. This is about all of us owning it. I don't care how you've gotten by, this is a moment of truth-telling in our community about what's needed and what's necessary."

Are there adults in this very room who can't read? People who have been shuffled along in Oakland public schools, cheated of the chance to connect letters and sounds in their own brains? Cheated of Faith Ringgold and Sandra Cisneros and Toni Morrison? Cheated of the chance to walk tall into job interviews without a curdling fear in their bellies that they'll be asked to spontaneously fill out a form with ten-dollar words?

Jumoke is building to a close: "And what I know is that the resistance, the pushback, is coming.... This is not about someone's job. This is not about a union. This is about young people and families being literate and being liberated. They're going to come after us, when you start talking about the liberation of Black people in this country, they will come after you. So stand up."

A stout Black woman with a denim cap and a black T-shirt that says I GOT MY KNOWLEDGE FROM A BLACK COLLEGE jumps to her feet and shouts, "We're ready! And I know I'm talking to some Black folks, but I'm really talking to some White folks in the room."

Is she looking at me? I try to meet her gaze with resolve.

"Be really clear, that if you're our ally, if you're going to be co-conspirators with us, *this* is the work of liberation for our people. Nobody can be free, right, unless all of us are free."

Applause erupts and she walks back to her seat.

This is about Darius and Maya, but this is also about their great-great-grandparents.

After Nat Turner led a slave rebellion in 1831, almost every Southern state passed laws against teaching slaves to read and write. Frederick Douglass, who was taught the alphabet in secret at twelve years of age by his White master's wife, famously described knowledge as "the pathway from slavery to freedom."

Teacher testimonies are up next. Kareem introduces Blair and the teacher she's been supporting. They get up from their front-row seats, and the teacher smooths out her pink floral skirt, looking nervous as she grasps the mic. Her high-pitched voice shakes a little, her Southern accent detectable but not strong: "My name is Janet, and I teach first grade. We are at the very bottom in reading and math."

"This is Blair," she says, pointing to her right and looking adoringly at her mentor.

When Emerson proved immune to Blair's powers of persuasion, she asked the district volunteer office where "her expertise could be put to use and the principal wouldn't be threatened," as she put it. They sent her to the absolute lowest performing school in all of Oakland. It has 323 students, 91 percent of whom are on free or reduced lunch (down from 97 percent the four previous years) and upward of 80 percent of whom do not do math or read at grade level. Not a single one of the students at the school is White. Blair thought to herself, "Oh, shit. They placed me here because nobody cares about this school.... And then I was like, okay, the Universe had a plan. I needed to get kicked out of Emerson so I could help kids here."

As she explained it to me: "I rolled up my sleeves and started teaching kids to read and teaching the teacher how to teach her kids to read. And for a teacher who has received zero support for two years and is on the verge of quitting, I was her angel. That means something to teachers when someone is willing to show up and help you learn to teach and get results."

At the church, Janet goes on: "I got by as best as I could last year with very little support. I was on my own. Then this year I got Blair. We started teaching small-group direct instruction with Blair's program..." She trails off and then says to Blair, "Do you want to explain the curriculum more?"

Blair takes the mic: "Hi. I'm joining her for moral support. I just want to emphasize that this is a second-year teacher, and it is pretty terrifying to be a second-year teacher and doing what you know your babies need but what you have not been empowered to be able to provide for them.

"I am also a former teacher myself and a parent in OUSD. I did all of my education work in New York City public schools and charter schools. and, um, wow, I thought New York City was . . . um . . . a hot mess."

The crowd laughs. She smiles, emboldened. "But let me tell you . . . New York City has their shit together compared to OUSD, and that is utterly terrifying."

The crowd now gasps quietly, but she doesn't hear it, because she's repeating herself loudly and emphatically: "Utterly terrifying."

She goes on, oblivious: "I know from my experience that Black children *can* learn to read, because I was a first-grade teacher in Harlem, and all of my babies learned to read. I started showing up to School Site Council meetings at my daughter's school and saying, 'This is not okay. What are we doing about this?'

"I got to spend two days volunteering in a first-grade classroom in my daughter's school before the principal then told me I wasn't allowed to work with them unless I wanted to do guided reading with them."

Now she's getting fired up: "And I said, 'Guided reading doesn't work! And I am showing up here, willing to help this first-grade teacher learn how to teach reading to his children, because it doesn't have to be this way! Children do not need to leave your school functionally illiterate!'"

I'm completely willing to entertain that there might be more effective ways to teach kids to read than how Emerson is teaching them. What bothers me is the way she talks about her approach as the answer, not an answer, but *the* answer to ending centuries of racialized illiteracy in our nation's schools. I'm not dismissing the idea that it has some validity, but I'm too old to believe in panaceas.

And I think it is just as cruel, maybe even more so in some ways, to claim that there is nothing standing in the way of all kids learning to read except curricula as it is to claim that some kids are incapable. All kids are capable, but curricula are not magic. We can and must do better to ensure that Black and Brown kids learn to read, *and* we will be capable of that only if we are honest about how we've failed and about the hard, worthwhile road of transformation. "Structured literacy" might be a part of that, but it's not the whole picture.

Blair goes on and on: "If your teachers are empowered with efficacious curricula and somebody who is willing to help them teach that curricula..."

Kareem starts creeping toward the pair of them, trying to signal Blair to wrap it up. Blair seems to get the message and hands the mic back to Janet mid-sentence like a hot potato.

Janet continues: "Okay, so, yeah, we've been doing it for six weeks now—we're pulling small groups, five different small groups, and, um, teaching them phonics and phonemic awareness, and I layered on shared reading, all while not teaching the curriculum I'm supposed to."

Jumoke creeps up to the stage and whispers something in Blair's ear.

"We have seen tremendous results," Janet says, getting a little sturdier. "We have multiple students who have already moved up to the next level. They're actually learning to read. We're rocking the boat. I'm a little bit scared of backlash, but we're getting results, and that's all that matters."

The crowd applauds. Blair grabs the mic back and, beet red, says, "I'm sorry I cursed. I'm very sorry."

A Black woman dressed to the nines, an executive of the local NAACP chapter, is behind the podium and says: "It's okay, girl, we're going to take the mic from you."

The crowd erupts with laughter, clapping and yelling out, "Preach! Tell her!"

"I appreciate her keeping it real, but that was too real for the church. Let's just remember that we're in a holy sanctuary. We're not mad at you, girl—now you know. I don't know what they do in New York, but we don't cuss in the church here."

An older Black gentleman slowly walks in then. He's wearing a velour tracksuit the color of milky coffee and has a bald head covered with freckles. He sits down gingerly in one of the back rows. "Well, look at that—we've got Oscar Wright in the house!" someone yells. The woman in the denim hat runs back and grabs Mr. Wright's arm, forcing him to come sit in the front row as the whole room cheers.

Oscar Wright is a ninety-six-year-old Oakland native who has been advocating for equal education for Black children since 1965. He's seen eighteen superintendents pass through OUSD, and countless campaigns and curricular controversies and strikes and protest movements come and go. As a child, Wright went to an all-Black agricultural school on a plantation in Coahoma County, Mississippi, where the students would sometimes be sent out of the classrooms and into the cotton fields for a couple of hours of picking.

We've come so far, and yet not far enough at all. It is all true at once.

81

I PICK UP MAYA and her new friend, Scout, from school, and we start walking home for a playdate. Scout is a White wisp of a little girl with thick pink-rimmed glasses who pretty much always has a skeptical look on her face. From what I can tell, she spends nearly 50 percent of her day doing a cat impression.

I met Scout's mom, who is almost always in workout clothes and a wide-brim brown wool hat, at morning drop-off. It felt easy to get her cell number and to text her about the playdate. We are part of the same White, feminist, exhausted-mom culture, which is a thing, as it turns out. A thing that helps you effortlessly strike the same tone about your kid who has two last names. You are amused, but never doting, as you schedule a hang that doesn't conflict with Zimbabwean dance or French lessons. Shared culture is the water—cool, soothing, and invisible. It's our food (those salty dried-seaweed packets, those squishy bags of organic goop), our persistent, performative friendliness ("Good morning! How are you this morning, Scout? I love your leg warmers!"), our thirty million words. It's amazing how utterly comprehensive and comforting it is, despite the fact that Scout's mom and I are perfect strangers.

As Maya and Scout and I are walking home, we realize that Darius and his dad, Andre, are walking about a block ahead. Andre, a lanky, dark-skinned Black guy with a head covering, always sort of hangs back during drop-off, leaning against the metal railing as the class marches by. Darius is a small boy with cornrows and an endearing* lisp, usually wearing jeans and a Spider-Man T-shirt. I've gotten to know him a bit during my library visits. We start to gain on them and realize that they live behind us on the same block, about two houses south. "Hi, Darius!" Maya shrieks joyously.

"Hi, Darius!" Scout parrots.

I lean in close and whisper to Maya: "Do you want to invite Darius over, too?"

"No, I just want a playdate with Scout," she says. "But another time."

"Okay," I say, waving at Darius and Andre as they enter the tall gate in front of their two-story pale peach stucco house and start walking up the concrete steps. There are wooden slats threaded through the chain-link fence. No bright accent colors or street number in a hipster font. No Prius. No BLACK LIVES MATTER sign in the window. All the things that would be dead giveaways in the neighborhood that a newbie has moved in.

"We live right over there!" Maya tells Darius, motioning in the direction of our house.

"What!" Darius shrieks back. "Really?"

"Yeah," Maya says, laughing, head thrown back.

"We should hang out sometime soon," I holler over my shoulder as the girls giggle and skip their way farther down the sidewalk. I don't hear a reply if there is one.

A few days later, we spot Andre and Darius walking to school, so I pop the question: "We were just talking about having a playdate with you, Darius. Would you like that?"

Darius nods his head and juts out his chin.

"How about Wednesday?" I ask Andre.

"We'll get back to you," he says, then looks at Maya and asks, "Are you Scout or Maya?"

---

* Dr. Dena Simmons: "Something about a White person saying *endearing* feels patronizing."

"Maya!" Darius yells, rolling his eyes at his dad, and we all laugh together.

That afternoon Maya makes a playdate checklist for her time with Darius—Legos, snack, art, dress-up—all with little crooked boxes next to them so she can check the items off. I worry she's getting her hopes up. I can't read Andre's interest.

The next morning, I check: "What do you think? I could pick the kids up after school and walk them home to our house if you want."

"We can't today," he says. "I need to get Darius's hair braided for picture day on Friday. Taking him to my sister's house."

"Ah, okay, no problem," I say while registering Maya's face fall.

"Next Wednesday would be good," Andre adds. Maybe also noticing Maya's disappointment?

"Great, let's plan on that," I say.

The next morning I notice that Darius's hair is not freshly braided. *Don't make meaning out of it,* I tell myself. *Mind your own business.*

Wednesday morning rolls around again. All the kids are hanging up their backpacks on hooks and unceremoniously throwing their lunch boxes into the laundry basket in the hallway outside their classroom, getting their last hugs and hair tousled. I brace myself for a no but ask anyway. "You all want to do the playdate today?"

"We'll tell you after school," Andre says.

It turns out to be one of the hottest days of the year, 92 degrees by the time I go to pick Maya up. I'm running just a few minutes late, as usual, sort of speed-walking and sweating and listening to a podcast, when a car pulls up alongside me. I look up and realize it's Andre. He rolls down the passenger-side window and smiles warmly. "Want a ride?"

"Sure," I say, and hop in. It feels strange to be sliding onto his leather seat, more intimate than I would have expected.

"Crazy hot, huh?" he says. He even drives gently.

"Yeah, so hot. I'm not used to this."

"You all want to go to a playground?" he asks.

I definitely don't want to go to a playground. It's uncomfortably hot,

which is very unusual for the Bay Area. The idea of baking in the sun
sounds terrible. Plus, as I quickly conjure up the full scenario, I realize
that doing a playdate at a playground means Andre and I will have to
make small talk. The whole time. Social anxiety fills my body. But as
I'm contemplating this, it's also dawning on me that Andre may not be
comfortable dropping his kid off with a perfect stranger.

I sit with Andre in a shady spot on a concrete wall, and we talk. "You
lived here long?" he asks.

"No, but I've already gotten used to the mild weather," I say. "We
moved from New York when I was pregnant with Maya. I can't believe
the heat and humidity I used to tolerate, but Oakland weather has made
me soft."

"I've lived here all my life," Andre says.

"Same house that whole time?" I ask.

"Nah, I've moved around a bit, but the house we're in now is my
mom's. It was my grandfather's before that."

"Wow, how cool," I say. That makes Darius the fourth generation to
live in that house.

"Darius and I moved in a few years ago," he explains. "I'm raising
Darius on my own for now. His mom's not around."

I don't ask why not, but my mind plumbs his word choice. Sounds like
she's still alive, or he would have said otherwise. Addiction? Incarceration?
I feel bad for what I know are stereotypical assumptions, but what else
keeps a mom from her kid?

"What kind of work do you do?" I ask, not sure where to follow the
single-parent thread without sounding nosy.

"I used to be a painter. Like houses and stuff," he says. "But I've had
major back problems the last few years, so I'm on disability now. They
told me I needed back surgery, but I didn't want it. My mom got it, and
it didn't end up helping her," he says.

"Yeah, I've heard that a lot—that the surgery doesn't seem very
effective. Have you ever tried acupuncture?"

"I'd like to try that, actually," he says. "I didn't like all the medication they had me on. About five different ones. I was on it for about a year but finally weaned myself off of all of it."

"Must be hard to parent such an active kid with back pain," I say, as we both watch the kids race up the metal steps of the playground slide and come back down fast. "Yeah, I'm kind of old for this. Fifty," he says, with a tinge of pride.

"No way!" I say. "You're fifty? You don't look it."

"Thanks," he says. "Darius's actually my third kid. I've got a son in his thirties and a daughter in her twenties."

"Wow, you're a pro. I should be asking you for advice," I say.

"Nah, we're all just doing the best we can," he says, smiling sweetly.

Then there's a lull. The first since we've sat down together. The kids are chasing one another around, sweaty grins on their faces. We focus on them for a minute.

"When's Maya's birthday?" he asks.

"November thirteenth," I tell him.

"Ooohhhh, a Scorpio," he says.

I laugh. "When I was pregnant and I would tell people my due date, they would get all wide-eyed just like that and say, 'You're in for it.' It was a little daunting."

"Scorpios are intense," he says.

"Yeah, they are," I agree. "She's very particular, very self-possessed. What about Darius—when is his birthday?"

"He was born right around Christmas. A Capricorn."

"Oh, me, too. I'm a New Year's Eve baby."

Andre raises his eyebrows and nods his head, impressed, as if I've done something. "Wow, a goat, huh. You all are grounded."

"Try to be," I say.

"And stubborn," he says, smiling.

"That, too, I'm sure. What about you?" I say. "What's your sign?"

"I'm a Sagittarius," he says.

"Ah, I dated a Sagittarius for a long time. Very chill dude."

"Yeah, we're laid-back," he says. "Curious. We like philosophy. We like our freedom."

"Sounds about right," I say. I'm about to ask him how he knows so much about astrology, when Darius comes bounding over.

"My tooth is really loose!" he tells Andre, wiggling it near his face. Then he runs back into the fray, gone as fast as he appeared.

"He's lost a lot of teeth," Andre says. "I think it makes his speech problems a little worse. That's what the therapist says. He used a pacifier a lot until just, like, five months ago. Way too long. But he'll be fine with time."

My brain is plumbing again. A pacifier until nearly six is really unusual.

He pulls me out of my investigation: "How long have you and your husband been married?"

"You know, I'm not even sure. I'm so bad at keeping track of that kind of thing. Let's see...I think seven or eight years. We met in two thousand nine."

"That's great," he says. "You done having kids?"

"I think so," I say. "Our lives feel really full. Not sure how we would fit another kid into the mix at this point. Being a father this time around must be so different."

He says, "Yeah, I didn't think I would get another chance at it. It's nice. He helps me notice things I wouldn't notice otherwise. Like the other day, we were walking over on Telegraph, and Darius saw a guy sleeping on the street, and he asked me, 'Why doesn't that guy have a home?' and I tried to explain it, but I also couldn't explain it, you know? I've never seen the homelessness so bad in all the years I've lived here," he says. "And yet, somehow I got sort of used to it until he said something. He's a good kid."

Darius and Maya are now wrestling in the grass, both trying to get a soccer ball that Darius brought. "Be careful with her," Andre yells.

"It's okay," I say. "She's tougher than you think."

But Darius stops wrestling with her, and they both stand up, grass clinging to their hair and clothes, and wander over to us. Maya looks so happy—that full-bodied happy that comes from playing hard and belonging. Darius, too.

"So, you all live in some kind of commune?" Andre asks.

I explain what cohousing is, and how we eat together twice a week, but all have our own private homes, too. "You should come to a common meal sometime," I say. "You'd be welcome."

"I've heard live music coming from over there sometimes," he says.

"That's the Prince boys!" Maya shouts with excitement. "They play music in the barn with their band. We dance to it on the grass."

"It's good," he says approvingly. "Really good music."

"Yeah, the owners of the house one house over from yours, Mary and Tom Prince, have twin sons and that's their band," I explain. "They use the barn as practice space."

"Oh, yeah, I've seen them, for sure," Andre says.

I feel like a gentrifying neighborhood is like a broken Magic Eye puzzle: a series of dots that should add up to a whole if you look at it right, but never quite comes together. No dimension. No context. As Andre and I sit here, naming people, tracing sound back to its source, it feels like we're shading things in. There's something relationally restorative about it, or at least grounding, even if it doesn't make the economic consequences of the last decade any less brutal.

"We've got a blackberry bush! And a garden!" Maya tells Darius.

"Like on Fortnite!" he says. "I built a big house and a garden on there with some watermelon seeds."

"We don't have watermelon, but we've got other things," I tell him. "We've got carrots and apples and basil and beans."

"Beans?" he says, eyebrows raised theatrically.

"String beans, those long green ones," I answer.

"Oh, my mom used to feed me those. Those are so good," he says. His mom. There she is again. Where is his mom?

"You should come over and eat some stuff out of our garden sometime," I say.

"I know what you need to garden—soil, water, and seeds," he says.

"That's right, Papa, and one other thing," his dad prompts him.

"Mmm," he says, thinking hard.

"There's a lot of it today," I hint.

"Sunshine!" he yells and we all smile.

82

I LOATHE A PIÑATA. The never knowing what to hang it on, the palpable violence that bubbles up in even the most gentle little souls, the cheap candy flying all over the yard, inevitably a few pieces rotting away in a garden bed or a gap in the sidewalk. But here we are. Maya's sixth birthday. We are manhandling the kids into a line—shortest to tallest. Stella and a few of the really little ones take pathetic little swings and don't connect with shit. We cheer maniacally. Maya takes her swing. I'm not hopeful. She gives the unicorn a gentle push, but doesn't even cause a scratch.

And then someone's cousin approaches—he looks to be about eight or so, with a competitive glint in his eye. He swings like a major leaguer and destroys the unsuspecting unicorn—half its body falls to the ground and a spray of tooth-decaying Laffy Taffy and misshapen Hershey Kisses flies across the yard. Children dive on top of one another in a savage scrum. Someone cries. Someone makes off with more than his share. Someone gets a kiss from her mother.

I told Maya that she could invite six friends for her sixth birthday. I heard some other parent say that, and it seemed manageable. Maya started making a list immediately. Among the friends that she needed, like, would die if they were not there, was Wyatt.

I'd seen Wyatt's dad gliding around the school. He was Black, had a winning smile, and usually had a pair of big over-ear headphones hanging around his neck. He seemed to drop off his two kids, and sometimes a nephew, pretty much every morning. I kept looking out for him as Maya's birthday quickly approached, but I kept missing him. Finally, a few days before the party, I spotted him heading down the hall and awkwardly chased after him. "Hey, you're Wyatt's dad, right?" I hollered.

He looked up from his cell phone and gave me that big-ass grin. I detected a little bemusement. "Sure am. What's up?"

"Maya would love to invite Wyatt to her birthday party. Can I text you the info?" I asked.

"Right on, sure, sure," he said, nodding.

"What's your cell?" I asked.

He told me, and I punched it in. "I'm Nick," he said.

Nick was the kind of guy I would have hung out with in high school—listening to hip-hop, laughing our asses off about stupid little things. But he would have no way of knowing that.

One of the worst things about being a White mom was being a "White mom." Sometimes when I'm pushing a stroller around the neighborhood, I can feel a bunch of teenage boys quiet down as they pass by me. *It's a White mom,* they are thinking. *Don't curse.* It makes me want to shout, "It's not what you think! Did you notice my vintage Jordans? I listen to Nas!" Or, well, I once listened to Nas. Mostly I listen to the *Coco* soundtrack now.

In any case, I waited a bit and then texted Nick: Party is on Monday night, 6pm at our house. You can come as a crew or feel free to drop him off.

Cool, cool. He wrote.

As the party approached, I realized I didn't actually know what that meant. Was Wyatt coming? And if he was, was Nick coming, too? I texted again on the day of the party: Just a reminder that Maya's party is tonight. Think you guys will be able to come?

He wrote back quickly: Yeah I told my wife. She's with him tonight.

At about 6:15 p.m., various friends of Maya's, most accompanied by an adult, start to wander in, including Andre and Darius. Darius hands Maya a princess watch, unwrapped, and a cup full of Halloween candy in a paper napkin with a unicorn on it. She freaks out at the watch.

It's exactly the kind of thing I would never buy her—plastic, purple, commercial. She loves it so much.

Shortly thereafter, four cars roll up to the front of our community, and Wyatt's mom hops out of one of them. "Hey, guys! Welcome!" I shout, opening up the gate. It's dusk now. The garden is bathed in beginning moonlight. The noise has reached a dull roar behind me.

She says, "Hey! Nick said you said we could roll with our crew. Is that true?"

"Of course!" I say. "Everyone's welcome!" I flash back to my original text but don't let my facial expression betray me. Crew. I used the word *crew*. That means family to me. That means FAMILY to them.

Four aunties and about seven cousins of various ages and heights come spilling out of the cars and walk through the gate with varying degrees of hesitancy, eyeing me up, looking around, and trying to make sense of the place.

I text John in a quiet panic: GET MORE PIZZA.

I had surprised myself by going sort of "Pinterest mom" on this birthday: ordering little canvases, paints and paintbrushes, aprons, and even little plastic palettes. But of course I'd ordered enough for, like, ten kids at the most. And now we had closer to twenty.

Maya had also insisted on making little gift bags for each kid. Now twelve-year-old strangers were coming up to me and asking, "Where's my gift bag?"

Shit. I don't know. I don't know what I'm doing, kid. I'm just a "White mom" trying to throw a halfway decent birthday party.

There also weren't enough canvases. There was barely enough pizza. But the big kids are super polite, retreating out to the courtyard to play soccer when they register the shortage. Some of them even start reading and playing with the toddlers milling about. I ask one, "Do you babysit? You're a natural."

"I would," she said, smiling at me, "but I live in Stockton. I'm just visiting."

"Ah, dang. My loss," I say. She takes a huge bite of salad. "You're good with kids and you eat salad! What a dream!"

"And I clean," she says, beaming.

Grace, who consistently has the best hairdos in all of kindergarten, gorgeous piles of braids arranged on her head with ribbons and barrettes, is here with her mother and grandmother. Her grandmother tells me that this is the first kids' birthday party she's been able to attend, because she works the graveyard shift cleaning over at Children's Hospital.

She says she loves the cohousing community. "Everyone should live like this," she says. "It's old school."

The next couple of hours fly by in a blur of pizza crusts on paper plates, metallic-gold-paint splatters, and aunties laughing. Intermittently, I look around to find Maya. Is she smiling? Does she care that there are a bunch of kids she doesn't know? Every time I spot her, she's surrounded by kids and has this satisfied little grin on.

When it's cake time, I thank my lucky stars that Maya rejected my suggestion of a homemade cake from my dear friend Allison. She wanted a Safeway cake—gigantic and stacked heavy with sugary white icing. There would be enough for a hundred kids, much less twenty.

John sets it before her, ablaze with six candles, and the crowd of best friends and perfect strangers sing their hearts out. My little girl closes her eyes tight and blows and wishes. Everyone cheers.

83

As I do every evening, I grab Maya's backpack and pull out her lunch box, inside of which is the half-eaten detritus of a too-short lunch period.

Tonight there is a new thing in her backpack—a purple vinyl bag with shoulder straps made of string. Inside is a one-gallon Ziploc bag and three small books. "What are these?" I ask her.

"Those are books that I get to read myself," she says, grabbing the first one out of the bag. *"Bub-bles,"* she slowly sounds out the title of the book.

"That's right!" I say, opening my eyes wide at her, my eyebrows shooting into the air.

Pride washes over her face. She opens up to the first page: "See the bubbles in the s-k-y. Sky. See the bubbles in the sky!"

"You got it!" I shout again. "You're really reading, Moo!"

See the bubbles in the pool.
See the bubbles in my milk.
See the bubbles in my tub.
See the bubbles in the sea.

Scrapping the phonics for the picture, she says *ocean* first.

See the bubbles in the fish bowl.

See the bubbles on the dog.
See the bubbles on me!

And just like that, my kid can read. Which is to say, she is practicing my religion for the first time. The world is hers.

84

TODAY, MRS. MINOR AND I are talking in one of the two bedrooms in her house that has been turned into the administrative office for the preschool, as well as a place where her two daughters can get work done. One of her daughters is curled up with a picture book that I brought, *Wonder Horse: The True Story of the World's Smartest Horse*. It introduces readers to a freed slave named Bill Key who became famous for training his horse to identify colors and all the letters in the alphabet, not to mention to add and subtract. It quickly became one of Maya's favorite books after we stumbled on it at the library.

While her daughter reads, I'm filling Mrs. Minor in on the latest developments at Emerson, as well as the new literacy campaign. Her energy is really warm today, like something has shifted between us.* Maybe it's consistency—this is my fourth time showing up in as many months. Last time I came, I brought Maya and Stella along, and we attended a special story hour that Mrs. Minor had planned with a local author. The kids shared snacks and then ran around in the backyard together while I chatted with Mrs. Minor's aunt and father in the Friday sunshine.

Maybe it's a warmth born of reciprocity. I've been texting her episodes of podcasts that I think she'll dig—local Black educational reformers discussing the Kaiser-Sankofa merger, the *School Colors* podcast out of

---

* Dr. Dena Simmons: "Was it not before? I feel like her honesty has been warm and a gift. What makes you feel there is such a contrast?"

Brooklyn, which is chock-full of some of her favorite themes, and an article here and there.*

In any case, today the air is lighter between us, and our conversation flows fast, punctuated by knowing laughter. I describe the meeting that I went to in the church basement and the confusion I've felt in the days after.

Mrs. Minor nods her head thoughtfully. She does all kinds of things in her preschool designed to seed her students' literacy—talking through the names and sounds of all the letters daily, practicing drawing those letters on whiteboards, surrounding them with books almost exclusively featuring Black characters. But she also recognizes that it's not just the mechanics that matter: "I feel like even the foundations of reading should be about 'Do you know there was a point when we weren't allowed to read? Do you know that they were afraid of how amazing and capable your ancestors were, so they didn't let them read? Your ancestors had to sneak to learn to read. They were killed for doing these things.'

"If we don't teach Black kids reading with this deeper context, then it's like a subconscious burden inside of them. They can't put their finger on it. It's the conversation that's never really addressed. It's a deeper knowing inside every person of color, and at some point you kind of wake up to it even if no one wants to discuss it."

"How did you wake up to it?" I ask.

She purses her lips, thinking for a moment or two, and then says, "From a very young age I had a sense of how unjust things were. It was just kind of inside of me. But I think it really started to come together when I was a teenager.

"I was inspired by Tupac Shakur—not all the music, but he had several songs and poetry that were definitely about our plight as a people. And his mom was a Black Panther, and I knew a lot of kids in the neighborhood whose parents were actually in the Black Panther Party. All of the sudden I was, like, 'Wait, I was taught a lie all my life.' I mean, when I

---

* Dr. Dena Simmons: "Why do you feel she needs this? Or, is this more for you? Your White guilt?"

learned about the Catholic Inquisition, and I was, like, 'Wait a minute, Grandma, why are we Catholic? They went around killing people?'"

We both laugh a bit at the thought of teenaged Artemis confronting her formidable grandmother with her newfound knowledge.

"That's why I teach for truth," Mrs. Minor says, the pride palpable in her voice. "Teaching can be a very radical thing, or it can be basically brainwashing everyone into the same false story."

I flash back to the Black History Month poem she shouted into that mic: *With knowledge of self, we have Pride but, Education is the key! / and when we raise Educated, Proud children they are free!*

"You did such an amazing job of teaching all the kids in Maya's class the facts about slavery and the civil rights movement, the sit-ins and the bus boycott," I say. "But I worry about the meaning White kids make of all that. Do they think racism happens in dramatic moments? How do we—as White parents—teach them that it's also systemic and on-going? How do we show them not just the potential for White harm but examples of White people being anti-racist?"

She's nodding, her lips pursed like she's really thinking through what I'm saying, trying to discern her truth in relationship to it.

"I'm just not sure we can teach White kids about *systemic* racism if we opt out of the system."

As I'm saying it, I glance over at Mrs. Minor's daughter, curled up on the futon around a sheet of paper, coloring. "I'm remembering you're homeschooling, so maybe you're, like . . ."

She fills in the blank before I can: "The system sucks!" We both laugh.

"I hear you, I hear you," I say. "But theoretically, public education is supposed to be there for everybody, like a public good. And I want to be a force for making that public good something better for everybody."

She nods and then says, "I get that, but it's also frustrating because it's almost like nothing gets done until, all of a sudden, the White people make a fuss about it. The system doesn't care unless you show up and say things are broken. Sometimes it feels like Black people don't even care enough. It's like we wait for the great White hope to come and join the march. Now we care?

"I can tell Black people all day, This is where we come from. This is who we are. This is our culture. But when a White person says, 'Oh, you all deserve better,' well, now that's true."

That hits me like a punch in the gut. It might be useful, ultimately, for my White kid and my White resources to be at Emerson, but why does it take that?

While I find Mrs. Minor's cynicism about the system deflating, I understand it. And I also see how it's a direct path from that kind of cynicism to the most optimistic act of all: world-building. Like the Black Panthers who didn't try to reform White America but rejected it entirely, she has left behind the trappings of White-defined success—a steady, albeit underpaid job—to create an oasis for Black children worthy of their inherent beauty and latent potential.

85

I'VE NEVER SEEN EVELYN so still.

She is usually not even on the carpet with the rest of the kids during library time. Instead, she'll be sneaking over to the computers and trying to check out a Fly Guy book, or she'll be out of the room altogether—in someone else's classroom (one of the teachers' shared strategies for dealing with behavioral issues is a change of scenery) or dawdling on her way to the bathroom.

But today is unlike any of those other days. Ms. Walsh has swapped classes for the hour. Evelyn is sitting at a Black teacher's feet, and the teacher is expertly kneading her head like dough. Evelyn's eyes are closed, and the look on her face is total and complete peace.

I flash back on Mrs. Minor's caution about the often underplayed, profoundly important gap between White teachers and Black students. It's not just a gap of expectations or cultural references—though those can be significant. It's also a gap of intimacies. Of Black hands in Black hair, pulling that hair around with just the right amount of gentle force to relieve the scalp, close the eyes, release the weights of the world. It's a gap born of something that could never and would never be taught in education school. It's a gap born of social location, not of good or bad intention. A gap born of Black love, which is to say not a gap at all but something elegant and infinite alongside so much trying.

IT'S ONE OF THOSE endless days with children. Not in the good way. In the bad way, where it feels like three p.m. at ten a.m. and you think that you will never make it until sundown.

We are at the playground, which is helping. It's January in Oakland, so the sun is beaming, the air crisp and kind.

Stella has convinced me to play airplane. I have a fantasy life in which my kids play with each other and small strangers at the playground, and I sit on a bench and read a novel, but six years in, it's basically never happened.

A text pops up on my phone: I'm so sorry about Courtney. I know she was your friend.

I think: *Courtney who? Why the "was"?*

Stella yells at me: "Buckle up! Buckle up! We're taking off!" She's the pilot, and I'm the passenger. We're headed to Milwaukee, where her pile of about a dozen cousins lives.

"Okay, buckled up!" I yell back distractedly while also texting back: I'm not actually sure what you're talking about. I haven't been online all day.

She sends me a link. There is a sunny photo of a steep residential street. And a little bit farther down, a picture of her: Courtney, smiling that warm, wry smile, her green square glasses framing her kind green eyes.

Stella: "What would you like to drink today, darling?"

"Um, ginger ale. I'll take ginger ale," I say, not looking up. "Thank you."

The article goes on to explain:

The victim of a fatal crash earlier this week has been identified as 46-year-old Courtney Everts Mykytyn, who was struck and killed in the street outside her home by a neighbor's car in what police are calling a "tragic accident."

My reading is having a hard time catching up to my knowing.

"And for your kid?" Stella asks.

"My kid?" I say, finally looking up at her. Her big puppy-dog eyes are so brown and oblivious. I feel like crying, but I don't. "My kid will take apple juice."

I flash back to the last text exchange I had with Courtney. I was in San Francisco for the night—a novelty. I'd put on a vintage sparkling orange dress that I once wore as a bridesmaid (the dress outlasted the marriage, good riddance), handed the kids off to the babysitter, and then taken BART into the city. I felt twenty-five again—light and happy and walking through the dark. I texted her about an article I'd read that day. We ended up in a rapid, funny exchange. When I got back in a car to head home, we texted some more.

We'll never have a giddy, slightly drunk text exchange again. I'll never be able to ask her if I'm doing the right thing at Emerson or writing the right book.

We weren't close friends. I've never been to her house or hung out with her family. I don't know a million things about her. But I'm so upset for so many reasons.

Courtney gave me social proof that I wasn't a bad mother for choosing Emerson; that it was a good decision, actually. Not heroic, but aligned. Weirding people out. Making them uncomfortable. Joyful. Radical. Joyful. Radical. And giving my kids a fighting chance of having a different journey from my own. Different battles. Her life, for me, is tied up in all of that humor and wisdom. Her death feels like a loss in so many dimensions.

87

OAKLAND UNIFIED SCHOOL DISTRICT BOARD
MEETING, JANUARY 22, 2020
TOTAL TIME: 2 HOURS, 48 MINUTES, 47 SECONDS

Denilson Garibo, student director: [1:18:47] We want to read a statement about why we haven't been present at previous board meetings. . . . As two Black and Brown youth growing up in East and West Oakland with less access to education, we take our job heavily. . . . During our last board meeting, we as student directors felt ignored and disrespected. When we tried to speak our point of view, no one, and I mean no one, would turn around to listen to what we had to say.

We want more clarity on what is the purpose of shutting down every board meeting. . . . We want to hear more from those parents who are not present in these meetings. . . . This decision to merge the schools was an attempt to give resources and supports to a school that has been neglected for so long.

The protesters are shouting over Garibo, but he persists.

Overall, we want to hear every person in the building, but if that's not even allowed, how are we, as students, going to be heard? We respect the purpose, but we don't see the cause.

Garibo throws his statement down on the table, an uncharacteristically dramatic move from a generally reserved guy.

School board member Rosie Torres: [1:29:41] At the end of the day, it's not just your physical safety, but it's also your emotional safety... that what happened with the arrests and so on with the protesters, as opposed to you just walking home from school and being subject to harassment by law enforcement is a whole 'nother story. And so that cuts really deep.

I hope that everybody understood what you were saying who is here tonight ready to protest because they don't have to walk home and worry about the police pulling them over.

The audience erupts in shouts and screams.

Saru Jayaraman: [off-mic but still audible] Excuse me! Look at my leg!

Jody London, school board vice president: Let's go now to the superintendent.

Protesters: No school closures! Oakland is not for sale!

Jumoke Hinton Hodge: Student directors, we want to center this on you and not them.

The chanting gets louder and louder.

Jody London: [1:30:38] We are now officially in recess.

The school board members slowly and reluctantly gather their papers and wander off the stage. The student board members look despondent as they also gather their things and leave. The only two who remain are Gary Yee, a second-time school board member, and Kyla Johnson-Trammell, the superintendent. I'm particularly struck by the look on Yee's face—he watches the protesters intently but with a sort of kindness behind his eyes that surprises me. I wonder what he's thinking.

The protesters chant: "We believe that we will win!"

I sit in my plastic folding chair, the smell of pizza wafting through the air, and wonder what it would mean to win.

I get up and snap a few pictures of a White boy blowing a trumpet straight toward Gary Yee's face. His mom leans in and tells him something and grabs his trumpet from him. She doesn't seem angry, but it's puzzling all the same. He walks out of the gym abruptly.

I walk into the cool January night to get a breath of fresh air, and I run right into the trumpet kid. "Are you okay?" I ask, a mother's instinct.

"Yeah, just waiting for Uber Eats," he says.

I laugh to myself. I laugh at the whole damn city. "What did you order?" I ask him.

"Starbucks," he says without an ounce of self-consciousness.

The meeting comes back to order in a private room upstairs, as it has every time since the school board ordered Kaiser to merge with Sankofa. The core folks who constitute the resistance to the merger have repeatedly shut school board meetings down, often encouraging their children to sit in the school board members' seats and playact as if they are running things. It is either great political theater or profoundly disrespectful, depending on your perspective.

Public comment begins with a union member requesting a moment of silence for Miesha Singleton, a forty-year-old Black mother of seven who was killed in a hit-and-run outside Elmhurst United Middle School the week before.

Vilma Serrano: [1:41:41] The OEA [Oakland Education Association—the teachers' union] would like to give their condolences to the family of Miesha Singleton, dedicated mother, an OUSD mother, and anti-violence advocate.

In the background, the protesters begin a call and response. At first their voices are quiet in contrast to Vilma Serrano on the mic, but they get louder and louder.

They are reciting a quotation from Assata Shakur's autobiography. Assata Shakur was part of the Black Liberation Army, a target of the FBI's COINTELPRO and convicted of the first-degree murder of a state trooper in 1977. She was also the godmother of rapper Tupac Shakur.

Protesters: It is our duty to fight for our freedom! It is our duty to win!

Vilma Serrano: We actually just wanted to have a moment of silence on her behalf in honor of her memory.

Protesters: We must love each other and support each other!

Vilma Serrano: So I'm going to take a couple of seconds right now...silence...in honor of her memory.

Protesters: We have nothing to lose but our chains!

The call and response continues straight through the moment of silence, and then the protesters begin clapping slowly, then faster and faster and faster.

I keep thinking about a line I read in James Baldwin's *Notes of a Native Son:* "Causes, as we know, are notoriously bloodthirsty."[20]

88

W E LIVE IN A little Craftsman house, and we wanted to do this backsplash that she'd seen in a magazine—little subway tiles, with various shades of green. Like a mosaic, you know?"

I say, "Yes, I can imagine it."

I'm talking on the phone to Roman, Courtney's husband, because I want to express my condolences and maybe say something about what she meant to me, what she has meant to so many people in the growing movement. But somehow we're not talking about that at all.

"Well, she looked it up and it was like five thousand dollars. So we sort of said 'Forget about it,' but then she did some research and came back to me a few days later, and she was like 'We're going to do those things. We're going to make them ourselves.'

"And I thought, 'You're fucking crazy, honey, but go ahead.'"

I laugh. Roman admits that much of the discussions on the podcast went over his head. That he wishes he'd listened harder when she was talking about it. But you can hear the profound admiration in his voice—for her political organizing, but even more palpably, for who she was at home.

He goes on: "Next thing you know, she bought herself little rectangular soap molds and started working with concrete and finding the right mix. She figured it out, and she started making these tiles and they were holding together. And then she went and she found a place, some industrial place where you stain concrete and tried a couple of different grains. And then she started staining them all and they were all a little different."

I can hear that he's crying now. "She suggested a scarab and I drew it on plywood, then used caulk to outline it. Then we poured the concrete on it to get the reverse, like inset..."

He trails off, realizing, perhaps, that he is talking to a perfect stranger in great detail about tiles his dead wife made. Surely he should be talking about integration instead. "Who cares?" he says. "I know it's just tiles, but it's emblematic of the kind of person she was."

"I care," I say. "I like hearing the story. It makes perfect sense. She was undaunted."

"Yeah, that's it," he says. "She was undaunted. She was a principled woman and a pain in the ass. She was a woman who said she was taking a thirty-minute phone call, and two hours later, she's still on. We're trying to have dinner here!"

We're both crying and laughing at the same time. I was maybe the person on the other end of the phone, delaying the family supper.

Later, I look up the scarab and find that it symbolizes immortality. This is what we leave behind—not just the grand plans and the social movements, but the backsplash, the dinner growing cold, our determination, our irritation, our love.

89

RIGHT AS WE WALK onto the blacktop the next morning, Coach blows the whistle and Maya and Stella both take a knee—along with all the other kids on the playground. About twenty feet away, a tall White guy in a gray sweatshirt and baggy jeans, who looks to be someone's grandpa, starts leaning toward the ground. He's not taking a knee; he's sort of folding in on himself.

And then he's on the ground, and it registers that he's having a stroke or a seizure. I drop the girls' hands and rush over, meeting a Black uncle who is a nurse and in his baby blue scrubs at the side of the old guy's curled-up body. "Should I get the office to call nine-one-one?" I ask him.

"Yes!" he shouts, putting his palm under the man's head. I race off, dodging kids and teachers and parents as I go. I throw open the office door and yell, "Please call nine-one-one! Someone's grandpa is on the blacktop—maybe a seizure or a stroke!"

Then I run back, and the nurse tells me and another mom, this one Black, who has joined us, to hold his hip so we can keep him on his side. He's seizing. I notice the white stubble on his chin and his big white tennis shoes. I notice the nurse's hand is bleeding a little, maybe from where he threw his flat hand under the guy's head as it was making contact with the concrete. I notice the surrender—strangers suddenly touching your body, working together, your voice only grunts, your point of view shoes and sky.

Someone runs to get his wife, who is waiting in the car. After what seems like quite a long time, she comes loping up, slowly, her face totally unworried. "It happens all the time," she says, the annoyance detectable in her voice. "If he has too much of his insulin, he has a seizure."

It's not adding up for the nurse. "What kind of insulin is he taking? I'm not sure that should be causing a seizure."

"Well, it does," she says, and I feel the weight of endless medical appointments and unhelpful doctors in her tone.

"Well, we're just glad he'll be okay, then," I say.

"He's fine," she says.

Suddenly my kids pop back into my mind. I dart into Maya's classroom next door and see that she is guiding Stella around. "You want an apple?" Maya asks her, and Stella says nothing, her gaze focused on the fish tank, her giant bike helmet still atop her giant head.

I give Maya a big hug and kiss and tell her, "The grandpa is going to be okay. The ambulance is coming soon. Thanks for your help, sweetie." She nods proudly and rushes off to her table.

"Okay, Stella, let's go. We've got to get you to school."

We walk outside, but Stella doesn't want to leave yet. "But I want to see the ambulance," she says. *Ambulance* sounds like "ambience."

Right then, a fire truck pulls up, and Stella's eyes expand to twice their normal size. We watch as a couple of people in uniform pop out and race over to the grandpa, still on the blacktop but covered up now with a blanket. I shuffle Stella over to our bike, parked outside the gate, and we hop on and ride away. The whole way to her school, she asks me questions: "Why the grandpa hurt?" "Why he fall?" "Where is the fire?" "Where is the ambulance?" "Is he going to the doctor?" "Where his doctor?" "Why the grandpa hurt?"

Then she starts listing every injury her own grandfather, whom she calls Didop, has ever had. When we arrived at my parents' house for Thanksgiving, my dad had a black eye—a midnight run-in with a door. Stella describes it in great detail now. She's sense-making as the wind whips past our faces.

I'm reminded of how much little kids take in. Sponges, we call them, but it doesn't seem quite right. There is no squeezing information out once they've absorbed it. They never unsee a thing. They absorb and question. Absorb and file. Absorb and connect.

Sometimes we, their parents, can control what they absorb (or so we tell ourselves), but there are also so many times that we have no control. The thing on the street. The emergency. The fight that bubbles over. The kid in class who has seen a lot of life or scary movies and is excited to tell about both.

I guess at today's absorption: Grandpas get hurt. People help. Not just firefighters, but moms and dads. And sisters, too. Black and White. In scrubs and jeans and yoga pants. Running and holding. Everybody is okay. Everybody is okay. Everybody is okay.

90

It's that time of year again. Parents in the neighborhood contact me—via texts and Instagram messages and emails—to meet up for coffee and discuss Emerson.

The tone is faux chill, unconvincingly masking the reality, which is that White and privileged people are touring and googling and spreadsheeting and LISTSERVing and sweating all the details. I have become another data point, a direct source to ask, in essence: *How messed up is it really?*

We go on walks and have cups of coffee and talk about the strengths and challenges of a community like Emerson, their own precious children, their resistant spouses. Sometimes they're sober about their kid—they talk about proclivities or fears but with a right-size tone. Sometimes they're drunk—on semi-conscious fears, on their own educational baggage, on their kid's brilliance. In these moments, I always think of the first biting paragraph in Roald Dahl's *Matilda:*

> It's a funny thing about mothers and fathers. Even when their own child is the most disgusting little blister you could ever imagine, they still think that he or she is wonderful. Some parents go further. They become so blinded by adoration they manage to convince themselves their child has qualities of genius. Well, there is nothing very wrong with all this. It's the way of the world. It's only when the parents begin telling *us* about the brilliance of their own revolting offspring, that we start shouting, "Bring us a basin! We're going to be sick!"[21]

I don't shout. I listen patiently. And after a bunch of these conversations, I notice that we tend to hit an impasse, wherein the person admits that she (it's usually a mom, though not always) feels like she is being forced to choose between her politics, which would put her kid at Emerson, and her responsibility as a parent, which would necessitate using her privilege to get her kid into the "best" school she can possibly access. When she gets stuck here—my politics or my parenting—I know we're done. She will not choose Emerson.

My default expectation must be that I will have these conversations and then get the sheepish email shortly thereafter in which I am informed that they are so grateful, and they seriously considered it, but ended up (*miraculously, magically*—fill in the blank with a word that conjures supernatural intervention, not structural privilege) getting into Peralta and/or Chabot.

And the thing is, I'm resigned to that. I know I can't convince people that this impasse isn't real; it's real inside them, and that's what counts. And further, I wouldn't want them to send their kids to Emerson if they saw it as a sacrifice.

Perhaps for the first time in my entire life I feel what it is to be pitied, to have someone get right up close to something you love, to a place you call home, and see it as something to pity.

The bitter pill is that I've been the flirt and the savior. I've thrown the pitying glances. I've complimented the courageous over coffee—turning my flattery into their labor. And I will do everything in my conscious power not to do that anymore.

I finally get how it is better to be unseen than to be seen through these particular eyes.

91

DR. GARY YEE AGREES to sit down with me. His name has come up, often with a sort of reverence, in a number of interviews I've done. Brian Stanley even sent me a chapter of Dr. Yee's badly photocopied dissertation from 1996.

I catch him as a small meeting about facilities winds down. We sit in some leather swivel chairs at the front of the room on a slightly raised platform, and I suddenly realize that we are in the same room where the board retreats when Oakland Not for Sale shuts the public meetings down. It's almost like finding myself on the set of a highly dramatic reality-TV show I've been watching.

We warm up by chatting a bit about my project and where Maya goes to school. His late wife, whom he is clearly still grieving, was the principal at Emerson from 2000 to 2002, so he has an intimate sense of the school (or at least the school as it was then). He and his wife met as teenagers at a fundamentalist Baptist church in Oakland's Chinatown and were married for forty-four years.

"What were you thinking at that last board meeting when you stayed behind and watched the protest?" I ask.

"In the church I go to now we're studying the prophets of the Old Testament. And so I was sitting there thinking about how I am now seen as the regime, you know, the kings and emperors, or at least the most accessible of the regime forces. Any kind of public citizen who's outraged could see me that way."

I chime in, "Although most kings don't get paid seven hundred and fifty bucks a month for thankless work," and we both laugh.

Dr. Yee goes on: "If you read the Old Testament prophets, you realize that they encountered the same kind of personal anguish that I'm experiencing."

"And you find some solace in that?"

"Yeah, I do, actually. Sometimes I think, 'Why did I do this? Was I really called, or was it arrogance?'"

He pauses for a few beats and then says, "But this is what I'm called to do. You're not called to make decisions in a perfect world. You're called to make decisions in an imperfect world.

"I want to assure you that if, in the end, next year or the year after that, you just decide you're going to send your kid to Park Day School, that's okay."

My whole body heats up. *What? Why is this man who has devoted his life to public schools telling me that it's fine if I abandon them?*

He goes on: "You would be super at Park Day School, because Park Day School wants to imbue in its student population pro-social, humane values. I think Park Day School probably does a great job in preparing those kids."

"I'm not sure it does, though. That's part of what I'm trying to push back against," I say. "I want my kid to be living *in* the questions instead of learning about them from a sanitized distance."

"But she will live in the questions because you're her mother," Dr. Yee says calmly, assuredly. "She can't help it. In the grand scheme of things, it's the values that you speak to, consciously and unconsciously, you know, the values that you provide for your daughter in all settings. It doesn't matter where she goes to school."

I love this man so much already, and I couldn't disagree more. Maybe he can see the shock in my eyes, because he keeps going: "Let's say your kid goes to Park Day and then she sees the disconnect between, you know, what you say and the fact that you're investing thirty thousand in a private school. And she says, 'Why am I going to Park Day?' Then you basically say, 'Because I was afraid. I was afraid that I wouldn't be a good mother, that ten years down the line, you wouldn't be the person that you are right now. You wouldn't be able to ask me this question.'"

"But I think she'll be better at asking those questions because of having been at Emerson, because she's living *in* the questions," I push back.

"That is totally true, but I'm saying in either path, she's going to be the same person. It's just the questions she asked would be slightly different."

I'm still confused. "And why do you have faith she'd be the same person? Because of your religious faith or—"

He cuts me off: "Because of you."

"Because of me?"

"Because if you sent her to Park Day, you would be anguishing over the decision for the next twelve years. She's so lucky because she has a mother who—"

Now I cut him off: "Who is in existential crisis all the time?"

We both laugh. "That's so funny you said *existential*. Did you study existentialism in college?"

"Yeah, a bit," I say.

"I hated philosophy until I discovered Kierkegaard. Then I became a total existentialist person. And that was just such a gift."

Kierkegaard, the guy who believed that objective truth is bullshit. I remember because I was seriously considering a career in journalism at the time but was troubled by the notion of Journalistic Truth. It seemed to me that no matter how many sources one had, there was a way in which journalists, themselves, were the sieves through which information was passed. Kierkegaard thought we were far less rational than we let on and that our highest calling was to reject dogma and institutional manipulation and instead make honest choices that honored our inner emotional lives.

"If Kierkegaard had been sitting at that board meeting Wednesday night, what would he have said about what went down?" I ask Dr. Yee.

"I think he would've said that there is no rational answer, that you face, like Abraham faced in the sacrifice of his son, that there is no rationale to it. There's only making the decision and trusting God that He will make it right, that He will honor the courage to do it even in the face of its irrationality."

He pauses then, looking up and thinking. "Yes, I think that's what he would say. The main thing that I've come to on the board is being willing to accept the negative consequences of decisions, that decisions don't always have just joy and delight."

"Like the Kaiser/Sankofa decision, as an example?" I ask.

"Yes, like that," he says, his expression falling. "I'm pretty good now, as an older person, you know, at just appreciating the fact that people come to the board—sometimes manipulating, sometimes not—but they come to the board, you know, with what they believe to be true. And that's truly existentialism. That's truly phenomenological. You know, that people come with what they are and that is their truth."

92

We're snaking into school like always, 8:30 a.m. on the dot. This morning, Maya, Stella, and I are right behind Wyatt, who is right behind Ms. Walsh. Wyatt does a little skip to get closer to her and then quietly says, "My great-grandfather died."

Ms. Walsh looks down at him with her piercing-blue Irish eyes and says, "I'm sorry, sweetie. You want to talk about it?"

"No."

"Well, you know I'm here if you do," she says, and grabs his hand.

After we get Maya's backpack hung up and her lunch box into the basket, Stella begs to visit the class fish. I relent, so we slide into the classroom alongside Maya and head for the tank.

The week before, we'd been asked to do a project at home: create a collage of our family and community. In the center are my parents, standing next to their first car—a 1955 mint-green-and-yellow Chevy convertible—in the desert. They look old, but young, too; the proximity to the car always does that for them. There are pictures of her other grandparents, too, and many, many cousins, our neighbors, a few friends, and lots of pictures of Stella as a brand-new baby. It is a sweet snapshot of the people who star in her heart.

I start wandering around the classroom, checking out other people's collages. Ms. Walsh has hung them from the ceiling, so they are floating around. The grandparents and the cousins, the aunties and the neighbors, all in mobile formation.

Some have photographs, like Maya's. Some have drawings. One of the recent immigrant kids has a bunch of sweet stick figures within the family circle and *I Love My Family* written in a labored scrawl. The circle dedicated to community is completely empty. Maybe she just ran out of energy, as six-year-olds so often do, but maybe the blankness says something more.

Little Angelo's family circle is filled with cute pictures of him and his little siblings, plus Mexican and Italian flags. The community circle is filled with Catholic symbols—a Christian fish symbol, many, many colorful crosses, and a sticker that says FAITH.

I stop in my tracks at one in the back of the room—the family circle has six photographs in it, with a big, beautiful dog at the center. The community circle features no people—only fast-food logos, like Burger King, Wendy's, and McDonald's, and a BART pass. As I peer closer at the photographs, I realize it is Darius's.

My heart sinks on first interpretation. Does he really think Carl's Jr. is his community?

But then I reason that maybe Andre and Darius interpreted it to literally mean what is physically in your community. It was concrete, honest—perhaps a correction to all the overly romantic pining for community among progressives in the neighborhood. What do we really mean when we say it, anyway? Nextdoor postings? The farmer's market with its artisanal sauerkraut? Queer night at the beer garden with the limited-edition designer cans? It's not that those things aren't community, but they aren't economically inclusive no matter how much we might like to pretend otherwise. We may live in the same neighborhood, but we don't inhabit the same space. Darius's mobile makes that plain. It cuts, not because it is untrue but because I so wish it were.

93

I have a headache brewing, John is out of town, and the task of getting my kids in and out of their car seats feels Herculean, but there's a district-wide meeting on next year's funding and no one else at Emerson is set to go. I'm the SSC chair. It's my responsibility to understand what might happen to our budget.

And thank God they've got childcare—as long as I can convince my kids to play with an old, shabby version of Candy Land with a couple of other small strangers.

There is a grand total of about seventeen parents there—all of them seem to be parents of color, with the exception of me, three other White moms, all of whom I know personally, and one White dad, in a district that serves forty-nine thousand students. I'm depressed before the meeting is even under way.

A Black guy—bald with thick eyebrows and a mustache, wearing a sweater vest over a blue button-down, plus black leather shoes so shiny they're showing off—sits in a kid-size plastic chair next to a humming projector. He tells us that his name is Ron Smith and he's the senior director of Strategic Projects. He tells us that he's a new dad, so he really understands what it means to come out on a Thursday night, and he thanks us all. Then he throws a Molotov cocktail into the middle of the room.

The district needs to cut $21.5 million from next year's budget.

He tells us this right after putting up a slide with a photo of three students—an East Asian–American girl, smiling but just barely, her stare seemingly going through me, and then a Black girl with a big smile and a mouth full of crooked teeth, leaning on another little Black girl with black tendrils and a purple velour hoodie. These words appear below them: WE WILL NOT LEAVE TOUGH DECISIONS FOR THE NEXT GENERATION.

Ron is talking to us like we, too, sweat over budgets in cubicles, moving around numbers on spreadsheets. Like we, too, understand the endless acronyms and the ways in which different pots of money—federal, state, county, city—all get added together but never ever seem to add up to anything like enough. Like we, too, are rational creatures.

He makes his right hand flat and cuts through the air with the tiniest elevation and says, "Our revenue is steadily going up, I mean just slightly. It's basically flat."

Then he uses his left hand to cut through the air, but this time it shoots to the right like a rocket ship. "But our costs are exploding," he says. He doesn't say the words, but his eyes say, *You know how it is.*

A White guy sitting next to me with a strawberry-blond beard and a black Cal cap is shuffling around on the bench. I can feel his body heat rising. Ron starts to move on: "We've got three ways we could meet our target reductions: efficiencies, reductions, or funding shifts, so we have to—"

The guy interrupts him: "Wait a minute. It's disingenuous to say that it's just kind of flat. I know we keep raising more and more money. Not all of us understand all the distinctions between all these different segregations—you gotta have this money only goin' to that, this, and that. . . . It's just all so confusing to us. We just want to know: Why do we have to make our kids suffer? That's the bottom line."

A White mom yells out, "We live in one of the richest cities in the state."

The White guy nods his head and chimes in: "Yeah, we got so much money coming in, and we still can't get it together?"

Another mom speaks up: "And what about the corruption that has been going on for forty years in OUSD? Why can't we get a handle on it after so long? It's not your guys' fault. It's so inbred in OUSD. The trauma is so there."

"I'm traumatized," the guy sitting next to me says, quietly this time.

Ron nods and nods. He's still sitting, but he's moving to the edge of his too-small seat.

He rattles off some county numbers, some city numbers, something about music and art in Palo Alto. Then he finally lands on something almost like acknowledgment: "We have problems. We have management problems. But there are problems bigger than our management problems that districts across the state are dealing with. I don't have any simple answers."

"We need you to bring this back to your finance people," a woman who appears to be Latinx responds. "This is why you're here, to bring back the sentiment. That's all, we're not making you answer everything."

The White dad next to me says, "They might have to get steel gates for the next meeting."

Another woman, who also appears to be Latinx, says, "Can we have a restorative justice process internally? We need to talk about the harm that has been created by the mismanagement. Is there an internal process for holding people accountable for that harm? There is trauma in this city, generational trauma."

"Write it down," says Troy, pointing to the woman behind him who is writing all of our questions on a giant sheet of paper. "I have no idea."

These district representatives, who are actual people, who are probably all parents, are forced in a way not to be human. They are forced to stand in front of us and tell us that in one of the richest cities in one of the richest states in the richest country on earth, we have to explain to our children why there isn't enough money for any of the things that we adults fully understand they deserve.

We know what they need to learn, to feel safe and fascinated and hopeful. We know these things, but we can't, no, we won't (and the *won't* is so painful I can hardly write it) get these things for our kids.

Or rather, for *all* kids. Some kids will get these things that we know they need in order to learn, to feel safe and fascinated and hopeful. But those kids will get those things because their parents will pay for them, because their parents *can* pay for them, with their own money in the form of giant piles of PTA cash or private school tuition.

I feel comforted by the parents yelling, because even though I know it will do nothing to get back the $21.5 million that is being taken away, it allows me to feel that I am still living in a reality where other people are refusing to accept that this is inevitable or, in fact, clerical. This is about small humans who are the only chance we have of being better than we were before, and we are fucking it up.

Later in the meeting, another OUSD employee, this one a White woman in a suit, gets up and tells us that she is currently working two full-time jobs, one at night and one during the day. She looks so tired. She looks like I feel.

She explains that each school will see its discretionary budget axed by half, and she encourages us to decide—as a school—whether we will focus on reading or math next year. We won't be able to afford new supplies for both subjects, so we'll have to choose. Or maybe we won't be able to afford literacy *or* math coaches, so we'll have to go without.

I shuffle through the papers in my folder and find one that is filled with bar graphs representing the kids' scores on math and literacy tests at our school, broken down by demographic. I stare at the red and yellow bars and actually feel like crying. The kids who read and do math at grade level at our school are by and large White and economically privileged—a small, lucky fraction of the whole. And this overworked district employee is telling me that I need to go back to the overworked educators at Emerson and explain why we have to pick math or literacy.

I shut my notebook and leave the meeting before it is over. I disentangle my kids from the kind strangers and the board games, and we head outside into the moonlight. "Can't we just play on the playground for one minute?" Maya begs. She's forgotten her coat at school. It's cold, but not too cold.

"You can pick one thing and do it," I say. "But just one. It's late. We gotta get home."

Maya climbs up and grabs on to the monkey bars, swinging from the first to the second, but she drops before she even gets to the third. Stella makes her way to the top of the twisty slide. "Want me to catch you?" I holler to her, making my way to the bottom just as she slides down, but she wriggles out of my grasp.

"One more time, just one more time!" she says, running as fast as she can back onto the equipment.

94

I COME INTO YOGA class heavy on this Sunday.

Why did I ever agree to write this book? White people are going to feel judged. People of color are going to be annoyed, maybe even offended. My daughter will hate me one day for exposing her. Anyone I write about will inevitably feel like I got it totally wrong. I'll lose friends. Maya will lose friends. And while we're on the subject: Why did I ever agree to be a parent, or a human, for that matter? People suck. We aren't rational or even kind to one another. We elect demented bigots and make it easy for angry men to get automatic weapons, and we warm the planet while putting our fingers in our ears anytime someone tries to tell us about it.

I roll my mat out, grab a blanket, and plop down, like Pig-Pen with a cloud of grumps all around.

Sitting next to me, I kid you not, is Angela Motherfucking Davis.

Yup, that Angela Davis—with the gorgeous head of brown and gray curls, and the big white teeth, and the iconic fist. That Angela Davis who was instrumental in the Black Panthers, spent over a year in prison under false charges, and cofounded Critical Resistance, the nation's preeminent prison-abolition group. That Angela Davis.

I try to be cool. I try to take subtle glances at her throughout the twisting and stretching and bending, just to be sure I'm not making this up. But it's definitely her. I am doing yoga next to Angela Davis, and she is planking like a pro at seventy-six years old.

If Angela Davis can get fired over and over, spend time in prison, write ten books, and still plank at seventy-six, then I can write one scary book at forty. Feeling overwhelmed is its own kind of privilege.

95

It's LIBRARY TIME AGAIN. Ms. Vetter is reading a book about all the different kinds of friends—school friends and church friends and family friends and work friends and neighbor friends, and Darius gives me a generous smile and says, "That's you!"

I feel like a million bucks.

96

I EMAIL AROUND A conflict-of-interest policy to the new School Site Council, and Blair texts me two seconds later: Was that directed at me?

It wasn't directed at you, I answer. It was directed at all the elected officers.

I had, in fact, heard rumors that some people were worried that Blair had nefarious aims—to make money through her own company by getting Emerson, and eventually the district, to adopt her curriculum. Some even wondered if she wanted to take over somehow, turn Emerson into a charter school, shine as the hard-driving principal. I had no idea how realistic any of that speculation was, but I figured an explicit policy would make clear that no one was allowed to use the council for anything other than grappling with the success and investment in our kids.

I resign, she immediately texted back.

As long as your heart is in the right place, you don't need to, I wrote. But I respect whatever decision you want to make.

I'm done.

And just like that, Hurricane Blair blew through.

Part of why Blair was rejected by the teachers and parents at Emerson was that she seemed disrespectful.

But another part of why Blair was rejected was not about her, but about Emerson. Close-knit communities, especially those that experience rejection by outsiders, are inherently defensive. Many of the White parents at Emerson chose it for our kids despite its reputation among our neighbors. We've had fights with our friends and in-laws about it; we've weathered the weird looks on the playgrounds. We've earned a kind of fierce loyalty.

And we are—at least in our own minds—contributing to the betterment of all kids, particularly the most historically marginalized in our society. In some ways, being a White parent at a Black and Brown school is uncomfortable. But in other ways, it's like the biggest possible pat on the progressive White back.

And then this White mom who isn't wearing the uniform of hipster jumpsuits, hoodies, and black-leather Vans, the mom who worships charter school maven Eva Moscowitz (not Nikole Hannah-Jones, our patron saint) teeters in those stilettoes onto our blacktop and tells us that we're not doing right by the kids. That *we* are collectively responsible for the low test scores and the dirty bathrooms.

She tells us this in terrifically unskillful ways. There are the annotated PowerPoints about said bathrooms, which are almost poetic in their disgust: "The mirrors are unusable. The soap dispensers are crooked and frequently empty of soap. The sinks are strewn with garbage."

There are the formal emails with a chastising tone sent to Black women who have worked at the school for decades: "I understand that the spit wads are going to be a daily battle, but I liken it to the broken windows theory (where signs of disorder induce more disorder). Will you be able to ensure that the custodian scrapes these nightly?"

And, of course, there is the way she participates in typically very casual and warm meetings as if she were the education czar of Planet Sorority.

I am most repelled by the harm she appears to cause the teachers and staff in our school. Her approach tends to be disrespectful at best, and racist at worst. She appears to believe that she has the answer to everything that befuddles them, that poverty is actually solvable through a regimented, well-appointed classroom and phonics instruction.

But for what it's worth, it is not the parents of color whom I hear becoming most agitated by her presence and style. It is the White parents.

Blair's presence, like Mrs. Minor's absence, calls us out: What *do* we make of the low test scores? Is there a bigotry of low expectations for kids of color on the part of White parents and teachers at our school? Or have we, as a multicultural community, collectively decided to honor other metrics? And if so, what are they?

It turns out that this is not just a matter of philosophical speculation for me, now that I've accidentally found myself the chair of the School Site Council. I have accepted primary responsibility for representing the parent community on achievement and the strategic investment of the budget at our school. Cue overwhelm.

Blair is not overwhelmed. She's underwhelmed. She's a whirling dervish of urgency. She comes in hot and arrogant, whereas I have been led to believe the righteous way is slow and humble. Don't take up too much space as a White person in a predominantly Black and Brown community. Acknowledge how tiny your reparative act is in light of the grand and complex wound of slavery and everything after.

And that still feels mostly right. But the rub is, well, Darius is already behind and Maya is already ahead, and what does that mean for their educational trajectory, their professional opportunities, their health outcomes way, way down the line? Does the fact that I light up when I see Darius, that I give him hugs and remember his favorite superhero add up to anything in the end *for him?*

Blair sees Darius, too. And she doesn't feel maternal toward him like I do. She believes she is fighting a great war of mediocrity on his behalf. When I interview her, she tells me, "I look at it from the standpoint of, like, fuck it! There isn't time to wait. There isn't time to waste. What I saw felt to me like a crisis. And I could not sit by and be quiet about it."

And it's not unlike what Mrs. Minor has told me. She speaks admiringly about strict behavioral approaches. Empathy should be encouraged, she says, but teachers shouldn't care so much for their students that they ultimately disenfranchise them. "The idea is basically 'I love you so much that I'm holding the bar high,'" she explains.

Mrs. Minor describes so many moments when she's had kids come in disheveled; maybe they've slept in the car last night, or they got shuffled from house to house and didn't have time to do their homework. She gives them big hugs, maybe keeps them in at lunch so she can see that they eat a square meal, get their teeth brushed, or put some deodorant on. But she doesn't then send them back out for recess. She demands that they sit next to her and finish their schoolwork from the day before.

As different as Mrs. Minor and Blair are, they have a shared diagnosis for what ails Emerson. Both see the school as a place where Black and Brown kids are being coddled in the name of compassion. Both see a lack of attention to detail and an absence of firmly held standards as a disservice to the kids who show up each day, especially those who experience a lot of instability outside school. And both suspect that this tyranny of low expectations is predominantly perpetuated by well-meaning White teachers and parents, though Mrs. Minor points out that even Black teachers can adopt a patronizing mentality with their struggling Black students.

Where they diverge, however, is in the remedy. From Blair's perspective, what a school like Emerson needs is a strict, achievement-obsessed school leader—perhaps like herself—who would "coach" the heck out of the teachers, holding their classrooms to a high standard on appearance, behavior protocols, and the test scores of their students. From Mrs. Minor's perspective, what a school like Emerson needs is school leaders and teachers who are both Black and committed to Afrocentric excellence—women like her, who express love through holding kids accountable to their own potential.

Blair gave up on Emerson. Sofia is going to Park Day next year. "Courtney, I feel like . . . I feel really guilty about it," she tells me. "Like, *really* guilty. But I also know it was not a healthy dynamic having her at Emerson."

She goes on: "I intentionally didn't choose Chabot, because if we're not going to go to our neighborhood school and we have the means to send her to a private school, maybe, just maybe, by our not taking that seat, somebody else outside that neighborhood gets the seat, and it could be a life-changing thing for them. That somehow makes me feel a little less guilty about it."

I can't even address those moral gymnastics. It makes me tired. "One more question?" I ask.

"Shoot."

"Do you think Emerson is uniquely broken, or do you think there are tons of schools that have a ton of potential but let kids down?"

Without a pause she answers: "Emerson is representative of many public schools across this country. It is, sadly, not unique at all."

I take a deep breath and consider all the Dariuses and Mayas, all the Andres and Courtneys and Blairs.

97

WE'VE COME TO MILWAUKEE, where John grew up, so the girls can revel in their twelve cousins under the age of twelve, eat Nana's Mickey Mouse pancakes, and—fingers crossed—play in the snow.

John's ninety-four-year-old grandmother, everyone's favorite family member, and I are sitting in the living room, shooting the shit. GG, as we call her, still lives in the small town where she was born, Oshkosh (yes, home to the famous overalls). We talk about what we've been reading and how much it sucks to watch all of your friends die ("You never get used to it"). Then she asks me to tell her about the school that Maya goes to.

"It's wonderful," I say. "Majority Black and low-income. Lots of newcomers from various countries, particularly North Africa and the Middle East. Maya seems really happy there. She's had great teachers and has made lots of good friends."

She says, "I think it's good she goes to a school like that."

"Why do you think it's good, GG?" I ask.

"Because if you live in this country, you shouldn't be estranged from anyone just because they're different," she says. And goes back to knitting in front of the fire.

98

WE'RE BACK IN OAKLAND. At breakfast I look over at Stella and see that her breathing is off. I'm more than familiar with labored breathing, having taken her to the emergency room twice in the middle of the night for croup, but I've never seen anything quite like this. Her upper lip extends out and her exhalations come in little labored puffs. It's like her trachea has become a straw instead of a tube. She's left her oatmeal untouched. I put my hand to her forehead. She's burning up. My own body fills with adrenaline and anxiety. "Not feeling so good, Stell Bells?" I ask.

She shakes her little head no, and I pull her into my lap.

Something in me knows this is different. Those little puffs are haunting. When John picked her up from preschool yesterday, the teachers told him that toward the end of the day, she just sort of faded—got super-tired and was flushed.

"Come look at her breathing," I tell John when he comes down the stairs, and he gets close and we both stare at her, my hand on her chest, his on my shoulder.

"Yeah, that's not good," he says. "I wish I could drop Maya off, but I've got an early-morning meeting. Think you can manage?"

"We'll figure it out. I probably can't get an appointment until later in the morning anyway," I say, and open up the app on my phone, still holding Stella close.

"But who's going to take me to school?" Maya whines.

"We'll figure it out, Moo. Don't worry."

I'm surprised to find that there's an appointment first thing—8:30 a.m.—but that means that I can't get Maya to school on time. Either I bring her with me to the appointment, or I find someone else to take her. Andre pops into my head. I text him: Any chance you could walk Maya to school this morning? Stella is sick and I need to get her to the doctor. Sorry for the last minute ask.

He texts me back within seconds: Of course.

I set Stella up on the couch in a cozy little nest and hustle to get Maya's stuff together for school—lunch, blue folder, purple bag filled with readers. Teeth brushed. Shoes on. My heart is racing, but I'm relieved that I can get to the doctor sooner rather than later. I put Stella in her stroller and walk Maya over to Andre's house. They're just heading down the front steps. "Good morning. Thank you so much for doing this. Can't tell you how appreciative I am," I say.

"It's no problem, of course. What's going on with the little one?" Andre asks, a look of sincere compassion on his face as he smiles down at her. Her eyes are at half-mast.

"I don't know. Her breathing is so weird. Never seen anything quite like it, so I want to get her to the doctor right away," I say.

I crouch down and give Maya a big hug, whispering in her ear, "Love you, Moo. Be a good listener for Andre, okay?" She nods and bounds off with Darius. They're like two puppies on their way to the park.

Andre blesses me with a reassuring smile and says, "Everything will be okay."

"Thanks. I needed that."

"Don't worry about Maya. We got you."

PART IV
RECKONING

Choosing an integrating school is not so much a sacrifice as it is reprioritizing what matters in building a world we want our children to be adults in.

—Courtney Everts Mykytyn

99

THE DOCTOR IS PERPLEXED by Stella's breathing. She keeps moving her stethoscope around and twisting up her face in an increasingly quizzical expression. "This is a strange one," she says.

"I know this is going to sound crazy, but you don't think it could be COVID-19, right?" The news of the coronavirus was just starting to hit the American press. It pains me to ask the doctor because I think it makes me sound alarmist, but I can't help myself.

"Nah," she says. "I wouldn't worry about that. But it doesn't sound great. We could send her to get an X-ray, or we could wait and see how this thing progresses."

"Okay," I say. Waiting for her to tell me the verdict.

"What is your feeling about it?"

I am sort of stunned silent. *My* feeling? This doctor looks like she could be my fraternal twin—White, long brown hair, about forty, mustard-colored tights and a mini-skirt on under her white coat, not your typical authoritative figure, but still...the white coat. *Isn't she supposed to be an oracle of my daughter's health? Aren't my feelings irrelevant in this setting?*

"Well, I guess I would like more information about what you heard when you listened to her lungs," I finally say, rising to the occasion.

"It definitely sounds like she's got something going on in there. It's a bit worse on one side than the other. It could be viral. It could be bacterial. We won't know unless we wait it out or get an X-ray," she explains. "But you know her best. What do you think?"

"I think we should get an X-ray," I say. "She's had plenty of colds, but I've never seen her breathe like that."

The doctor nods and then starts typing away, placing the order, and sends us to the basement of the hospital. The radiologist's late mom had been called Estella, so he is especially excited to meet my indefatigable, labored breather. She gets to wear a "shield" over her little belly, which is very exciting, and so many people in official-looking medical uniforms tell her what a brave kid she is. In other words, it is a really good day... other than the pneumonia, of course.

"The radiologist is perplexed, too," the doctor tells us when we get back to her office. "It's showing up in a strange way, but we think it's pneumonia. I'll send you home with some antibiotics, and you can either give them to her right away or wait on it a few days and see how her breathing progresses."

I know the danger of overuse of antibiotics, and in that moment I don't give a shit. I want to see my little girl breathe normally again. I would do anything to make that happen right this very minute—lift a car, slay a dragon, pop a pill.

It took about a week for her to feel better—a much longer recovery period than most of her toddler sicknesses. Another week after that, I'm walking down the street to grab a coffee, when Dawn texts me. Are you considering keeping Maya home from school?

Hadn't even crossed my mind. Stella was home for a whole week, so I had a ton of work to catch up on. I open a tweet thread she's sent me: some epidemiologists are talking about controlling COVID-19 by, and I'd never read this phrase before, *social distancing*.

In Maya's new favorite book series, Polly Diamond, Polly loses her little sister at a science fair and says, "A worried feeling goes through me like a slippery eel."

That's how the text feels. By the following Thursday, school is canceled. Dawn had been keeping Linden home since the previous Monday. I flash back to so many conversations we've had in which I admired her preparedness but thought her focus on possible calamity (the threat of nuclear attacks or the effects of climate change on our food supply mostly) was a little much. It's good to have a worst-case scenario thinker in every group but only because they help paint a picture of how bad it *could* get, not how bad it actually will get.

Suddenly Dawn isn't a little much; she's an oracle. And the earthquake kit in the attic that we got for donating to NPR is not going to protect us. For a couple of nights in a row I get the kids to bed and then turn into an amateur coronavirus researcher. I am reading a Q&A with a Stanford pediatrician, and she says that pneumonia often occurs along with COVID-19 in kids. There's that slippery eel again.

I message the doctor: You don't think Stella actually did have COVID-19, do you?

The doctor calls me first thing in the morning. She says a thing you never want to hear a doctor say to you in the time of a pandemic: "I've been thinking about your family for the last few days."

Stella's X-ray did, as our doctor understands it now, look a lot like COVID-19. She had all the symptoms. As my doctor and I keep speaking, I sit at my kitchen table, staring out the window at the last petals of the cherry blossoms falling off the tree in front of our house.

When I ask the doctor whom we should be communicating with about the possibility that we could be carriers, she says, "That's a judgment call." One more reminder that we are all, even the experts, new to this.

I take a deep breath. I try to explain to the girls, who can no longer go to school, why I am so distracted when playing school. I sit down next to them and say something like "I just talked to Stelly's doctor, and it turns out she might have had the coronavirus after all."

"I know she had it!" Maya says.

"How?" I ask.

"Because she stayed home from school for five days! I've only gotten to stay home for one day!"

I call John, and he bursts into tears. We decide we will communicate with the communities we are a part of—his small staff, our cohousing, and preschool, in particular. I write careful notes about what we know and what we don't. Have a few phone calls. Text Andre. Text friends. I am heartbroken that we may have exposed anyone, even though unknowingly. I try to forgive myself. I feed the kids lunch and wipe their butts and build forts with them. I FaceTime with my mom and finally cry, myself.

I remember Andre's calm expression and words that morning when he took Maya to school for me: *everything will be okay*. On one level, he was right. Stella is okay. We are okay. For now. But for how long? And have we made anyone else sick? The danger of our mutuality has never felt so raw.

100

Ms. Walsh emails families about various apps—confusing even for me, a person who spends many of her days swimming around the Internet, looking up things. Buried beneath the log-in information is a subhead labeled RESOURCES, and it cheerfully reads:

> Myself and several other teachers are doing food deliveries on Monday and Thursday mornings for families who need food. If you would like to be added to our drop-off list, simply let me know how many children under the age of 18 you want food for, your address, and the best number to text when food has been dropped off by your front door.

In the time of the coronavirus, teachers are tech support, food-delivery workers, distance-curriculum designers, online influencers (many of them have started their own Instagram and YouTube accounts, where they read daily stories), and social workers.

Unsurprisingly, there is some controversy over how the district is handling the pandemic. So many Oakland families depend on schools for meals, so when everything shut down, keeping families fed was a top priority. From the very first day of sheltering in place, the district has provided both breakfast and lunch at twelve drop-off locations for kids who need it. According to Preston Thomas, chief Systems and Services officer for OUSD, about thirteen thousand Oakland students and their families show up to get food every day.

On the curriculum front, OUSD appears less coordinated. Shortly after the stay-at-home order came down, I got an email from my friend, a father at Peralta, concerned about how equity was being interpreted in the midst of all this. He was incensed by their principal's message to the school community, which he forwarded. In part, it read:

> Here at Peralta, consistent with the district's approach, we will continue to offer our students supplemental activities that they can do at home.... We will not be offering any new content while schools are closed. This is worth noting again, we will not be offering new content, only opportunities for students to review and practice what has already been taught so far this year. I know that many of you will find this a challenging idea. I encourage you to think broadly of the equity issue that is at play if only students of well-resourced families continue to receive new content while others do not. We are a public school district and we must be mindful of this context-driven reality.

My friend, as predicted by the principal, found this to be a "challenging idea." He wrote to a handful of other Peralta parents: "What does this say about us—as parents especially—if we can't work with school leadership to mobilize and ensure students with less access actually get more in a time like this? While positioned as an act of equity, it feels much more like an outright act of resignation."

If we take, as a proxy, that 15 percent of kids at Peralta might not have a laptop or Internet access (the same number of kids on free or reduced lunch), that sounds like a pretty easy gap to fill. Meanwhile, Emerson—which has 323 kids, 71.5 percent of them on free or reduced lunch—was anything but idle. Principal Palin and the teachers were busy devising a full-scale Chromebook distribution plan (by mid-April, two hundred had been distributed to families), checking in with every single student to assess their needs (Internet? food? books and supplies?), and in constant communication with the district and one another about which online learning platforms were the best fit for our kids. Emerson will distribute $14,000 in $400 cash disbursements to forty-five families, most of them either undocumented and therefore unable to access stimulus money or experiencing short- or long-term homelessness. We show up for one another—intellectually, emotionally, and also materially.

It was hard not to feel a little smug. The school that our neighbors coveted was treading water, while Emerson educators were diving into the dark and turbulent waters headfirst. We operate within chronic crises all the time—homelessness, displacement, food insecurity, unemployment.

A mother stomps through the playground for pickup, clearly high on something (known for being high on something frequently), yelling at random teachers to tell her where her kids are. The staff quickly communicate and figure out a way to keep her kids for afterschool so she can sober up a bit, maybe minimize a little bit of harm.

A new parent shows up to the office with her ten-year-old kid, who speaks only Tigrinya, one of the dominant languages of Eritrea. The attendance clerk triages: Which other mothers in the community speak Tigrinya? How do we make sure this kid gets into a class where he has a fellow Tigrinya speaker whom he can rely on for a few weeks while he starts to wrap his mind and tongue around English for the first time?

Our school has strong muscles for crises.

101

W<small>E HAVE OUR PARENT-TEACHER</small> conference with Ms. Walsh over FaceTime. We pile onto our bed, Maya characteristically mute in the light of the glowing screen, especially one with her teacher's face on it. Stella immediately sparks up her sheltering-in-place performance-art routine—a mix of yoga, gymnastics, and weird noises. At least we all manage to keep her clothes on.

Ms. Walsh has sent Maya's report card ahead of time; she got mostly 3s on a 1-to-4 scale in categories like Reading and Informational Text and Operations and Algebraic Thinking. John has noticed that she got a 2 in a category called Geometry and immediately brings it up, theoretically as a joke, but Ms. Walsh dives right in, explaining that Maya knows all the basic shapes but not some of the more advanced ones, like parallelogram. ("Fuck parallelograms," he will say later after we get the kids to bed, and I will laugh.)

Before we sign off, I say to Ms. Walsh: "Hey, we live right around the corner from Andre and Darius. I thought I'd just let you know in case there is anything you think of that we can do to be supportive. I've been checking in with texts."

Ms. Walsh lights up. "Oh, wow, that's so great to know! Actually, we're trying to figure out Internet and a laptop or an iPad for them right now."

"We've got an extra laptop," says John. "We can clean it up and take it over."

We hang up and give Maya some big parental squeezes. "We're so proud of you, Moo!"

"But you said that you don't really care about report cards," she says, never one to let me get away with a contradiction.

"Well, we don't really. I mean we don't care about the grades. There are so many ways to be smart, and report cards measure just a few. But we're proud that you love learning and you're good to your classmates," I explain. "That makes us really happy."

102

I KEEP THINKING ABOUT the fact that the teachers are doing ten different jobs while also trying to wrap their minds around this pandemic. I ask Principal Palin what the parent community can do to support them. "Ask them," she says.

So I do, and they say, essentially, "Can you do that thing you do where you ask people a question and then make them sit in silence for a while and think about it and then talk to one another about what they thought?" It is a thing I do, I realize.

We start meeting on Friday afternoons on Zoom. I read them something and then give them a prompt. Sometimes it's Buddhist nun Pema Chödrön, sometimes it's trauma specialist Resmaa Menakem.

Usually it's poetry. We read "Five A.M. in the Pinewoods" by Mary Oliver, about the time she stumbled upon two deer that reminded her of "two mute and beautiful women." The poem ends: "I was thinking: / so this is how you swim inward / so this is how you flow outward / so this is how you pray." We do a free write on the questions: *How are you swimming inward, flowing outward? How are you praying?*

One week we read Dilruba Ahmed's gorgeous poem "Phase One"—"For leaving the fridge open / last night, I forgive you. For conjuring white curtains / instead of living your life."—and then free write on the question: *For what do you forgive yourself right now?*

We talk about what comes up. Or just how their week is going. Or what's heavy on their hearts. Basically it's a way of asking, "How are you? No, how are you *really?*" in fifty-two different ways.

It's between us—this space and what has surfaced. For me, it's been another lesson in just showing up, shushing up, and staying put. The listening was supposed to be for them, but it has also been an anchor for me. It has expanded me in a year of contraction. It has been a study in the texture of teaching—the delight and frustration and exhaustion. It has been a holy thing, a joy, another totally unexpected gift of this shunned school.

103

THERE WILL BE NO standardized tests this year. Much-maligned Secretary of Education Betsy DeVos has made it so. Millions of kids don't even have access to the Internet. Some are being juggled between family members and households while their parents attempt to show up to work at assisted-living facilities, grocery stores, and via Instacart and Amazon. Everyone is on a steep adaption curve. Trying to fit anxiety-producing testing into the middle of all that makes little sense.

In a letter to the state school chiefs, DeVos emphasizes that the exemption wasn't taken lightly, writing of standardized tests: "They are among the most reliable tools available to help us understand how children are performing in school."

In fact, they aren't a very reliable tool at all. Only 20 percent of a test score appears to be about what is happening inside the classroom; the other 80 percent is about what's happening at home.

Test scores matter, not because they are an accurate evaluation of what a kid knows but because—seen in aggregate—they say something about the kinds of kids who have been trained to take life-defining tests at a given school and those who have not. And doing well on tests means getting access to more opportunities, particularly for kids coming from families without economic or racial privilege.

I can have my kid opt out of taking a test, or shrug my shoulders at her decent scores on a standardized test, saying, "It's not really a measure that I care about." I genuinely feel that way. But I also understand that it's a privileged thing to feel safe saying. We can rail against the tests. And we should. In addition to being an inaccurate measure of intelligence or knowledge, they constitute a $400 to $700 million industry, depending on which studies you rely on.

But meanwhile, we'd better not stick it to the man so hard that we forget the kids right in front of us. Educational opportunity is currently structured as a gauntlet of various tests. Until that's not the case, it's my civic duty to care about them.

Gloria Ladson-Billings, the first Black woman to become a tenured professor in UW–Madison's School of Education, made a speech when she became the president of the American Educational Research Association in 2006 in which she argued that what she and her colleagues had referred to as the "achievement gap" was actually a misnomer. It mistakenly pointed people in the direction of yearly test scores and meaningless fluctuations instead of toward "the historical, economic, sociopolitical, and moral decisions and policies that characterize our society," what she calls an "education debt."

She argued that the achievement gap is equivalent to our national deficit—the amount each year that we owe versus what we've spent. "Yearly fluctuations in the achievement gap give us a short-range picture of how students perform on a particular set of achievement measures. Looking at the gap from year to year is a misleading exercise," she argues.

Our "educational debt," on the other hand, is equivalent to the national debt—the cumulative amount of our annual deficits. "Educational debt," Ladson-Billings lays out, is profound—our genocidal and exploitative beginnings as a country, our racist economic and housing policies, our differentiated funding in schools, and what she calls "our moral debt."

Ladson-Billings doesn't explicitly lay this last one at the feet of White and/or privileged parents, but I do. It's that jar of coins buried in the backyard. It's that guilty feeling that we are continuing to pass our moral failings on to the next generation, hoping they'll be the ones clever enough to solve for inequity. But it's not a solve. And it's not a test. It's a societal wound that keeps festering generation after generation.

This year seems like it could be an opening to finally address those wounds—not theoretically but practically. The whole education system has been destabilized so profoundly that even a conservative secretary of education gave a pass on standardized testing.

In the absence of flawed data, in a position of deep humility and creativity born of crisis, what elegant measurements might we imagine instead?—the *we* here being, importantly, not just a few particularly vocal White parents but a genuinely representative group. How might we begin to heal the educational debt? How might we hold ourselves—the adults, not the kids—to a higher standard of not accruing so much in the first place?

104

IN OUR SPRING WALKS around the block, Maya, Stella, and I discover a loquat tree. With little else to do, we become loyal citizens of this particular tree. We eat its little sweet fruits—almost more pit than flesh. We paint it. We research it and plant some ill-fated seeds of our own. We play hide-and-seek within its drooping branches. We run into neighbors there and evangelize about the tree's special properties. I give Maya her first taste of real freedom; she can ride her bike to the tree and back home alone.

John has found an old MacBook in our attic, wiped it clean, and charged it up for Darius. I text his dad that we've got some stuff to drop off, and he writes back to let me know that they're home.

"You girls want to drop some stuff off for Darius with me?" I ask. They are running around the courtyard in front of our house while I drink a beer and try to gather the last bit of stamina for the dinner and bedtime shift.

They leap at the chance to get out, even if it's just a few houses away. Over the last couple of days, I've been assembling a bag of things I think might help Darius and his dad weather the long days—paintbrushes and paint, some paper, coloring books, stickers, a bunch of books.

"Is it Darius's birthday?" Stella asks, when she sees the bag full of goodies in my arms.

Maya laughs at her little sister: "No, Silly Bella."

Maya has discovered that for some unknown reason, it makes Stella seethe when she calls her Silly Bella, so now she's weaponized it to great effect.

"Maya, don't call me that! My name's not Bella!"

"Okay Silly Bella, relax."

"Darius doesn't have an iPad like we do," Maya says. I don't know why I'm still consistently surprised to discover that she listens to John's and my conversations even when I think she's totally absorbed in her own little projects.

"How does he watch shows?" Stella asks, suddenly very worried for Darius.

"He has a huge TV!" Maya shouts.

The one time we crossed the threshold to his house to give Darius his birthday present—a Spider-Man Duplo set—I noticed that his very spare living room had a worse-for-wear leather couch, a pit bull, and a giant TV in it. (A Zillow search later revealed that their home is a two-bedroom, one-bath, just shy of a thousand square feet; it was valued at $898,502.)

"Hey, guys," I greet them when they emerge. "Hey, Darius, how you doing, bud?"

He smiles sheepishly. I realize I miss his lisp. "Say hi, Darius," Andre urges him. "How you guys doing, Courtney?"

Andre is one of those guys who always uses your name. It would seem like a politician's move, except he's ~~the most~~ gentle ~~creature~~.*

Nothing he says ever sounds politic in the least.

"We're hanging in there, you know," I say. "This is all so crazy."

"So crazy," he says, shrugging.

I hand him the bag, noticing the beer still in my hand as I do. I hope it doesn't offend that I'm traipsing around the neighborhood with my open container (such a White woman thing, not to fear any reprisal for drinking in public). "There's just a bunch of stuff in there that we thought might be fun for Darius," I explain. "And the laptop is in there. It's all charged up, and you should be able to use Internet Explorer to access the stuff that Ms. Walsh is asking us to do with them—Clever [a digital learning platform] and all that."

---

* Dr. Dena Simmons: "Maybe let's not call him a creature, especially from a White narrator."

"Okay, great, thanks so much, Courtney," he says. "Internet Explorer, you said?"

"Yeah, do you all have Wi-Fi?"

"We don't, but I think I can use the hot spot on my phone. I'm going to try that," he says.

"Okay, just let me know if you need to troubleshoot. I found logging into all the apps kind of confusing," I explain.

"All right. But you guys doing okay?"

"Yeah, I mean we're taking it one day at a time," I say.

"Yeah, we're picking up food at Sankofa, so that's been good," he says.

"Oh, good, that's great. I'm so glad they're doing that," I say. "Let us know if you need anything, too. We've been sharing food with a lot of our neighbors. Sarah, who lives over there"—I motion to a neighbor's house—"made us some insanely good cake, and we've been getting bread from another neighbor."

I realize as I'm doing it that I'm trying to normalize the sharing of food. Meanwhile, picking up crappy free lunches from Sankofa is not equivalent to eating Sarah's almond-cardamom cake or Rick's artisanal bread.

"Ah, that's so nice," he says. "Well, you all take care. Thanks again for this. It's a big help, Courtney."

"No problem at all. Bye, Darius! We miss you!" I shout up to the doorway.

105

B<small>LAIR TEXTS ME TO</small> check in. I tell her I'm hobbling along like everybody else. She offers to forward me her homeschool schedule in case it's helpful. She's sent Sofia's entire class her schedule.

Sure, I say. Why not?

Daily Schedule

8 a.m.: Breakfast: After she eats, she has to dress herself and brush her teeth.

8:15 a.m.: Calendar, Weather, Morning Message

8:30 a.m.: Reading Lesson

9:00 a.m.: Handwriting Practice: If your child already knows all their uppercase letters, start having them practice lowercase letters. I've found that using a whiteboard and dry-erase markers makes this more enjoyable.

9:15 a.m.: Read Aloud

9:30 a.m.: Snack: Scheduling snacks has been a lifesaver. She now knows she only gets food at certain times and isn't bothering me every five minutes for something to eat.

9:40 a.m.: Free Choice: Drawing, playing with toys, etc.

10:00 a.m.: Math

10:15 a.m.: Puzzles: I pulled out all the puzzles and they're in a stack so she can self-serve. Puzzles are good for foundational math skills. Block play, Legos, Marble Run are all good options as well.

10:30 a.m.: Outdoor Play: Biking, scootering, walking, etc.

11:00 a.m.: Lunch

11:15 a.m.: Science Show: I look for something on demand that she can watch for free that's about nature. I turn on closed captioning so she's also seeing words on the screen.

12:00 p.m.: Independent Reading: Because she's learning to read, she can sit and read to herself during this time, but she also enjoys looking at picture books. I set the timer for 30 min and tell her that she can look at any books she wants to look at in the house.

12:30 p.m.: Snack

12:40 p.m.: Clever Free Choice

1:00 p.m.: Free Choice

1:30 p.m.: Outdoor Play

2:00 p.m.: Yoga: This is actually for me, but I roll out another mat and she messes around on it until she gets bored.

3:00 p.m.: Movie: This is a privilege she has to earn by doing all of

322 • COURTNEY E. MARTIN

her work, not throwing temper tantrums, and not driving me crazy when I'm trying to do my work.

4:00 p.m.: FaceTime with a Friend: Some much needed social interaction so she isn't a weird only child.

Every day has been a little different in our house, but mostly it seems we eat a million bowls of dry cereal, watch copious amounts of *Wild Kratts* and *Octonauts,* and wander up to the aforementioned loquat tree. Early in the mornings I hide in our bright orange 1975 VW bus parked next to our house so I can get writing done. If we do anything educational, it usually involves googling odd questions: *Who invented the cup? How many people can a hot-air balloon hold? Do fish have feelings?*

There are no fifteen-minute increments in our house. There is a sort of eerie and sweet suspension of time, of life as we knew it. We're trying to fill the days without freaking out. Andre and Darius are trying to get online. There is no one pandemic, really.

I'm reminded of sociologist Annette Lareau's analysis of class differences when it comes to parenting. In her 2003 book, *Unequal Childhoods,* she writes about the ways in which middle-class parents tend to approach parenting with a style she calls "concerted cultivation"—structuring their children's lives with great intention and controlling how their days play out.[1] They have a clear idea of the exact skills, knowledge, and values they want their kids to have and a plan to execute. Working-class parents, on the other hand, tend to take an approach she calls "the accomplishment of natural growth"—fewer organized activities, more free play. For the working-class parents, this is not just a philosophical but also a practical choice; they've got shit to do. Concerted cultivation takes a lot of attention and effort.

In the absence of school, in the presence of so much anxiety—the difference in our parenting styles is turned up to a 10. And I can't help but wonder, Who will we be when all this is done? And more important, Who will our children be?

106

I SPEND QUITE A bit of time replaying the laptop drop in my head. The fact that Andre told me they were picking up food from Sankofa seems like a pretty big deal. Or is it? Was he planting a seed with me—letting me know that they are needing food so I might help?* Or does he see picking up lunch at Sankofa as sort of a neutral thing? Are they otherwise fine on food, just grabbing school lunch because it's there and available?

The problem is, I don't know. And I don't feel close enough to him to ask.

A friend wisely suggests that offering a bag of groceries sends a different message than simply saying, "Hey, we've got extra soup. Can we drop some off?" So first I try the latter. A few days later I text at around six p.m. and say, We've got some extra dinner (pasta with tomato sauce). Can we drop it off for you guys?

I don't hear back.

A week passes. On one of our daily walks around the block, I see that workers appear to be tearing out some concrete around their house. I text him to check in. He writes back that the city is finally getting around to replacing their pipes.

A few more days pass. The girls and I put together a little Easter basket filled with translucent green tinsel and pastel jelly beans for Darius and leave it on his steps. Andre texts: Thank you guys for the basket. He really loves it!

---

* Dr. Dena Simmons: "Dig into this more? How does this call out your White savior? Why do you think he would 'work' you like that?"

I rarely try to get Maya to do anything remotely academic these days, but when I do, she sort of melts under my insistence; she slides off her chair, starts making weird animal noises. In short, she drives me crazy. And then I think, "She's six. She's fine. She can already read. I'm not going to push this."

And then I think: *But what about the kids who can't read yet? Will this make it even harder for them to catch up?*

Ms. Walsh tells me that Darius is at level A, so I can drop off the appropriate books. I've watched Darius look at a sight word with a blank stare. I've seen his handwriting—still a series of shaky marks on a water-stained page rather than the careful, proud letters found in those blank books with the dotted lines.

My neighbor Tom, the master reading teacher who sent his son Dave to Emerson twenty years ago, lives just one house away from Darius. Here is a kid who really needs reading support so he doesn't fall further behind, and here is a man who knows exactly how to give it to him. Both trapped in their homes. Fifty feet away.

Tom has met Darius's grandmother, who owns the house, but has never met Andre or Darius. He says he'd be happy to help if they're up for it. I text Andre: My neighbor Tom says he has some books he could offer for Darius at his reading level if you all need them. He also said he'd be happy to work on his reading if you all are interested. He's a real sweetheart. Helped Maya learn to read.

I hear nothing back.

Danielle S. Allen, a professor at the University of Chicago, wrote a book called *Talking to Strangers: Anxieties of Citizenship Since "Brown vs. Board of Education"* in which she argues that interracial distrust between citizens is at the heart of our political failings. She writes, "Distrust can be overcome only when citizens manage to find methods of generating mutual benefit despite differences of position, experience, and perspective. The discovery of such methods is the central project of democracy."[2]

She also writes: "Friendship is not easy, nor is democracy."

Andre doesn't owe me anything. Certainly not friendship, and not even a text back. I'm learning how to disentangle my expectations for community from my expectations for friendship. You can be a functional, and even beloved, community without being close friends.

Maybe Andre senses my need to feel helpful and is rejecting the role. I sure as hell get that. I recall the day he walked Maya to school for me. I was pretty desperate. It helped me a lot. I was shy to ask but glad I had. But in a crisis like this, I'm the one with the resources—the laptop, the pasta, the stupid jelly beans.

To give Darius a taste of the same power would now require an awkward FaceTime call between strangers—an older White guy with a chartreuse beret and a little Black boy with cornrows—brought together by me, a persistent, possibly to the point of annoyance, neighbor.

To stop writing Andre these self-conscious texts would feel like a defeat, prioritizing my own dejection over the possibility that something might be helpful. But to keep writing them also feels a little desperate and unwise. He's gracious, but never the one to reach out. Should I just get the hint and fade back into my little world, grown even smaller during this surreal period of staying at home? Or should I keep sending out smoke signals, hoping one of them makes sense?

Allen writes: "Friendship is not an emotion, but a practice, a set of hard-won, complicated habits that are used to bridge trouble, difficulty, and differences of personality, experience and aspiration."

Allen urges her readers to understand that the kind of friendship that can save democracy is not born of Pollyanna plots, but of sturdy humility and solemnity. White people like me have to prove ourselves trustworthy. "But in order to prove oneself trustworthy," she writes, "one has to know why one is distrusted. The politics of friendship requires of citizens a capacity to attend to the dark side of the democratic soul."

I resolve to be patient with the dark side. His silence speaks. I don't know what it says. And that makes two hundred years of sense.

I write him sporadically to check in: You all hanging in there? Crickets.

And then the next day, a Sunday, I get this: Good morning, Courtney. Darius and I would like to wish you a happy mother's day. May you have a wonderful, joyful day!!!

107

I HIT THE ZOOM link that Ms. Walsh has sent us, and there she is, her makeup and hair impeccable as always. A few other kids are on, too. All of them, I realize as my heart sinks, White. The kids are giddy and bizarre—making silly faces at one another, shouting about light sabers and Nerf guns, waving maniacally. Eventually Wyatt hops on. Then Angelo. Six in all will join the inaugural hour of kindergarten Zoom.

Ms. Walsh has each kid check in: What has been fun, and what has been hard? Scout has turned her apartment into a hotel. She put numbers up next to all the bedrooms and is telling her family where they get to sleep each night. Wyatt, who joined late, is missing burgers from his favorite local joint, but he loves spending so much time with his parents. Ida is pissed that she can't see any trees in her courtyard. Maya says that she has loved making art, and it's been hard to be with her little sister so much.

Then Ms. Walsh shares her screen, and there's a grid with each student's name in one of the squares. She walks us through selecting the "annotation" function on Zoom and encourages the kids to write their names in their respective squares, then draw a tree. The kids love it—they can pick the colors and thickness of the line, stamp hearts and stars. Little Mikey reprimands his dad for taking a cell phone call and not helping him figure out the drop-down menu. Wyatt and Nick also banter, unmuted, about how a computer works. Max's little sister continually fills the whole screen with scribbles, which his mom then erases. It's a Dada collective performance art piece by overwhelmed parents and stir-crazy six-year-olds.

Ms. Walsh reads a book in her theatrical style and then signs off. Maya shuts the laptop and we go downstairs.

On the one hand, it was sweet to see a few of the kids' faces and remember their weird little personalities. And yet the exuberance and physicality of kindergarten-age creatures flattened by the dull glow of the screen feels empty and sad.

We decide to take a walk around the block. Maya can't find her sparkly boots that Nana gave her for Christmas, the ones that match her cousin Sally's, and she starts melting down. Within seconds, she is sobbing uncontrollably on her bed upstairs. She used to lose her mind like this when she was three and four, but it's rare these days. I go up and pull her into my lap and give her a big hug. "You okay?"

She sputters and sobs; her whole body is feeling it. "What's going on, Moo?"

She cries and cries. No words coming. I'm trying to learn not to push her to be so verbal, not to use so many words myself in moments like this.

"I miss my friends," she finally manages to blurt out. "I want a hug from Wyatt."

"Oh, love. Me, too. I get that. Did the Zoom call make you sad?"

She says nothing, just nods her head and lets out another sob from her gut. I hold her close, tears welling up in my own eyes. This sucks. This is not how it's supposed to be. I don't want this for her. I don't want this for any of them. Any of us. We rock and rock and she cries and cries.

108

I AM LOOKING BACK through old notes and run across this: *Reach out to Dave for an interview.* It makes me smile. At the time I wrote it—over three years ago—I didn't know Dave at all. I was interviewing Tom and Mary, and they were telling me about how "rough" Emerson had been on their youngest, most tender child. That child was an abstraction to me then—a story. Now he's a twenty-eight-year-old man whom I know.

Dave moved back home. Stella quickly fell madly in love with him, begging him to sit next to her at dinnertime, make forts with her, read to her. And he not only obliged but seemed to genuinely enjoy her exuberant energy.

We meet up at the firepit on a random afternoon and fall into easy conversation about his favorite movies. He's a cinephile, spending many evenings in the common house watching old movies on the projector screen with a couple of other adult kids in the community. "Where was your love of movies born?" I ask.

He explains how he first became obsessed with *A Bronx Tale,* watching it more than a hundred times. It's a classic tale of good versus evil: a son is torn between his own father, an honest, hardworking bus driver, and his mentor, a Mafioso with a dog-eat-dog worldview.

Dave worships the bus driver. Dave *is,* as far as I can tell, the bus driver. When I explain the premise of my project and ask him about his own time at Emerson, he quickly says, "I blocked it out."

"Oh, really?"

"I mean, it's not just that. I blocked out most of my childhood."

"Why?"

"For most of my life, um..." Dave is struggling with how to answer me. The wind chimes nearby make a glittering noise. The voices of the kids fighting next door waft over the fence.

"I'm still learning, to this day, how to find joy in moments. I'm in a constant battle with sadness. To this day, I'm just trying to understand how to live and exist in a decent way, and I find I'm completely uneasy with what I've seen and been through.

"I have never been at a place of comfort or peace of any kind," he goes on. "It's always been a really deep internal struggle."

"And you remember feeling that internal struggle even as a really little kid?" I ask.

"Yeah, I think it all started with church.... This idea of good and evil, and heaven and hell, is torturous. And then your sensitivity to your environment."

I notice myself doing this in therapy sometimes—using the second person, *you*—when I'm talking about something that's particularly hard. I look it up and learn that some psychologists call this "splitting the mind"—a mild form of disassociation, an unconscious way to get a bit of distance from difficult emotions.

Dave goes on: "You see all this brokenness and you see violence, and you see poverty and you see homelessness, and you see people are being killed. Family members of people you know are being killed. And kids are talking about sex in elementary school, and this and that... and these two worlds don't even come close to being in balance with each other."

I assume that he's talking about the world of his family and the world of the city, but I don't interrupt to ask. He's being so vulnerable. I want to be gentle.

"It makes you feel kind of like you're floating in the abyss. Like, how do I fit into all of this? Like, I don't even belong here. And even if you're not even partaking in what's going on in your environment, just the pain of the existence of it.... You want it to be better, and the burden of feeling like you have to do something about it or you need to change it is great. But then how can you change it when you're a broken sinner yourself?"

He pauses then, so I ask: "Do you think you felt that sense of floating in the abyss because of Emerson, or do you think you would have felt that even if you'd been at a different school but still lived in the city?"

"Due to my nature, at some point, this is what would have come to be," he says. "Because your awareness, even if you're not in it—the awareness of pain and suffering and injustice hurts the sensitive person, regardless if it's in your face or not."

As I sit here, listening to this sweet guy describe his daily struggle so openly, I am reminded of my jar of coins, of that little girl who marched around the block and then buried her instincts in the dirt. For Dave, there is no burying.

The way he talks makes me remember the part of myself that is this way, too.

"Pain is so real. Oppression is so real. And suffering is so real," he goes on. "But as a human being, being aware of that means, well, you're a part of it, right? I can't be cool with that."

"So, what choice do you have? What action do you take?" I ask.

"I'd be lying if I said there was a way to make it okay. It's never been okay. I don't know if it'll ever be okay." He pauses then. Rubs his head. Takes a deep breath. "I don't see it ever being okay as long as we live the way we live."

Dave starts shaking his head slowly. "One of the most oppressive things you can do is try to say, 'I'm going to go do this for these people.' When ninety percent of the time they never asked you to come do nothin' for them. Right? And you might not even be able to sustain whatever it is that you're doing. It might cause more harm than good."

He squints his eyes, almost as if he's worried his words are hurting me. He's trying to speak his small truth but not offend me. "And so for me—and I'm not talking about you, it's just for me—it all comes back to the simplest practices of decency and kindness. Just being there and showing up for whoever is right in front of you."

When Dave discovered flying airplanes as a teenager, he fell in love with it. He got his pilot's license and spent much of his twenties flying small charter planes for hire in Hawaii and Alaska. I guess in some ways, it's the opposite of getting incarnational. He got some genuine relief from floating high above the suffering of the world. He has left the saviors and the hypocrites down below.

"I think it's really up to the individual," Dave says. "I don't think it should be a thing of 'We all should do this.' Because, like, say, for instance, you're a person who has mental health problems. Your daily battle, maybe for the rest of your life, is just trying not to cause any harm to anyone else. That's your greatest devotion to society. And that takes all your time and all your energy and all your work.

"And for someone else, his daily battle is not beating his wife because his father abused his mom. Like, that's his life's work—he was so hurt, he saw this, and it takes so much for him not to hit his wife. Right?

"What I'm trying to say is, I think heroes come in all shapes and sizes. Whether you're a Muhammad Ali, or whether you're a guy who doesn't beat his wife like your father did, and you're overcoming that to hopefully free the next generation. That might have taken just as much work as Muhammad Ali doing whatever it was that he did."

But I still believe that movements, as flawed as they can be, matter—that it's worth trying to get people en masse to be more awake to the suffering that cuts Dave like a knife.

He nods and says, "I think you should raise your child to be the most upstanding individual she can be, to understand injustice and oppression and the brokenness of this world, and prepare the mind and soul mentally to be able to go out into the world and deal with those things. But not necessarily to raise her in that battlefield."

"Do you wish your parents had made other educational decisions at the time?" I ask.

"No, no, no," he says.

"Do you blame them for the decision they made?"

"No, I have no blame or anger or anything, ever, toward my parents," Dave says, his eyes filled with tears. "They're, to me, angels."

109

M AYA AND I ARE snuggled into our queen bed, reading her bedtime book. She's chosen *Dangerous Jane,* a children's book about Jane Addams, cofounder of Hull House in Chicago and winner of the Nobel Peace Prize. In response to World War I, Addams also started the Women's Peace Party. I turn to a spread depicting it; there are about a dozen women sitting at a long table on a fancy-looking stage. I read the words. I flip the page.

"Wait a minute," Maya says. She turns the page back. "How can that be a group of women that represents the whole world if they're all White?"

I scan the women again, and, indeed, there aren't just a dozen women sitting at a long table, there are a dozen *White* women. I hadn't even noticed.

I am filled with a feeling I don't even know the name for. Is it gratification? Delight? Some combination of the two? She hasn't been in school for months, and yet, her vision has not narrowed. In just two years, Emerson has set her expectations and trained her eye.

110

8 MINUTES AND 46 seconds. 8 minutes and 46 seconds. 8 minutes and 46 seconds. 8 minutes and 46 seconds. 8 minutes and 46 seconds. 8 minutes and 46 seconds. 8 minutes and 46 seconds. 8 minutes and 46 seconds. 8 minutes and 46 seconds. 8 minutes and 46 seconds. 8 minutes and 46 seconds. 8 minutes and 46 seconds. 8 minutes and 46 seconds.

111

JOHN HAS RESPONDED TO the pandemic with an almost PTSD-like fear and an out-of-character submission to authority—taking every directive from Governor Newsom as gospel. We wear masks wherever we go. We don't let a soul cross the threshold of our home. We wipe down the groceries. Whereas I struggle with the social isolation and awkwardness of keeping our distance, he is comforted by it.

But I won't compromise on this: I want to go to the Black Lives Matter protest being organized by the youth of Oakland following Ahmaud Arbery's and Breonna Taylor's and George Floyd's murders. I want to bring the girls. I know it makes no epidemiological sense, and I don't care. It matters too much. We can show up in the safest way possible: masks on, maybe riding our bikes, staying briefly. But I want to show up.

"I want to go to the protest this week at Oakland Tech, and I want to take the girls," I say.

"Agreed," he says.

I'm shocked. "Really?" I say.

"Yup," he says.

When I put Stella down for her nap, I explain that when she wakes up, we will be going to a protest. Maya and I have been talking about police and George Floyd and Breonna Taylor for the last week in the winding, weird ways one has an ongoing conversation with a six-year-old. "I don't understand," Stella says after we try to explain it to her.

"You will," Maya says. And then she spends her quiet time listening to an audio book and making our sign. It's beautiful—BLACK is in huge letters across the top in bright, bold colors with hearts and rainbows all around it; LIVES MATTER is below in one long line.

We tape it to the rack around the cargo bike and load the girls in—masks on, helmets on. Even though it's nearly 80 degrees, Maya refuses to get out of her pink llama-adorned flannel footie pajamas, a fight I decide not to have. John bikes with the girls. I hop on my own bike. We head down our street with what feels like hundreds of people, mostly on foot, making their way to the high school nearby.

I feel a rush of emotion—like elation but different because there's grief in there, too. I'm so relieved that all of these people came out, that their story of this country is like mine. One of the great discomforts of Trump's presidency is feeling like I have such a wildly different story about America than so many other Americans.

As we get close to the high school, the density of people increases, and I can feel fear creep in. The girls go silent, looking around in shock, it seems. We haven't been in a crowd since January. It is June 1. We have purposefully avoided anything even remotely like this. But we're here for a reason. All these people are here for a reason.

We snake our way to a resting spot across the street from the school. Every one of the fifteen thousand people who surround us seems beautiful to me in that moment—most are younger, but a few are in their seventies and maybe even eighties (real protest veterans), White and Black and Latinx and Asian-American and every racial identity and size and shape and gender and ability you can imagine.

We run into a young White family we've met who are trying to start a new Christian church in the neighborhood. The mom has a sign that reads LET JUSTICE ROLL LIKE A RIVER, and her baby in an Ergobaby on her chest.

We run into a few Emerson teachers. I'm struck that it's like finding a needle in a haystack, seeing this crew of still familiar though masked faces in their red Emerson T-shirts. We lament not being able to hug but try to Care Bear stare at one another so we can feel the mutual love. Ms. Grill hands me a white cloth, like the one each of the teachers is wearing safety-pinned to their backs; it's got a raised fist spray-painted on it. I feel like I've been initiated into a sacred club.

Everyone is wearing masks. Everyone is peaceful. We even navigate getting out of the way for a few lowriders who want to bump through the calm scene and make a bigger noise.

The young people are organized—they have water and masks to hand out (notice: not sell), marshals who are on the lookout for any violent behavior (which is not to be tolerated), and plenty of historic context to bring to bear. I've missed this kind of leadership, and here it is, emanating from the kids who usually hang on the corner, waiting for the bus near the high school and flirting with one another. They have masqueraded as TikTok-ing teens, but as it turns out, they are warriors (of course, they are both, and that's perfect). In the tradition of their mothers and grandmothers, their great-grandmothers and great-great-grandmothers even, these young Black Oaklanders are remaking the world right in front of me.

112

JOHN AND I WAKE up at the same time, our bodies filled with panic. "What was that?" I say.

"I don't know," he answers, as he stands on top of our bed to try to look out the small window above it—his typical post for middle-of-the-night sounds, which are so frequent these days. It feels like the noise of our society disintegrating is most audible after eleven p.m.: fire engines, but also what sound like police announcements being made over a loud-speaker, glass breaking, shouting. He can't see anything from here. The sounds are getting louder.

We both slip on sweatpants and decide to go look. I remind John, "Let's just keep our distance from whatever is going on."

We don't know what's around that corner. . . . Until we do: a garbage fire. I almost laugh to myself, thinking of all the memes about 2020 being a dumpster fire of a year. But the fact that these powerful orange flames are shooting out of an actual garbage can just a hundred yards from my sleeping children quashes any chuckle I might have enjoyed.

We spot a few White kids in all-black clothing coming out of the paint store, where they've evidently just smashed a window. They throw an open paint can against the wall, leaving a big, bold streak of white paint. It would have been beautiful were it not for the circumstances.

Lights bounce off the buildings, their source a bunch of fire engines and cop cars parked to block off the main intersection a few blocks away. Police are ordering people to disperse. Protesters scurry down the street in pairs and little groups beyond where John and I are standing and disappear into the dark of the underpass nearby. Someone wanders down and shoots pictures with a high-end digital camera of the flames rising into the air. We see the firefighters starting to make their way down the street and decide to head home. I grab John's hand and pull him close, nudging his arm around me. "Jesus," he says.

I look up at the stars. There are so few visible.

113

It's August—a new school year, though it's hard not to think of it as a new "school" year. What is a school without the restless bodies of children, the sounds of whistles and shouts, the density of little backpacks on hooks?

Maya is in first grade now, with Ms. Aviles. She's new to Emerson, a biracial woman (her dad is Puerto Rican, her mom is White) with a theatrical flair like Ms. Walsh but a calmer essence. Despite the limitations of the medium, she is thoroughly engaging. She teaches the kids about Dolores Huerta and math reasoning; they play freeze dance and share their "peaks or pits" each day. They write thank-you notes to firefighters as the California sky darkens eerily and the air quality plummets. They make beautiful cards for elders trapped in nursing homes. They paint self-portraits inspired by Frida Kahlo, while listening to cumbia music.

I am catching up on emails when Maya comes bounding down the stairs. "Guess what, Momma?"

"What?"

"We went on a *real* field trip! We saw a *real* walrus!"

"Wow!" I say, and reach my arms wide for a hug. She bounds into them, genuinely happy.

I can't stop thinking about it all day. On the one hand, Ms. Aviles is a genius. She is using the live cams set up at the San Diego Zoo as incentive for good behavior. If the kids stay on mute, raise quiet hands, keep their "Zoom bodies" on—more new language of this strange moment—then they get to take a "field trip" at the end of the hour.

She picks a stick with a student's name on it out of a jar, and that kid gets to choose which animal they'll check out. Sometimes the animal is lazily draped over a rock, at an unflattering angle; other times there is real action—the elephants are being bathed or the cheetahs are pacing around their habitat.

On the other hand, it depresses me. What is my daughter learning about what is real in this moment? If she is excited about it, I suppose that's all that really matters. But it's hard not to plant one more seed of worry next to all the others. On top of social isolation and germ phobia, unbreathable air and a racist president, she is being shaped by this—the reward of a 2D experience of a 3D world.

A big part of why we sent her to Emerson was for the 3D social experience, and now it's unreachable, pixelated, flattened out, always hampered by some technical difficulty or another. Even months into school, there are certain students who go off mute, and it sounds like they are in a hurricane. No one can hear what they're saying above the ear-splitting noise of the broken technology.

114

STUDENTS IN HIGH-POVERTY districts were the most likely to start the year with fully remote learning,[3] and 30 percent of all K-12 public school students, about 15 to 16 million children, live in homes that don't have an Internet connection or an adequate device for distance learning at home.[4] An early study by McKinsey & Company predicts that the pandemic will exacerbate existing achievement gaps by 15 to 20 percent at least.[5]

But as I've already explored, "the achievement gap" is an unsophisticated way to think about educational disparities in this country. "Educational debt," Gloria Ladson-Billings's framing, which takes into account the "historical, economic, sociopolitical, and moral decisions and policies that characterize our society," is far wiser, and it's never been more apt. Jack Schneider, author of *Beyond Test Scores,* writes: "The covid-19 outbreak...may be the best time to actually see educational debt in action....An outgoing tide has lowered all boats. Yet, some students will make significant educational progress during this hiatus from school, even as many of their peers lose ground."[6]

Individual schools have never been as worthy of our scorn or our praise as we pretended they were. Now, as so many are forced to cope at home, the great leveler, we can see that more clearly than ever. The question is, What are we going to do about it?

The Oakland REACH, an organizing force for Black and Brown families, didn't wait around to find out. From the minute distance learning kicked in, they were talking to families about what they wanted and needed. The answers they got were money, technical support, and culturally relevant, higher-quality curriculum. So Oakland REACH created an emergency fund and distributed more than $400,000 to about a thousand families for rent and food, handed out two hundred laptops and sixty hot spots, and created a five-week virtual summer program that included structured literacy for the youngest learners. They had an astonishing 83 percent attendance rate, with kids jumping up, on average, two levels in reading.

When the district announced that they'd be virtual in the fall, the Oakland REACH stepped up to support their parents once again—doubling the size of their virtual programming and offering it after school, but also adding a new component: the family liaison. Family liaisons—50 percent of whom are bilingual—help parents make sense of distance-learning requirements, platforms, and assessments, and get their kids the best possible education available.

While the Oakland REACH is listening to Black and Brown families (92 percent of whom qualify for free or reduced lunch) about what they need and designing for it, White and/or privileged folks have been creating committees to pressure districts to reopen schools, often claiming that they are acting on behalf of the less fortunate. Lakisha Young, the co-founder and CEO of the Oakland REACH, told me, "White and privileged folks think they have the answers to our problems. Speak from what you know. Ask questions from what you don't know."

Only 20 percent of families that the Oakland REACH surveyed in November said they would go back to in-person learning, and 15 percent of those said it was because distance learning was actually working really well for their families. "A lot of our kids can learn online, and they have been," Young explains. "It's not so much that we're pushing for distance learning, but what we're saying is that distance learning actually can close achievement gaps for kids."

She said that some parents of color have experienced this moment as a real wake-up call about the quality of instruction their kids were getting all along: "By the way, we're not about to take that shitty-ass education we were getting in person either," she says. "Either which way, nobody's off the hook for stepping up their game now."

115

I CATCH UP WITH Susan, whom I'd first met at Peet's all those years ago, to hear more about how things are going at the newly formed Sankofa United, as the merged school has been named. There are about two hundred students in total—half of them Black; it's a massive shift from the year before, when three-quarters of the kids were Black. We chat over Zoom while in the background her kids tussle over still-warm chocolate chip cookies they've just baked.

In the beginning, Susan explains, it felt like "COVID challenges overwhelmed merger challenges."

Everyone was just trying to get the technology straight and get used to the newness of online learning; the parents who came from Kaiser were largely people who had been "merger-curious" from the very beginning but often kept quiet so as not to endure the wrath of the Oakland Not for Sale folks. They were interested in being part of an integration experiment. Many of them felt this was a chance to repair, to grow together, to prove that the vitriol of the school board meetings was not representative of the whole community.

The Kaiser teachers who did end up coming, many of them the same ones who stood up in that school board meeting and testified that they refused to be part of any design process, have been surprised by the palpable challenges at the school. The fourth graders had had a different principal every single year of their Sankofa journey; one school year, they had four principals. Many kids couldn't read at all. Some were coming from families struggling with housing and food insecurity, addiction, and unemployment—the kinds of challenges typical of a student body with high free or reduced lunch numbers. Remember, Kaiser, while multiracial, was economically homogenous and richer than the district population as a whole.

Susan explains, "In my mind, the promise of school integration is as much about visibility and creating opportunities for empathy as it is about bringing resources more directly. Most people just don't have any real sense of the reality at a school with high levels of poverty and trauma, inexperienced teachers, and several years of unstable leadership. And since it's not in front of them, they're not going to show up at a school board meeting about it, or donate to that school's PTA, because, you know, their school needs aides, too. They don't know."

Once you've seen it, you can't unsee it.

Parents and teachers at a more highly resourced school really hadn't seen it. And now they have. One former Kaiser teacher told Susan: "I mean, I knew, but not really. But now I know these kids. And I care about them. And I'm mad as hell."

116

We're having our nominating meeting of the new school year, on Zoom, of course, and I'm trying to figure out how to make sure the School Site Council doesn't end up being mostly White parents again.

I decide that I'll just be super explicit. Anti-racist parenting experts say that we have to stop pretending that race doesn't exist among children, when we know they damn well see it and make meaning out of our silence. Why would it be any different among adults?

I put it in the PTA newsletter and the principal's letter and all of the copy for the various newsletters: not just the meeting info (date, time, link) but an explicit call for more parents of color to join us and run for office. No experience necessary. I ask the teachers if they'll announce it in their online classes, in case any parents are listening, and reach out to parents of color who they think might be interested.

People start logging on. And then more people log on. And then more people. And before I know it, there are nearly forty people at our monthly SSC meeting—the most the school has ever had. They are driving home from their hospital shifts in their minivans, snuggled into their beige couches with their squirmy kids, and cooking empanadas in their tiny kitchens.

Principal Palin gives a few updates on more technical aspects of our duties as a committee, and then we get right into the nominations.

A Black dad whom I've never met whose camera is off nominates himself: "I chose Emerson for my babies because I wanted them to be in a diverse community, where staff supports learning and focuses on the whole child," he explains. "I want to be on the SSC because I feel that it should represent the makeup of the student population."

He pauses then, looking for a good metaphor: "I think we're like the triangle offense in basketball: you have the parents, the teachers, and the support staff... all working together to ensure that all of our children are successful."

I'm beaming. I love this. Then a Latinx mom whom I've never met formally but have been in some breakout rooms with speaks up. Her kids are in second and fourth grades—their second year at Emerson—and she was on the PTA of their former school. "The biggest question on my mind," she shared, "is how are the kids doing emotionally?"

Then, to my total surprise, a Black mom I've been hounding over email because I knew she had deep professional expertise in community outreach in schools nominates herself, even though she told me previously that she didn't have the bandwidth. I have no idea what prompted her change of heart, but I'll take it any way I can get it.

We give everyone one more chance to nominate—themselves or others.

Crickets.

I'm fascinated by the silence. There is no Blair here. These White parents, even those with expertise to offer (and I know some of them personally, so I know what they do professionally), keep their mouths shut. The parents of color got the message, but importantly, the White parents did, too.

Everyone sends me a private chat with their votes. As they talk about the challenges of distance learning in small groups, I tally the votes. The Black dad is in the lead by a bit, and the Black and Latinx moms are tied for second. I realize that if Scott, the all-knowing acronym oracle, will step aside, we can welcome all three, with Julia and me serving the second year of our terms. Julia is a Chinese-American mom whose son has autism. With the exception of a parent from one of our recent immigrant families, this is basically a representative body of our real community.

I frantically text Scott: Hey Scott, would you consider becoming an alternate so we can welcome three new parents? We've got a tie for second place.

Sure.

The full group comes back together, and I announce the new slate. People thank Scott in the chat for his long and faithful tenure. He beams magnanimously.

I log off and sit there on our bed for a minute, stunned with what just transpired. "Parent engagement" is a buzzword in educational circles, but really, getting parents involved, showing up at meetings (all these dreaded meetings), and feeling comfortable to speak up about their ideas regardless of their educational or professional background is the holy grail of true integration.

Most schools that are desegregating end up just like Emerson has been for the last few years: White and/or privileged moms run things despite the wide variety of parents who are actually part of the community.

In other words, even in racially diverse schools, the nodes of power—the PTA, the SSC, other spaces and times where power accrues and influences how the school runs and what it cares about and invests in—are often dominated by White and/or privileged women. The only way to truly disrupt that is for White and/or privileged women to cede leadership to parents of color. Which sounds simple enough, but in my experience, it's not.

Leadership is time-consuming, and time is a luxury a lot of working-class parents don't have. Plus, the structure requires confidence, fluency with English, and a willingness to wade through a lot of bureaucracy and legal formality. It shouldn't be this way. Maybe with this crew on board, we can subvert the structure altogether.

117

THE KIDS HAVE BEEN good for another morning meeting and math lesson online. They get to go wherever they want on Google Earth. Ms. Aviles picks a stick out of the jar: "Emani!"

"I want to go to Yemen! My home. I miss it." Emani and her cousin, Fahad, are both in Ms. Aviles's first-grade class. Emani has an amazing poof of hair that always seems to be taking up much of her little square of screen. She loves to talk. Her cousin is quieter and loves to dance. The kids dance a lot during distance learning, another stroke of genius on Ms. Aviles's part.

"That's a wonderful idea," Ms. Aviles says. "Let's go to Yemen so you can show the whole class your home."

She expertly navigates to what looks like the edge of the Red Sea. People are walking along the edge of the rough water—some in the traditional dress of ankle-length, loose-fitting shirts called *thoobs,* some in T-shirts and pants. The architecture nearby is light, mirroring the color of the sand; building upon building upon building, all reaching for the cloudy sky.

"It's beautiful, Emani!" Ms. Aviles says. "Look at that sea!"

"Yes, it's very beautiful," Emani says proudly.

118

Maya is eating a piece of toast with cherry jam and constructing long nails for herself with Scotch tape, totally tuned out to the morning meeting on the iPad propped in front of her. I'm half-listening as I empty the dishwasher and think through the day's juggle. I hear Ms. Aviles say, "Good morning, Darius! Where are you, at the school?"

I wander over and find his little square, and, indeed, there he is, the blue sky and the unmistakable entrance to the school behind him. "Our hot spot isn't working," Darius says.

"Oh, okay," says Ms. Aviles. "Thanks for finding a way to log on!"

I'm actually relieved to see him. I hadn't heard him in Maya's daily Zoom meetings for weeks, and she told me that Darius was no longer in her class. I didn't know whether he'd been transferred to another class or had left the school. When Stella and I walked by their house on our "night walks"—just little strolls around the block after dinner—we could usually detect signs of life inside or sometimes outside. Then we noticed a FOR SALE sign on the fence, and my heart sank.

As class wraps up, Ms. Aviles asks Darius to put his dad on, but Darius says he's waiting in the car. She tries to explain to Darius that there is a teacher who can help with the technology, that she might even be at the school, but it's not clear how much Darius understands. I unmute and chime in, "Ms. Aviles, we're happy to have Darius come use our Wi-Fi, too. We live right around the corner."

She looks relieved. "Oh, that would be so great. Can you text Andre?"

"Yeah, no problem."

Andre and Darius wander over, paper masks falling off their faces, and we sit in a little outdoor hang spot behind our house and log on for the librarian's story time. I bring out some oranges and goldfish crackers, and the kids dig in, giddy to be in the physical presence of each other. Andre opens up his laptop—which I notice is not the one we gave him—and shows me the hot spot. I've never used one before, so I'm not really sure how to help.

"The thing is that it doesn't even make sense to get Wi-Fi at our house because we're moving next week," he says.

"Oh, really? I was wondering when you all would be moving out. I saw the sign."

"Yeah, my mom has to sell the house. We gotta go."

"You have a next spot figured out?"

"Nah, we might go to Alameda, or maybe East Oakland. We're looking. Haven't really figured anything out yet," he says. "But we will."

"I wish I knew of something," I say.

"Yeah, we'd love to stay in the neighborhood, stay at Emerson. It's been so great," he says.

"I'll keep an eye out," I say, but even as I'm saying it, I feel hopeless. What could I possibly recommend to Andre, who is out of work with a bad back, in this neighborhood?

"And you all really are welcome here anytime to use our Wi-Fi. We love seeing you," I add.

"Thanks, Courtney, we appreciate that. How have you all been?"

"We're hanging in there. My car got stolen, so that sucks." We'd woken up one morning and found that my Prius had just vanished into thin air.

"Oh, no! I'm so sorry. That's awful. That Prius?"

"Yeah. The mechanic said someone would've needed a flatbed to steal it. I don't know how we didn't wake up. It feels like we hear everything."

"Maybe it will turn up? I've heard that happens a lot. Might not be in great shape..."

We both manage a laugh at that. "I can't figure out why someone would steal my Prius when there are Mercedes and other fancy cars on the same block," I say.

"Probably sold it for parts," he says.

It feels good to laugh. Library time is winding down. Maya and Darius are talking about books, and Maya is boasting, "I can read like a hundred books now."

"That's great, Maya! Good for you," says Andre. "Darius, you gotta start reading like Maya!"

"I don't know about a hundred books, Miss Moo, that seems like a bit of an exaggeration," I say, embarrassed at her bragging, and not wanting Darius to feel compared. "Darius, do you like those Elephant and Piggie books? Those are the ones Maya really took to reading with."

"I love those!" Darius says. I duck inside to see if I can find some.

When I come back, Darius and Maya are telling Andre about all the plots—physical comedy and misunderstandings that hit the spot for six-year-olds. There are only a few, fairly simple sentences of dialogue on each page, so it builds early readers' confidence. Or at least that's been the case with Maya, who reads them to her grandparents on FaceTime.

I hand Darius a copy of one of the stories and say, "Here, you can have this one. We've got an extra."

"What do you say, Darius?" nudges Andre.

"Thanks!"

119

I ORDERED AN ORIGINAL copy of *The Purposes of Education in American Democracy*—a treatise of sorts written by the National Educational Policies Commission in 1938. It was published to get all American educators on the same page about what schools were really for. The cover has a drawing of a book on it, spread open, at the feet of a dignified-looking bald eagle. The pages are yellowed and satisfying. It reads: "Every major change in the structure of human society from tribal government to nationalism and from chattel slavery to capitalism has been accompanied by profound changes in educational purposes."[7]

We are at another crossroads. In some ways *Brown vs. Board,* and the immediate resistance and decades-long retreat that followed, was predictable. The policy was ahead of the culture. We weren't ready to love one another's children. We weren't anywhere near straight about our own adult shame.

But the world is largely different now. A not insignificant number of White Americans are trying to quit compartmentalization and rationalization. We're trying to get straight about our own excesses and impact. We're trying to exorcise our inner savior, be less toxic in proximity. We're trying to tell the truth about how tired we are of winner-takes-all whiteness and the narrowest and most individualistic definitions of success. We're trying to do things differently than our overtly racist grandparents and our well-intentioned parents did. We're trying to tell a different story.

Those yellowed pages also say, "Social institutions are convenient systems of relationships among individuals, the lengthened shadows of groups of individual men and women."[8]

We are the lengthened shadows of a healing nation. Some of us, not all of us but some of us, are ready to try again. Try harder this time. And easier, too.

Thirteen Ways of Looking at the White Moral Life

an impossibility
an imperative
a cookie, a street Oscar, a status bestowed by a Black deity
the next right thing (h/t to *Frozen II*)
an inner journey
a lifetime project
a generational project
solipsism
transformation
humble listening
urgent action

ANDRE KNOCKS ON THE door, Darius by his side. They have a big plastic red Radio Flyer wagon with them. "Hi, Courtney, we just wanted to drop this off for you guys."

"Oh, my gosh, thank you!"

"I got this for my third birthday," Darius says. "I'm not a baby anymore and you have a baby, so I wanted you to have it. It swells my heart to give it to you."

"Oh, man, that is the sweetest. Thank you, Darius! Did you hear that, Maya?"

Maya emerges from our house, where she was knotting a friendship bracelet. Her babysitter taught her how to secure the threads in a piece of cardboard. She smiles widely at Darius and shows him what she's been making.

"You want one?" she asks.

"Yeah!" says Darius.

"Pick six colors," she says, bringing out her Tupperware container of thread. He picks a range of blues and greens.

"We're officially moving out today," Andre says.

"You all find a place?" I ask.

"Nah, we haven't figured it out yet. We got a room for tonight." His voice is calm, but I sense the worry underneath.

"Did you have any luck connecting with that guy I texted you about, the landlord for those apartments behind us?"

"Nah, I haven't had the chance. It's been really hectic."

"Yeah, I can imagine. Is it helpful for me to send those? I don't want to bombard you."

"Yes, yes, please keep sending them. We'll figure something out," he says.

I look at the kids examining the lettuces in a garden bed that Maya and our eldest neighbor planted recently. "Darius has gotten so big," I say.

"Yeah, I think he's been eating too much from all the stress," Andre says. "We're going to the doctor soon. I know he's going to notice."

Darius and Maya wander back over to us. "Closing circle is in a couple of minutes. You want to hang out here and do it with Maya? You guys can sit right here where the Wi-Fi reaches outside," I offer.

"Sure, sure, closing circle. Let's do it," says Darius.

"But you said you'd help me, Darius. I need help," Andre says. And then to me: "I'm all by myself over there, doing the final boxes."

"Are you okay?" I ask. "I remember you had back problems."

"I'm hurting," he admits. "But I'm going to the hospital on Sunday to get an epidural shot. That will help a lot. Will you tell Ms. Aviles we're moving, and that's why we can't be on?" Andre asks.

"Of course."

"Darius, you're welcome here anytime to do classes outside with Maya," I tell him. "We're really going to miss you if you move out of the neighborhood."

"Well, we might stay close, or we might go far," he says. "We just don't know yet."

"That's right, Darius, we just don't know yet. Thanks, Courtney!" Andre is creeping down the driveway, headed back to finish his packing.

"Thank you for the wagon! That was so sweet of you all," I holler after them.

"Be sure to send us a picture of Stella in there," Andre says, his smile wide and sweet.

"We will," I say, and watch them walk away.

122

WHITE PEOPLE IN AMERICA are raised to believe that we are the authors of our own lives. We are born into a family, sure, but really we are born into an ethos—that we live in a place where we can spend a lifetime figuring out who we are, what we love, and then pursue a life around those loves. That we are entitled to this kind of authorship, this kind of control and safety. And that ours is an innocent, solitary pursuit—that our job and our house and our kids and our dream have nothing to do with anyone else's. We've conjured them up from the thin air of the ethos. Our blood, sweat, and tears (though really, there's not much blood). Our beginning, our middle. Eventually our end.

But when you start to look closely at race in America, and you are White and well-meaning, you often have this sense of the story coming apart. Part of it is a loss of innocence, a reckoning with your authorship. You realize that, all along, you have not been writing the story; you have been choosing your own adventure in a prewritten, fairly unimaginative young-adult fiction series where no one ever really grows up.

I didn't ask to be born into a White family in Colorado Springs on the last hour of the last day of the 1970s. I didn't ask to be made of sensitive stuff, filled with "color-blind" ideology by ex-hippie parents and teachers, and then pickled in Biggie Smalls and a study-abroad program in South Africa and September 11. Maya didn't ask to be born to a White mom in Oakland who can't keep her damn hands off a keyboard. It's disorienting and sometimes off-putting to be asked to place yourself within a larger national history, some of which you hardly have the stomach to even look at, in still, grainy black-and-white photographs, much less 8-minute-and-46-second videos.

But indigenous folks have the premium on "didn't sign up for this." Black Americans definitely have a profound claim on "didn't sign up for this." For many of them, it started on a slave ship in 1619. It led to a colony in 1719. A cotton plantation in 1819. A Chicago beach in 1919 (see the "Red Summer"). A city street anywhere in America in 2019.

Imagine how much a single mom contending with homelessness, sitting in a government office for four hours only to be disrespected by the underpaid bureaucrat, feels *I didn't sign up for this.* Or the flood of immigrants showing up at our southern border out of economic desperation or fleeing violence. Did they sign up for camping out, unwanted and unwelcomed, in the desert? Did they sign up for living in a land whose terrain and words are unintelligible, whose people may be openly hostile, where money is easier to come by, perhaps, but still never enough?

Part of the mental journey of White America is a painful realization that we are not the benevolent center of the universe, even if we are good and watched the right documentaries and gave the right end-of-year gifts. We are part of systems—economic, educational, medical—that were designed by unabashed racist patriarchs who prioritized profit above all else. These systems have been tweaked over the years to appear less racist, less sexist, and sometimes less capitalistic, and some of these tweaks have altered individual lives.

Despite the performance of reform, these systems have remained largely intact from our founding, causing profound harm to people of color and limiting the White American imagination. So White people do what White people have done for generations. We are kind, or so we think, to individual people of color (this is where we feel we have control), while participating in the systems that disenfranchise, exploit, and sometimes even kill them (this is where we pretend we have no control).

So, what do you do when you wake up in the middle of your life and realize you have been dropped down in the middle of a story, in the middle of unjust systems, in the middle of a country's profound reckoning?

Stop looking away.

"We live in very broken times, times with lots of gaps between the difficult realities of life and what we know to be possible, humanly," says Quaker author Parker Palmer. "One of the most important qualities a person can have in our time—a person who wants to make this a better world—is the capacity to stand in the tragic gap between corrosive cynicism and irrelevant idealism, between what is and could be."

The gift of the gap is that it's honest. There is liberation in letting go of the delusion that your choice doesn't matter in the face of such vast tragedy, a liberation in understanding you are not the center of the universe, but neither are your actions insignificant. As my late friend Courtney said, "You're either contributing to school segregation and concentrations of whiteness and privilege, or you're making a choice to not have that as a priority."

Integration isn't *the* answer. But it's a wildly worthy quest—personally and politically—in these beautiful, broken times. It's a way to practice being brave, to collectively build a nation as we wish it were. It's a way of finally growing up.

123

It's MORNING MEETING, AND I overhear Ms. Aviles. "We each get to choose what pronoun feels most comfortable for us, which one feels like it most fits what gender we are," she says. "Yes, Ella?"

"I read a book about this. If you were born a boy, but you don't feel like one, you could tell people you want to be called *she*. Same with if you were born a girl."

"Exactly," says Ms. Aviles. "Linden, you have something to add?"

"And if you don't feel like a boy or a girl, you can go by *they*," he says.

I'm sort of blown away by the kids' sophistication. Maya chimes in. "Like I have a friend who was born a boy but likes wearing dresses and skirts."

"Right," says Ms. Aviles. "I bet many of us have friends like this. Some of us might not, and that's okay, too. What do you do if you're not sure what pronoun a person wants to use? Henry?"

"You ask them!"

"Exactly," says Ms. Aviles. "Darius, I see you've got a quiet hand raised. Do you have a thought to add?"

"I've got an answer," he says. "What about *us?*"

"Is that how you want to identify?" Ms. Aviles asks.

"Yes!" Darius says enthusiastically.

Coda

KAMALA HARRIS BECAME THE first female, the first Black, the first South Asian vice president in American history. She attributes much of her success to her radical parents and her early experience with desegregating schools. In her own words: "There was a little girl in California who was part of the second class to integrate her public schools, and she was bused to school every day, and that little girl was me."

Lucille Commadore Bridges, Ruby's mother, died of cancer in her home in New Orleans on November 10, 2020. Of the protesters who once made her family's life very challenging, she said, "All those people calling us names, you just have to charge that to their ignorance and just go on. Be yourself, and God will bring you through."

Representative Bobby Scott, chairman of the Committee on Education and Labor, submitted a statement into the Congressional Record to honor Courtney Everts Mykytyn. Among much else, it said: "Unlike many school integration efforts that place burden solely on families of color, Courtney's mission was also to challenge white families to integrate schools. Courtney was always intentional in her efforts as she boldly stated: 'We're [white people] the ones who kind of made it all [school integration] fail. Really fixing it has to be on us.'"

I have cofounded an Oakland chapter of Integrated Schools with my friend Rachel Latta. She pulled her kids out of Peralta and now drives them to West Oakland to be part of a Black-majority school. We meet quarterly and try to have real conversations about the art of showing up as a White and/or privileged parent in an integrating school. There are now more than twenty-five chapters of Integrated Schools across the nation and one in London.

Prop 15, which would have ended a corporate tax loophole and pumped nearly $5 billion back into California public schools, lost by the slimmest of margins in the November 2020 election.

GreatSchools.org reconfigured how it scores schools in an attempt to better translate what is valuable about schools that serve lower-income students and, therefore, tend to have lower test scores. Emerson Elementary is now a 2 out of 10 instead of a 1 out of 10.

Mrs. Minor's preschool closed for only three days, for cleaning, after the initial shutdown in March and then promptly welcomed all the kids back, including some new kids of essential workers. She also expanded, creating Set Apart Scholars, a distance-learning option for homeschooling Black families. (Homeschooling was already on the rise among Black families before the pandemic, but many experts believe there has been a real spike during it.) Set Apart Scholars already has families from North Carolina, Texas, Florida, and Canada. Finally, Mrs. Minor welcomed a new baby into the world on August 20, 2020, a boy named Ra'amyah—which means "thunder of God."

Zaya and Aaron go to a majority-Black Catholic school now.

Brian Stanley's son attends Sankofa United. Online learning has been a challenge, but they're getting through. Brian texts me: Honestly, the school would be fine if they were in person.

Saru's children attend a new school. According to Saru: "My children are up all night depressed. They are really broken. . . . The pandemic has been hard on all children, but my children are twenty thousand times more isolated than other kids because they're not even seeing faces they know or teachers they know. . . . It's a disaster." Her lawsuit is still pending.

Sofia is thriving and in person at Park Day School. Blair is unsatisfied with the curriculum: "I've talked with the Head of School and she is aware the core programs leave much to be desired. . . . And I like that because I am paying I can't be dismissed when I have a concern." The outdoor learning tents went up on the lush grounds right before Thanksgiving. The district remains closed.

Our Emerson School Site Council is reimagining how we define success. First we asked the kids. They said success feels like the wind in your hair when you finally learn to ride your bike. They know they've been successful when a grown-up puts their picture on the wall. The grown-ups are thinking a lot about how to get their wisdom reflected in the way we measure success and how we structure the budget; though there is never enough money, there is always enough love.

The teachers and I continue to meet every Friday from four to five p.m. on Zoom and ask, "How are you? No, how are you *really?*"

Maya is fine. She has bouts of grief. She misses going to school in person with her friends. She misses hugs from Wyatt. But she's fine. She's covered most of our kitchen walls with collages, paintings, and math problems (surprisingly, she has fallen in love with math).

Andre and Darius now live in Hayward, a twenty-five-minute drive away.

Stella adores her wagon and can't wait to become an Emerson cheetah.

ACKNOWLEDGMENTS

First and foremost, I must thank the 1975 bright orange VW bus parked in the driveway next to our house. It was the one place where my kids would leave me alone during the dumpster fire that was 2020 so I could write.

I benefited so much from the wisdom of a wide variety of experts while writing this book. The authors that most influenced me were Eula Biss, Eve L. Ewing, Margaret Hagerman, Nikole Hannah-Jones, Jennifer Harvey, Cathy Park Hong, Rucker C. Johnson, Dani McClain, Elizabeth Gillespie McCrae, Resmaa Menakem, Noliwe Rooks, and Jack Schneider. I hope this contribution to their stunning chorus is useful and beautiful.

Locally, I was most influenced by the genius and straight talk of Shari Davis, Jeremy Gormley, Albert Hong, Rachel Latta, Thomas Maffai, Artemis Minor, Tom Prince, Brian Stanley, Dirk Tillotson, and Gary Yee. I also had influential conversations with Jon Deane, the person I describe as Elizabeth, Nancy Lai, Emily Murphy, Jonathan Osler, the person I describe as Blair, Brooke Toczylowski, and Charles Wilson.

I had a deep bench of friends that gave me feedback on different parts of the book, or talked through various issues with me, including: Mia Birdsong, Laurel Braitman, Garrett Bucks, Allison Cook, Louise Dunlap, Natalie Foster, Gabe Kleinman, Jon Korn, Kate Levitt, Amanda Machado, Wendy MacNaughton, Alexis Madrigal, Patrice Martin, Amanda Nadelburg, Samin Nosrat, Tom and Mary Prince, Pam Scott, Rebecca Skloot, Sandy Speicher, and Kate Madden Yee. Special thanks to Twilight Greenaway and Malia Wollan for their eleventh-hour editing and Selena Sermeno for helping me understand trauma and resilience. Sarah Wheeler and Allison Cook, you have made even the hardest days somehow less lonely and more joyful. Meet you at the base forever.

I am so grateful to all the parents who spoke with me about their experiences—too many to list here. I am especially indebted to those in the Kaiser and Sankofa communities, who talked openly about the pain and possibility of the merger, and those in the Emerson community who have worked alongside me as I've learned. Special thanks to Nicole Hunter for her quiet modeling and the person I describe as Andre for his quiet friendship.

I would not be the same organizer, activist, or parent if it weren't for Courtney Everts Mykytyn and the whole Integrated Schools community. Special thanks to Anna Lodder, who was on much of this journey, and Andrew Lefkowitz for the huge blessing that is the podcast.

My early sense of being unaccompanied burned away in the bright light of a few critical friendships in these past few years. Thanks to Twilight Greenaway, Rachel Latta, the person I describe as Jack, and the person I describe as Susan for being my comfort in the midst of productive discomfort.

It's impossible to sufficiently express my gratitude toward the Emerson staff, particularly the wise and steady principal, Heather Palin, and the teachers who have helped me see the gorgeous hearts of those who choose the profession: especially Dexter Coleman (honorary), Sydney Dexter, Hannah Galvin, Allie Grill, Peter Limata, Mikayla Logan, Jessica Price, and Jennifer Vetter. Special thanks to Maya's teachers—Artemis Minor, Laura Aviles, and Kassondra Walsh—whose magic I have had the honor of witnessing most closely. See you in the field at sunset.

Thanks to the staff at Stella's preschool, Home Away from Home, who are family—Katie, Jacob, and Ty, and the late, truly great Lauren. Without you all, this book wouldn't exist. I don't take you all for granted for one second.

Kari Stuart, you believed in the power of this book, not just as an agent but as a mother, and that meant everything to me. Thank you for taking such good care of it and me. Vanessa Mobley, my fate in a green dress, thank you for being so tenacious about getting this book in the right shape and for cheering me on all the while. You are what every writer craves—an editor with teeth and heart. Little, Brown is bursting with people who really care about books, and the ideas and values that animate them; thanks to Massey Barner, Liz Gassman, Liz Garriga, and Pamela Brown for doing all the things—visionary and detailed—that helped this book make it out into the world. Thanks to Lisa Dusenberry for checking my facts so fastidiously.

I am so grateful to my mentor and friend Parker Palmer, who helped me hear my own voice when I was most conflicted about the prospect of even writing this book. And to Krista Tippett, who has championed my writing, but even more my way of moving through the world, in a way that keeps me true. I am braver because of you two.

Dena Simmons, this book would not be what it is without you. I would not be who I am without you. Thank you, dear one.

Thank you to my parents, who moved the generational work forward with their own kind of courage, and to my big brother, for being a radical-thoughts-and-feelings partner on this and all things. Mary, your artistic sensibility and your moral clarity have always been a gift. Thank you to the entire Cary clan, especially John and Mary, who provide cousin cuddle puddles, endless encouragement on my writing, and a great study in showing up. Megan, thanks for seeing me and my girls so clearly and lovingly.

And of course, thank you to John, without whom I wouldn't have this life to compose in the first place. Thank you for stepping back in the face of some of my convictions, and stepping forward when we need it most. Thank you for caring for our children and my calling so passionately. Thank you for wearing the crab costume.

Maya and Stella, I hope this all makes sense one day. Thank you for choosing me. You are unfolding blessings magnitudes beyond anything I could ever have imagined.

NOTES

PREFACE

1   Aristotle A. Kallis, "Race, 'Value,' and the Hierarchy of Human
     Life: Ideological and Structural Determinants of National Socialist
     Policy-Making," *Journal of Genocide Research* 7, no. 1 (March 2005):
     5–30.

A NOTE ABOUT THE MAKING OF THIS BOOK

1   Eve Ewing. "I'm a Black Scholar Who Studies Race. Here's Why I
     Capitalize 'White.'" *Zora,* July 1, 2020. https://zora.medium.com/
     im-a-black-scholar-who-studies-race-here-s-why-i-capitalize-white-
     f94883aa2dd3.
2   Linda Martín Alcoff, *The Future of Whiteness* (Cambridge, UK: Pol-
     ity Press, 2015), 140.
3   Abraham Joshua Heschel, *God in Search of Man: A Philosophy of Juda-
     ism* (New York: Farrar, Straus and Giroux, 1955).

PART ONE: CHOOSING

1   Deidre McPhillips, "How Racially and Ethnically Diverse Is Your
     City?" *U.S. News,* January 22, 2020, https://www.usnews.com/
     news/cities/articles/2020-01-22/measuring-racial-and-ethnic-diver
     sity-in-americas-cities.

2 "QuickFacts Oakland City, California," United States Census Bureau, July 1, 2019, https://www.census.gov/quickfacts/oaklandcity california.

3 Gary Kamiya, "When WWII Brought Blacks to the East Bay, Whites Fought for Segregation," *San Francisco Chronicle,* November 23, 2018, https://www.sfchronicle.com/chronicle_vault /article/When-WWII-brought-blacks-to-the-East-Bay-whites-13417228.php.

4 Richard Rothstein, *The Color of Law: A Forgotten History of How Our Government Segregated America* (New York: Norton, 2017), xiv.

5 Jack Schneider, *Beyond Test Scores: A Better Way to Measure School Quality* (Cambridge: Harvard University Press, 2017), 76.

6 https://archive.org/stream/americanbabylonr0000self#page/170 /mode/2up/search/23%2C000.

7 *Tract Housing in California, 1945–1973: A Context for National Register Evaluation* (Sacramento, CA: California Department of Transportation, 2011).

8 Joshua Bloom and Waldo E. Martin Jr., *Black Against Empire: The History and Politics of the Black Panther Party* (Berkeley: University of California Press, 2016).

9 Ibid., 184.

10 Oakland Wiki, Local Wiki, https://localwiki.org/oakland/History.

11 Richard Florida, "The Rise of the Creative Class: Why Cities Without Gays and Rock Bands are Losing the Economic Development Race," *Washington Monthly,* May 2002.

12 Emily Deruy, "Rents Jump in Oakland, Drop in San Francisco," *Mercury News,* January 23, 2020, https://www.mercurynews.com /2020/01/23/rents-are-up-in-oakland-down-in-san-francisco/.

13 *Bay Area Affordable Housing Survey Report,* Prepared for the Non-Profit Housing Association of Northern California by Hertz Research, Bodega Bay, California, January 28, 2010, http://ebho .org/wp-content/uploads/2011/09/poll_report.pdf.

14 Robert B. Cialdini, *Influence: The Psychology of Persuasion* (New York: HarperCollins, 2006).

15 Alain de Botton, *Status Anxiety* (New York: Knopf, 2005).

16 Hanif Abdurraqib, "It Is Once Again the Summer of My Discontent & This Is How We Do It."

17   Nikole Hannah-Jones, "Choosing a School for My Daughter in a Segregated City," *New York Times Magazine,* June 9, 2016.

18   Alison Gopnik, *The Gardener and the Carpenter: What the New Science of Child Development Tells Us About the Relationship Between Parents and Children* (New York: Farrar, Straus and Giroux, 2016).

19   Rucker C. Johnson, *Children of the Dream: Why School Integration Works* (New York: Basic Books, 2019), 64.

20   Ibid., 62.

21   Ibid., 64.

22   Ibid., 65.

23   Ibid., 209.

24   Ibid., 60.

25   Ibid., 65.

26   Janet Helms, *Black and White Identity Development: Theory, Research, and Practice* (Westport, CT: Greenwood, 1990).

27   "The Secret Shame: How America's Most Progressive Cities Betray Their Commitment to Educational Equity for All," *Brightbeam,* January 2020, https://brightbeamnetwork.org/wp-content/uploads/2020/01/The-Secret-Shame_v4.pdf.

28   *My Story: Mrs. Lucille Bridges* (The Power of Children), https://www.youtube.com/watch?v=CoJ1NXclO4w.

29   When I showed Mrs. Minor sections of this book, admittedly terrified of what she might think, the one change she requested was that her name be written as *Mrs.* Minor, not Ms.: "Although I've never minded when students called me *Ms. Minor,* being a married black woman (I just celebrated my ten-year anniversary) is a badge of honor in today's society. Using *Mrs.* gives a deeper view of who I am."

30   Eric Torres and Richard Weissbourd, "Do Parents Really Want School Integration?" *Making Caring Common Project,* Harvard Graduate School of Education, January 2020, https://static1.squarespace.com/static/5b7c56e255b02c683659fe43/t/5e30a628 0107be3cf98d15e6/1580246577656/Do+Parents+Really+Want +School+Integration+2020+FINAL.pdf.

31   "Market Signals: Evidence on the Determinants and Consequences of School Choice from a Citywide Lottery," *Mathematica Policy Research,* June 15, 2016, https://www.mathematica.org/our -publications-and-findings/publications/market-signals-evidence

-on-the-determinants-and-consequences-of-school-choice-from-a
-citywide.

32 Johnson, *Children of the Dream,* 53.

33 "A Call for Reparations: Nikole Hannah-Jones on the Wealth Gap,"
Fresh Air, June 24, 2020.

PART TWO: ARRIVING

1   Harvard professor Evelyn Brooks Higginbotham first argued in her
1993 book *Righteous Discontent: The Women's Movement in the Black
Baptist Church, 1880–1920* (Cambridge: Harvard University Press)
that Black women in the twentieth century were forced to adopt a
"politics of respectability"—polite, sexually pure, demure—in order to disprove the racist stereotypes. This puts the burden on Black
women—the victims of oppression—to shift the oppressors' false
ideas about them rather than putting the burden of disproving racist
ideas on the racists themselves.

2   Pam Houston interview with Toni Morrison, *O, The Oprah Magazine,* November 2003.

3   Bill Ware, "Black Power," Reprint of a position paper for the
SNCC Vine City Project, United States National Student Association, April 1966, https://www.crmvet.org/docs/6604_sncc_atlanta
_race.pdf.

4   *2018–2019 Alameda County Grand Jury Final Report,* County Over-
sight of Community, June 21, 2019, http://grandjury.acgov.org/
grandjury-assets/docs/2018-2019/2019.FR.pdf.

5   Courtney Mykytyn, "Reflections on the LA Teacher Strike—and the
Podcast is Back!" January 31, 2019, https://integratedschools.org
/reflections-on-the-la-teacher-strike-and-the-podcast-is-back/.

6   Linn Posey-Maddox, *When Middle-Class Parents Choose Urban
Schools: Class, Race, and the Challenge of Equity in Public Education*
(Chicago: University of Chicago Press, 2014).

7   Jennifer Harvey, *Raising White Kids: Bringing Up Children in a
Racially Unjust America* (Nashville: Abingdon Press, 2017), 199.

8   Ibid., 200.

9   Jennifer A. Richeson, "Thin Slices of Racial Bias," *Journal of Non-
verbal Behavior* (January 2005).

10 Harvey, *Raising White Kids,* 206.

11 Kyla Johnson-Trammell, "Oakland Superintendent: District Must Choose 'Imperfect Solutions over Strife,'" *EdSource,* February 20, 2019, https://edsource.org/2019/oakland-superintendent-district -must-choose-imperfect-solutions-over-strife/608857.

12 *Financing California's Public Schools,* Public Policy Institute of California, November 2018, https://www.ppic.org/publication/financing -californias-public-schools/.

13 "Spending: Does California Spend Enough on Education?" *Ed100,* August 2017, updated and reworked January 2021, https://ed100.org/lessons/californiaskimps.

14 Rucker C. Johnson, *Children of the Dream: Why School Integration Works* (New York: Basic Books, 2019), 81.

15 Dirk Tillotson, "The 'Good,' Bad and Really Bad News on the OUSD Budget," *Great School Voices,* June 2018, https:// greatschoolvoices.org/2018/06/good-bad-really-bad-news-ousd -budget/.

16 "Early Reading Instruction: Results of a National Survey," *EdWeek Research Center,* January 2020, https://www.edweek.org/media /ed%20week%20reading%20instruction%20survey%20report-final %201.24.20.pdf.

17 Cathy Park Hong, *Minor Feelings: An Asian American Reckoning* (New York: One World, 2020), 74.

18 Barbara Johnson, "The Critical Difference," *Diacritics* 8, no. 2 (summer 1978): 2–9.

PART THREE: CLASHING

1 http://www.acphd.org/media/401560/cumulative-health-impacts- east-west-oakland.pdf.

2 Katy Murphy, "Oakland's Small Schools Movement, 10 Years Later," Stanford Center for Opportunity Policy in Education, May 6, 2009, https://edpolicy.stanford.edu/news/articles/899.

3 Kyla Johnson-Trammell, "Oakland Superintendent: District Must Choose 'Imperfect Solutions over Strife,'" *EdSource,* February 20, 2019, https://edsource.org/2019/oakland-superintendent-district -must-choose-imperfect-solutions-over-strife/608857.

4 Thelma Cayne Tilford-Weathers, *A History of Louisville Central High School, 1882–1982* (General Printing Co., 1982).

5 Dunbar High School, GreatSchools.org, https://www.great schools.org/washington-dc/washington/62Dunbar-High-School/.

6 Elizabeth Gillespie McRae, *Mothers of Massive Resistance: White Women and the Politics of White Supremacy* (New York: Oxford University Press, 2018), 168.

7 P. J. Williams, *The Alchemy of Race and Rights* (Cambridge: Harvard University Press, 1991).

8 Eve L. Ewing, *Ghosts in the Schoolyard: Racism and School Closings on Chicago's South Side* (Chicago: University of Chicago Press, 2018).

9 Some of those who spoke identified themselves by name. Some didn't. I have included the names of those with whom I followed up in my reporting, particularly those who identified as professional organizers. I have not included the names of most parents and students, but I have included information about their school affiliation and their racial identity, as this feels critical to understanding the context in which they speak.

10 Presumably she is speaking to the fact that transgender kids are far more likely to die by suicide than other kids, according to the American Academy of Pediatrics. See Russell B. Toomey, Amy K. Syvertsen, and Maura Shramko, "Transgender Adolescent Suicide Behavior," *Pediatrics* 142, no. 4 (October 2018): e20174218. Will moving Kaiser's kids to Sankofa's campus harm transgender children at both of these schools? Her assumption appears to be that (a) there are no transgender kids at Sankofa currently; and (b) it is not a safe place for them.

11 Between 2004 and 2019, OUSD closed nineteen schools, all of which were in the flatlands of East and West Oakland and served majority-Black and -Latinx populations. Note that in this case, the proposal is to close *a building* and move the community that once learned there to another site, merging with more students.

12 The volunteer hours contributed and money raised by parents in individual schools deeply exacerbates inequity within districts. In 2017, according to the PTA's tax information on their IRS 990 form, Kaiser privately raised $143,597, and Peralta, $376,395. Sankofa has no PTA and therefore has no 990, but parents there told me they raised less than $5,000 at most.

13 Kaiser's specialness was invoked repeatedly throughout the public comments. I began to think of it through the lens of "terminal uniqueness," a term from Alcoholics Anonymous to describe the false belief that your experiences with substance abuse are unlike anything any other addict has ever experienced. Those who testified on behalf of Kaiser seemed overwhelmingly convinced of their own cloistered specialness.

14 Brian Stanley, "Yes, It's About Race," *Noteworthy: The Journal Blog,* https://blog.usejournal.com/yes-its-about-race-ad9129eebc1b, September 25, 2019.

15 I found the Kaiser students who testified, and there were many of them, to be the most revealing part of the Greek chorus. They were empowered and rebellious—qualities I deeply admire. They were also mocking, incurious about Sankofa students, and disrespectful of their elders—qualities I came to loathe.

16 Jack Schneider, *Beyond Test Scores: A Better Way to Measure School Quality* (Cambridge: Harvard University Press, 2017), 90.

17 James Q. Wilson and George L. Kelling, "Broken Windows: The Police and Neighborhood Safety," *The Atlantic,* March 1982, https://www.theatlantic.com/magazine/archive/1982/03/broken -windows/304465/.

18 "How a Theory of Crime and Policing Was Born, and Went Terribly Wrong," NPR, November 1, 2016, https://www.npr.org/2016/11/ 01/500104506/broken-windows-policing-and-the-origins-of-stop- and-frisk-and-how-it-went-wrong.

19 Bruce Hartford, "Notes from a Nonviolent Training Session," Non-Violent Action Committee/CORE, 1963, https://www.crmvet .org/info/nv1.htm.

20 James Baldwin, *Notes of a Native Son* (Boston: Beacon Press, 1955), 15.

21 Roald Dahl, *Matilda* (New York: Viking, 1988), 7.

PART FOUR: RECKONING

1 Annette Lareau, *Unequal Childhoods: Class, Race, and Family Life* (Berkeley: University of California Press, 2003).

2 Danielle S. Allen, *Talking to Strangers: Anxieties of Citizenship Since*

"Brown vs. Board of Education" (Chicago: University of Chicago Press, 2004).

3   Betheny Gross, Alice Opalka, and Padma Gundapaneni, "Getting Back to School: An Update on Plans from Across the Country," Center on Reinventing Public Education, August 2020, https://www.crpe.org/publications/getting-back-school-update-plans-across-country.

4   "Closing the K-12 Digital Divide in the Age of Distance Learning," Common Sense and Boston Consulting Group, 2020, https://8ce82b94a8c4fdc3ea6d-b1d233e3bc3cb10858bea65ff05e18f2.ssl.cf2.rackcdn.com/9c/0b/62d34d674c979876e9b13be353df/common-sense-media-report-final-6-26-7.38am_WEB.pdf.

5   Emma Dorn, Bryan Hancock, Jimmy Sarakatsannis, and Ellen Viruleg, "COVID-19 and Student Learning in the United States: The Hurt Could Last a Lifetime," McKinsey & Company, June 1, 2020, https://www.mckinsey.com/industries/public-and-social-sector/our-insights/covid-19-and-student-learning-in-the-united-states-the-hurt-could-last-a-lifetime.

6   Jack Schneider, "How Covid-19 Has Laid Bare The Vast Inequities in U.S. Public Education," *Washington Post,* April 14, 2020, https://www.washingtonpost.com/education/2020/04/14/how-covid-19-has-laid-bare-vast-inequities-us-public-education/.

7   The National Educational Policies Commission, *The Purposes of Education in American Democracy* (Washington, D.C.: National Education Association of the United States and the American Association of School Administrators, 1938), 3.

8   Ibid., 17.

LEARN MORE

BOOKS

Beyond Test Scores: A Better Way to Measure School Quality by Jack Schneider

Children of the Dream: Why School Integration Works by Rucker C. Johnson

Cultivating Genius: An Equity Framework for Culturally and Historically Responsive Literacy by Goldy Muhammad

Ghosts in the Schoolyard: Racism and School Closings on Chicago's South Side by Eve L. Ewing.

Minor Feelings: An Asian American Reckoning by Cathy Park Hong

The Purpose of Power: How We Come Together When We Fall Apart by Alicia Garza

Raising White Kids: Bringing Up Children in a Racially Unjust America by Jennifer Harvey

The Sum of Us: What Racism Costs Everyone and How We Can Prosper Together by Heather McGhee

We Want to Do More Than Survive: Abolitionist Teaching and the Pursuit of Educational Freedom by Bettina Love

Why Are All the Black Kids Sitting Together in the Cafeteria?: And Other Conversations About Race by Beverly Daniel Tatum

PODCASTS

Integrated Schools

The Promise

Nice White Parents

School Colors

ORGANIZATIONS

National Council on School Diversity
The Abolitionist Teaching Network
Barnraisers
LiberatED
Integrated Schools

QUESTIONS FOR DISCUSSION AND REFLECTION

1. Are the schools in your community segregated? When did you first notice? What do you know about the ways in which segregation was historically set in motion in your city? What questions do you have about it?

2. Martin tells her story of racial formation through Dr. Janet Helms's framework for racial development. How did this make you reflect on your own racial formation? When did you realize you had a distinct racial identity?

3. Martin's neighbors tell her that they regretted sending their kid to the neighborhood public school, and she found that damning Great Schools.org score (1 out of 10), and she chose to send her kid anyway. What did you think about that choice initially? Would you have, or have you, made a similar one?

4. What do you think about the advice Martin gets to "show up, shush up, and stay put"?

5. Martin reflects on the way being raised in segregated communities shows up in White bodies. She writes, "Sometimes at school, I feel almost trapped in my White, awkward body" (page 142). If you are

White, do you relate? If you are a person of color, do you pick up on this in White folks, as the research she cites suggests?

6. Throughout the book, Martin reflects on what it's like to try to create friendships across racial and class lines—the understandable distrust, the different cultural references, the joy and confusion. She quotes Dr. Danielle Allen: "Friendship is not easy, nor is democracy" (page 324). What did these reflections make you think about in your own life?

7. White parents throughout the book describe how unique and/or special their children are, or their school communities are, as a way of explaining their choices. What do you make of this? If you're a parent, do you think of your kid as unique and/or special? How has this question influenced your choices, and how have those choices affected larger systems (which is to say, other kids)?

8. Martin often writes about how unknowable our children are to us. If you're a parent, do you wrestle with this feeling? In what ways? If you're not, have you felt known by your own parents—particularly at moments when they made big choices on your behalf, like where to send you to school?

9. Assuming you didn't go to an integrated school, how might you be different if you had? How might your children be different if they had? And if you did go to an integrated school, how has that shaped you—personally, professionally, as a voter and neighbor?

10. A lot of this book is about a young family defining its values. How has your family gone about identifying and living your values? Where do you fall short? Where do you feel in alignment?

ABOUT THE AUTHOR

COURTNEY E. MARTIN is a writer living with her family in a cohousing community in Oakland. She has a popular Substack newsletter, *Examined Family,* and she speaks widely at conferences and colleges throughout the country. She is also the cofounder of the Solutions Journalism Network, FRESH Speakers bureau, and the Bay Area chapter of Integrated Schools. Her happy place is asking people questions. This is her fourth book.